EDEN Dublin Annual Conference 2023

"Yes we can!" - Digital Education for Better Futures

Concise and Other Papers

Dublin, Ireland
18-20 June 2023

Editors:

Josep M. Duart
Elena Trepule

ISBN: 978-1-7138-9068-3

Printed from e-media with permission by:

Curran Associates, Inc.
57 Morehouse Lane
Red Hook, NY 12571

Some format issues inherent in the e-media version may also appear in this print version.

Printed with permission by Curran Associates, Inc. (2024)

For permission requests, please contact European Distance and E-Learning Network (EDEN) at the address below.

European Distance and E-Learning Network (EDEN)
Budapest University of Technology & Economics
H-1111 Budapest, Egry J. u.1.
Hungary

Phone: +36 1 463 1628
Fax: +36 1 463 1858

secretariat@eden-online.org

Additional copies of this publication are available from:

Curran Associates, Inc.
57 Morehouse Lane
Red Hook, NY 12571 USA
Phone: 845-758-0400
Fax: 845-758-2633
Email: curran@proceedings.com
Web: www.proceedings.com

EDEN Annual Conference Proceedings

"Yes we can!" – Digital Education for Better Futures

EDEN 2023 Annual Conference

hosted by

Dublin City University (DCU), Dublin, Ireland

18-20 June 2023

Edited by

Josep M. Duart, Elena Trepule

on behalf of EDEN Digital Learning Europe

EDEN Annual Conference Proceedings

2023 Annual Conference | Dublin, 18-20 June 2023

ISSN: 2707-2819

Published by EDEN Digital Learning Europe

Editors:

Josep M. Duart

Elena Trepule

Editorial co-ordination:

Gabija Kvieskaite

Carlos Madrid

EDEN DLE Secretariat

Kuklase tn 16-12, 13423, Tallinn, Estonia

E-mail: secretariat@eden-europe.eu

https://eden-europe.eu/

Supported by the Erasmus+ Programme of the European Union

The publication reflects the authors' view, the EACEA and the European Commission are not responsible for any use that may be made of the information it contains.

Acknowledgement and thanks are given to the Program Committee

Josep M. Duart, EDEN DLE President, Spain

Mark Brown, Vice President of Strategy and Communication, Ireland

Denise Whitelock, EDEN DLE Vice-President for Research, UK

Sandra Kučina Softić, Vice President of Open Professional Collaboration, Croatia

Orna Farrell, Ireland

Airina Volungevičienė, Lithuania

Helga Dorner, Hungary

Alfredo Soeiro, Portugal

Mart Laanpere, Estonia

Antonella Poce, Italy

Wim E.A. Van Petegem, Belgium

Vlad Mihăescu, Romania

Elena Trepule, Lithuania

TABLE OF CONTENTS

CONCISE PAPERS

TRANSFORMATIVE EDUCATION

FUTURE PEDAGOGIES

GASTA PAPERS

TRANSFORMATIVE EDUCATION

FUTURE PEDAGOGIES

NEXT GENERATION TEACHERS AND LEARNERS

DIGITAL CITIZENSHIP FOR SUSTAINABLE FUTURES

CONCISE PAPERS

LISTENING TO STUDENTS ON ACCESSIBILITY AND INCLUSION IN ONLINE LEARNING MODULES: A 'FROM THE TRENCHES' CASE STUDY

James Brunton, Dublin City University, Ireland / University of South Africa, South Africa
Chloe Beatty, Sophia Pallaro, Dublin City University, Ireland

Abstract

Online education is transformative for students with diverse learning needs who would otherwise not be able, or would prefer not, to attend on-campus higher education institutions (HEIs) (Lee, 2017). While such programmes have improved access to HEIs for this cohort, various aspects of our teaching and learning approaches can impact negatively on the degree to which the student experience is accessible and inclusive (McKeown & McKeown, 2019). Although progress has been made in recent years around accessibility and inclusion (A&I) in HEIs, it is necessary to continually improve aspects of teaching and learning practice in order to improve accessibility (Batanero-Ochaita et al., 2021). To achieve this goal, we require greater insights into learner needs, especially those with specific conditions, impairments, or disorders (CIDs). Fortunately for educators, we frequently receive such insights from students in the form of formal and informal feedback. We just need to be open to listening to these student voices.

Early in the 2021/2022 academic year, students with CIDs reported some issues with aspects of the undergraduate, online learning modules they were studying. In response to this, a project was initiated with the aim to:

1. respond to the student reports and put in place actions that could be implemented in the short-term, based on the feedback received, advice from a senior occupational therapist, and a rapid review of best practice accessibility toolkits in an effort to see where the gaps were in our existing practices;
2. review and redevelop online learning materials, module organisation and structure, and related teaching and learning practices, for the next academic year to address issues students had highlighted that required more time to address.

The project employed an action research methodology centered on obtaining more in-depth feedback on accessibility and inclusion in online learning modules from stakeholders such as staff and colleagues within the institution with expertise in the area, but most importantly from students. The feedback sought related to topics such as:

- making A&I information more explicit and normalised in the programme;
- changing practices around discussion forums to make them less overwhelming for students;
- improving structure, organisation, and direction in modules;
- reviewing assessments in light of UDL principles and reasonable accommodations.

Data were gathered through written feedback, interviews, and focus groups with these stakeholders. The aim of the study was to include stakeholders, especially the students, as co-designers of online learning, where research was done with, rather than on, those in minority groups. Before any changes were fully implemented into the modules, written feedback on these changes was again sought from the stakeholders to ensure that no further learning barriers were inadvertently created while implementing the suggested changes.

The current session will present the analytic findings of this project, and the implementations made in undergraduate online learning modules as a result of the project. The goal of disseminating these findings and resources is to help make a step toward a higher education where education is accessible to everyone, and where the diverse nature and needs of higher education students are recognised.

Keywords:

Universal Design for Learning (UDL), disability, learning design, distance learning.

References

Batanero-Ochaíta, C., De-Marcos, L., Rivera, L.F., Holvikivi, J., Hilera, J.R. and Tortosa, S.O. (2021). Improving Accessibility in Online Education: Comparative Analysis of Attitudes of Blind and Deaf Students Toward an Adapted Learning Platform. IEEE Access, 9, 99968-99982.

Lee, K. (2017). Rethinking the accessibility of online higher education: A historical review. The Internet and Higher Education, 33, 15-23.

McKeown, C. & McKeown, J. (2019). Accessibility in online courses: Understanding the deaf learner. TechTrends, 63(5), 506-513.

National Forum (2016). National Professional Development Framework for all Staff Who Teach in Higher Education. National Forum for the Enhancement of Teaching and Learning.

HIGHER EDUCATION FOR GOOD: TEACHING AND LEARNING FUTURES

Laura Czerniewicz, University of Cape Town, South Africa

Catherine Cronin, Independent, Ireland

Abstract

This concise paper provides an overview of a new book from 70 authors in 18 countries regarding what a better future for higher education would look like. Considering both transformative education and future pedagogies, *Higher Education for Good* is a diverse, theoretical, and practice-based collection of imaginative, searing and inspiring insights in multimodal formats.

Keywords:

higher education, futures, future pedagogies, social justice, equity, hope

Higher Education for Good

It is a truism that the pandemic has profoundly altered the practice and trajectory of higher education. In many ways it has amplified existing pessimism and despair about higher education's future. Even prior to the deep disruption of Covid-19, the nature and role of higher education institutions were under scrutiny; it was already clear that teaching and learning, in particular, had to change for an increasingly uncertain future.

Most predictions about the digitized, datafied future of higher education are steeped in homogeneous neoliberal discourses; while they claim to offer alternatives, many foundational assumptions remain intact. Profit-making as the main driver has proceeded apace too often through thinly disguised "open washing" and "equity washing". At the same time, there are challenges to this hegemony: pockets of resistance, sites of innovation for social justice, glimmers of alternative futures. These are too often below the radar, unshared and unknown. Intent on surfacing these, and cognisant of the general atmosphere of pessimism, even despair, in the sector, in early 2022 we invited responses from the global higher education community to the question: "What can be done?".

The result is *Higher Education for Good: Teaching and Learning Futures* (or *HE4Good*), a book comprising 27 chapters, due to be published in mid-2023. The book offers ways of thinking, conceptualising and creating possibilities for making and remaking higher education, focusing on futures that foreground inclusion, equity, social justice, care and sustainability. *HE4Good* offers ideas regarding the role of higher education in addressing "wicked" problems that require multiple solutions, resolutions, experiments, and imaginaries.

The book exemplifies diversity in several ways. Seventy authors from 18 countries and multiple disciplines have contributed. Authors range from established academics and researchers to learning professionals, early career scholars and students. Chapters are written in a range of forms: critical reflections, conceptual essays, dialogues, speculative fiction, poetry, graphic reflection, image and audio, as well as newly created artwork.

Considered together, the chapters in *HE4Good* make a powerful claim for higher education that is just, humane, and globally sustainable – as well as acknowledging that "goodness" is relational and contextual, deeply interwoven with ideological, political and social realities. There are numerous examples in the book of both calls to and enactments of resistance. To change knowledge and understanding in the sector means re-centering and bringing in from the margins voices and views that are at the periphery. It means intentionally crossing borders of all kinds: geographic, disciplinary, status and "accepted genre".

The book includes a range of theoretical lenses and imaginaries to make sense of and reconsider the profound present, unfolding dilemmas. Theoretical work is included in areas such as design justice, data justice, decolonising knowledge, critical pedagogies, ethics of assessment, and open knowledge. These lenses illuminate a range of relevant topics including humanising learning design, infrastructures of care, blended and online learning ecosystems, and new teaching and learning business models. The book also includes chapters that offer ways to vision and imagine better futures, as a step towards bringing alternative realities into being. It exemplifies Davis et al.'s (2022) exhortation: "we will dream our way out; we must imagine beyond the given" (p. 16). Treating the future as a site of "radical possibility" (Facer, 2016), *HE4Good* shows how a range of players can bravely imagine and share fresh possibilities and alternative higher education futures, beyond existing realities and hegemonic discourses.

A thread through all the chapters is about change, how it happens and how it can be possible. It is clear that effective progressive change is strengthened by communality and is most powerful when forged through coalition. After all, "it is in the many acts, small and large, acting in constellations and collectivities, over time and place that bear results" (Sultana, 2022). The focus is on teaching and learning, offering a collection of diverse and creative ways that educators and students have used to make changes in teaching and learning —with examples from HE sectors in ten countries— as well as ways to embed long-term change through systemic and structural changes at institutional and national levels.

Summary

Overall, *HE4Good* identifies avenues for thought and action and offers hope as an antidote to despair and regret. Together the authors provide inspiration towards possible manifestos for "higher education for good" which can be tailored to specific contexts. The possible tenets for a Higher Education for Good which emerge from this collection are: (1) name and analyse the troubles of higher education; (2) challenge assumptions and resist hegemonies; (3) make claims for just, humane and globally sustainable HE; (4) courageously imagine and share fresh possibilities; and (5) make positive changes, here and now. Jonathan Jansen notes in his foreword that *HE4Good* "works with an unspoken proposition, that we cannot wait for the neoliberal university to transform itself. Universities can change 'because of their capacity for challenge, critique, invention and intellectual growth ... but it has to be fought for' (Connell, 2019, p. 10)". Through multimodal narratives, the book's principles counter despair and provide inspiration to all engaged in higher education.

References

Connell, R. (2019). *The good university: What universities actually do and why it's time for radical change.* Zed Books.

Davis. A. Y., Dent, G., Meiners, E. R., & Richie, B. E. (2022). *Abolition. Feminism. Now.* Hamish Hamilton.

Facer, K. (2016). Using the future in education: Creating space for openness, hope and novelty. In H. E. Lees & N. Noddings (Eds.), *The Palgrave international handbook of alternative education* (pp. 63-78). https://doi.org/10.1057/978-1-137-41291-1_5

Sultana, F. (2022). The unbearable heaviness of climate coloniality. *Political Geography*, 102638. https://doi.org/10.1016/j.polgeo.2022.102638

AI TUTOR PILOT: A SCALABLE SOLUTION FOR 1:1 SUPPORT?

Tim Hall, University of London Worldwide, UK

Abstract

Research has shown that one-on-one tutoring is an effective means of improving student outcomes (Bloom, 1984). However, with increased workloads for academics, large class sizes, and in the case of the University of London Worldwide, the fact that students are studying all over the world – traditional one-on-one tutoring is not always a scalable solution.

According to Lai (2021), when considering AI in education, studies have found that students preferred AI as a tool to assist their learning. The University of London is piloting the use of Noodle Factory's Walter (Noodle Factory, 2022) to find out whether an AI Tutor, or *smart personal assistant learning tutors* (Winkler & Roos, 2019) approach could help us achieve our goals of improving student performance on our courses, increasing student engagement with study materials, and empowering our educators and programme teams.

We will use the pilot to trial AI in answering FAQs, preparing formative multiple-choice questions, and providing personalised and rapid feedback to University of London students. The purpose of the pilot is to assess the suitability of these opportunities and to assess whether they could be rolled out more widely across Worldwide programmes.

The primary objective of this pilot project is to evaluate the suitability of these AI-based tools and to determine their potential for wider implementation across University of London Worldwide programmes, particularly in relation to: Increased student feedback opportunities, Assessment of quality of software (i.e., is it fit for purpose), Required amount of any human intervention (i.e., does it save any time?), Assessment of staff and student opinion of the AI Tutor, and Implications for non-academic enquiry management.

We'll also consider what the future holds for the continuing development of AI assistance and its place in education.

Attendees can expect to see a real-world example of an AI Tutor implementation and will learn about the approach to the content generation that this example takes. They will have an opportunity to ask questions about the pilot and hear about the lessons being learned during this ongoing project.

Keywords:

AI tutoring, chatbot, natural language processing, machine learning, educational technology, e-learning, adaptive learning, intelligent tutoring systems, conversational agents, educational chatbot, educational AI.

References

Bloom, B. S. (1984). The 2 Sigma Problem: The Search for Methods of Group Instruction as Effective as One-to-One Tutoring. Educational Researcher, 13(6), 4–16. https://doi.org/10.2307/1175554

Lai, C.-L. (2021). Exploring University Students'Preferences for AI-Assisted Learning Environment: A Drawing Analysis with Activity Theory Framework. *Educational Technology & Society*, *24*(4), 1–15. https://www.jstor.org/stable/48629241

Noodle Factory. (2022, December 12). *Walter - Intelligent Automated Tutor for Teachers*. Www.noodlefactory.ai. https://www.noodlefactory.ai/intelligent-automated-tutor-for-teachers

Winkler, R., & Roos, J. (2019). Bringing AI into the Classroom: Designing Smart Personal Assistants as Learning Tutors. *ICIS 2019 Proceedings*. https://aisel.aisnet.org/icis2019/learning_environ/learning_environ/10/

THE USE OF RUBRICS FROM TEACHER AND STUDENT PERSPECTIVE – THE CASE OF DOBA BUSINESS SCHOOL

Mateja Brejc, Marko Divjak, DOBA Business School, Slovenia

Abstract

The aim of the paper is to present a case study of the use of rubrics at DOBA Business School (DBS), a private online business school in Slovenia. DBS runs 11 study programmes (BA, MA, PHD) with currently over 1800 students enrolled, studying from over 40 different countries. Study programmes are delivered by 103 teachers with the support of 97 online mentors, 4 programme managers and 5 academic advisors. The case study of the use of rubrics from teacher and student perspectives is aimed at gaining insight into how rubrics are perceived, how they are used, and what perceived benefits and challenges they present. Internal monitoring shows that over 50 % of teachers at DBS already use rubrics.

In the 1st phase (February 2023), data was gathered using a survey and focus group with teachers. Survey's preliminary results (n=49) indicate that teachers find rubrics to be a useful tool for assessment, helping them to evaluate students' work more objectively, precisely and to provide better, more focused and on-time feedback to students (personalization). The main challenges are related to time-consuming creation of the rubrics, the overall definition of criteria that clearly reflect the specifics of different assignments as well as student motivation in using the rubrics as a helpful tool in their study process. Also, the expected benefits for teachers in terms of time savings during assessment and provision of feedback are not clearly recognised. In the 2nd phase (April, 2023), current data will be complemented by additional data among students at DBS regarding their perspective on the use and usefulness of rubrics.

Along with the final results and the conclusions of the study, the activities at DBS will be briefly presented in terms of encouraging and supporting teachers as well as students in using rubrics for better quality of the study process and study achievements.

Keywords:

Rubrics, online study, case study teachers, students

References

Bregar, L., Zagmajster, M. and Radovan M. (2020). *E-izobraževanje za digitalno družbo.* Andragoški center Slovenije.

Bregar, L and M. Puhek. (2018). *Razvoj modela uporabe učnih analitik na DOBA Fakulteti.* Poročilo projekta Smart DOBA. Interno gradivo. DOBA Fakulteta.

Brookhart, S. M. (2013). *How to create and use rubrics for formative assessment and grading.* ASCD.

Andrade, H. (2000). Using rubrics to promote thinking and learning. *In Educational leadership* (57 ed., Vol. 5, pp. 13-18).

Chowdhury, F. (2019). Application of Rubrics in the Classroom: A Vital Tool for Improvement in Assessment, Feedback and Learning. In *International Education Studies.* (12 ed., Vol. 1, pp. 61-68).

Reddy, Y. M., & Andrade, H. (2010). A review of rubric use in higher education. In *Assessment & Evaluation in Higher Education*, (35 ed,. Vol. 4, pp. 435-448).

FROM DATA TO ACTION: DEVELOPING A LABOUR MARKET INTELLIGENCE SYSTEM TO ASSESS SKILL NEEDS IN A SPANISH ONLINE UNIVERSITY

Federico Christmann, Àngels Fitó Bertran, Marina Muñoz Martínez, Carmen Pagés Serra, Universitat Oberta Catalunya, Spain

Abstract

Rapid technological change, artificial intelligence, the transition to a green economy, and the effects of the COVID-19 pandemic are transforming how we live and work. This paper discusses the implementation of a Labour Market Intelligence (LMI) system called "Labor Market Intelligence for Educators" by a Spanish online university. This tool aims to track the demand for skills in online job vacancies (OJVs) with a focus on updating existing educational programs and identifying new offerings. LMI tools can help higher education institutions (HEIs) to stay relevant and ensure that their offerings meet the labor market needs (Sparreboom, 2016).

The "Labor Market Intelligence for Educators" shows how HEIs can use LMIs to catch new labor market insights to improve students' employability. Data used in this tool is obtained from Lightcast (https://lightcast.io/), ESCO (https://esco.ec.europa.eu/en), and other secondary sources. Lightcast scraps data from OJVs and applies AI algorithms to classify postings corpus into occupation, skills demand, economic sector, geographic location, educational requirements data, etc. This information serves to analyze the latest labor market trends from the employers' revealed preferences-i.e., their stated skill needs. On its part, ESCO provides information about a complementary set of skills associated with each occupation based on experts' recommendations.

The data files received from Lightcast are transformed and combined with ESCO-based data. This data is stored in the data repository system of the university using Snowflake (a cloud database platform). Then, each program director is tasked with identifying those occupations that students could perform in the future and those hard and soft skills that students must master. With this, we obtain the potential market of a program from vacancies that meet both criteria. Therefore, it is possible to identify which skills are requested in the market and provide information about the skills gap of each program. By doing this, we can assess how up-to-date programs are.

The data is visualized and shared with faculty through the Power BI Service. This app allows for interactive navigation: users can customize their visualizations selecting data filters. Figure 1 shows an example of the capabilities of this tool, using a dashboard from the report of the School of Arts and Humanities. By applying different data filters, users can get quick insights into the skills demand of vacancies associated with the Arts Degree. Those skills requested in the labor market but missing in the Arts Degree program are marked with flags (hard skills) and exclamation marks (soft skills). We provide information to each School in different reports, updating all the contents periodically.

Figure 1 - An example of the skills analysis associated with the Arts Degree (GA in the university's main language). Report for the School of Arts and Humanities, 2018-2021.

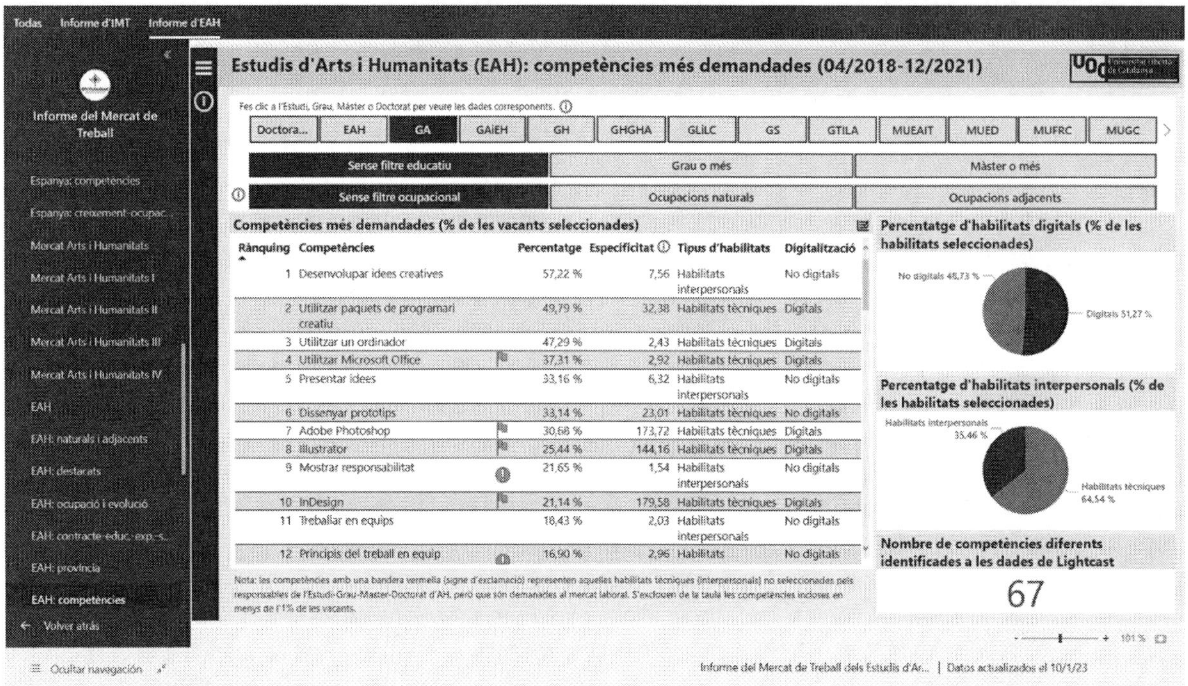

The "Labor Market Intelligence for Educators" depicts how HEIs can use LMI to foster competitiveness in creating and updating educational offerings to meet market needs. Beyond internal uses, this LMI system could be the basis of other solutions that provide updated labor market information to external audiences such as students, alumnae, and society. It is noteworthy that institutional governance factors are crucial to ensure that such information is used for decision-making. Then, there should be a strong mandate from university officials to place LMI tools at the center of the institutional strategy.

Keywords:

Higher education institutions, labour market intelligence, online job vacancies, meeting skill needs.

References

Sparreboom, T. (2016). Labour market information and analysis systems. Perspectives on labour economics for development. Geneva, Switzerland: International Labour Organization, 255-82.

FROM VIRTUAL LABORATORIES TO MICRO-SKILL BADGING: DIGITAL TOOLS TO DEVELOP AND EVIDENCE SKILLS AND COMPETENCIES FOR STUDENTS IN THE CHEMICAL SCIENCES

Frances Heaney, Denise Rooney, Trinidad Velasco-Torrijos, Carmel Breslin, Maynooth University; Ronan Bree, Bernard Drumm, Dundalk Institute of Technology; Eric Moore, University College Cork; Aoife Morrin, Blanaid White, Dublin City University; Brian Murphy, Technological University of the Shannon, Ireland

Abstract

This paper will discuss the introduction of Virtual Laboratories as a pedagogic tool across five partner Higher Education Institutes in the Republic of Ireland (Virtual Laboratories in Higher Education, 2020) and the inclusion of such activities within a badging project messaging the employability value of skills and competencies developed within a laboratory curriculum.(Velasco-Torrijos et al., 2022) The Virtual Laboratories initiative is developing best practice for a blended approach to practical science where virtual training supports and reinforces the in-lab experience; inquiry-based learning, teamwork and development of work-place transversal skills are key pillars of this enterprise informed approach. Irish Higher Education students are acutely aware of the importance of work-readiness and "developing skills to maximize employability" dominants their perspective of success.(National Forum, 2019) It is thus important that educators support students not only in developing key discipline-specific and transferrable skills but, at the same time, empower students by instilling a recognition that the skills acquired within their curricula can improve their competency for employment.

Gamification is gaining traction as a pedagogic tool with digital badging and leaderboard approaches being adopted in educational settings at various levels, and across a wide range of disciplines.(Balci et al., 2022; Braxton et al., 2019; Fulton, 2019; Hennah & Seery, 2017; Noyes et al., 2020) The effectiveness of digital badges, typically used to recognize skill or competency acquisition is reported to depend both on the type of badge and the stage of the learner.(Abramovich et al., 2013) In this project, working with students taking undergraduate organic chemistry modules, a series of in-course 'micro-skills-learning-opportunities' were clearly signposted and regularly rewarded in the form of digital badges. The focus was not on in-depth mastery of a single technique, instead it targeted microskills/competencies which were integral to the existing laboratory programme and assessment practices. For each skill short-term goals were set, and engagement regularly rewarded by transfer of a digital badge system via our VLE (Moodle); awarding criteria included training with virtual laboratory resources LearnSci sims and in-house vidoes, quizzes, in class practical work and independent experiment reporting. Moodle Badges smoothly integrated with the activities and assessments assigned for each skill development and importantly facilitated automatic badge award. Openbadges.me and Badgr.com were also key enabling digital tools used respectively for badge design, and back-packing and sharing badges as a digital passport or on a social media profile.

This paper will report on the integration of virtual laboratory training into undergraduate chemistry modules and the inclusion of such activities as one of a number of assessment components of a microskill-badge award system. It will share initial findings on the student perspective of the impact of virtual laboratory resources and the badging initiative on their technical experience, knowledge and confidence as well as on how it impacted on their wider appreciation of the value of said skills/competencies for employment.

Keywords:

Virtual Laboratories, micro-skills, digital badging, signposting and evidencing skills, enhancing awareness, employability, chemistry, STEM.

References

Abramovich, S., Schunn, C., & Higashi, R. M. (2013). Are badges useful in education?: It depends upon the type of badge and expertise of learner. *Educ. Technol. Res. Dev., 61*, 217-232. https://doi.org/10.1007/s11423-013-9289-2

Balci, S., Secaur, J. M., & Morris, B. J. (2022). Comparing the effectiveness of badges and leaderboards on academic performance and motivation of students in fully versus partially gamified online physics classes. *Educ. Inf. Technol., 27*(6), 8669-8704. https://doi.org/10.1007/s10639-022-10983-z

Braxton, S., Bohrer, J., Jacobson, T., Moore, K., Leuba, M., Proctor, C., & Reed, A. (2019). *7 Things You Should Know About Digital Badges*. Retrieved Feburary 2023 from https://library.educause.edu/resources/2019/7/7-things-you-should-know-about-digital-badges

Fulton, C. (2019). Innovating with Digital Badges in Assessment: A Case Study Using Digital Badges in an Undergraduate University Module. *AIJHE-J 11*.

Hennah, N., & Seery, M. K. (2017). Using Digital Badges for Developing High School Chemistry Laboratory Skills. *J. Chem. Ed., 94*(7), 844-848. https://doi.org/10.1021/acs.jchemed.7b00175

National Forum. (2019). *Towards a National Understanding of Student Success*. Retrieved February 2023 from https://hub.teachingandlearning.ie/resource/towards-a-national-understanding-of-student-success/

Noyes, J. A., Welch, P. M., Johnson, J. W., & Carbonneau, K. J. (2020). A systematic review of digital badges in health care education. *Med Educ, 54*(7), 600-615. https://doi.org/10.1111/medu.14060

Velasco-Torrijos, T., Heaney, F., Cleary, A., Joyce, O., Collery-Walsh, R., Stephens, J., & Elmes, R. (2022). *Maynooth University Teaching and Learning Fellowship.*

Virtual Laboratories in Higher Education. (2020). *The project is funded by the Higher Education Authority, The Department of Further and Higher Education, Research Innovation and Science, and the National Training Fund as part of the Human Capital Initiative Pillar 3 under project reference number [16698436].*

A CONCEPTUAL MODEL TO ADAPT MICROLEARNING TO DESIGN DIGITAL TEACHING AND LEARNING PROCESS IN HIGHER EDUCATION

Vindya Senadheera, University of Kelaniya, Sri Lanka / University of Peradeniya, Sri Lanka
Dileepa Ediriweera, Thilini Rupasinghe, University of Kelaniya, Sri Lanka

Abstract

Microlearning is an innovative pedagogy that is practiced in current higher education. It is the method of learning through small-sized, well-organized learning units and short-term learning activities (Hug, 2005; Allela, 2021). Each microlearning unit is designed to achieve a single learning objective (Wagner, 2002). A systematic review and meta-analysis conducted on the effects of microlearning in academic performance of students has showed a higher academic performance when microlearning is used compared to the traditional learning ($p = 0.03$). The overall mean difference in academic performance in relation to post-test scores in theoretical examinations between microlearning and traditional learning groups has been 12.6 (95% *CI*: 1.2 - 23.9) (Senadheera et al, 2022c). This can be attributed to reducing cognitive load, providing flexible learning environment, promoting self-directed learning and by providing timely feedback (Senadheera et al, 2022c). Currently, university teachers are working towards re-designing the traditional teaching and learning activities (TLA) to digital courses using digital pedagogies, to address the learning needs of current students. Undoubtedly, this digital transformation of formal higher education should be accompanied by a sound conceptual model to provide a meaningful education. The aim of this paper is to present a conceptual model to adapt microlearning to design digital teaching and learning process in higher education. A comprehensive analysis of literature was carried out in order to identify the components that should be integrated to adapt microlearning, to achieve the best outcomes in relation to performance and students' satisfaction. Accordingly, the 'CAA model' was designed which is presented in Figure 1.

Figure 1: CAA model to Adapt Microlearning to Design Digital Teaching and Learning Process in Higher Education

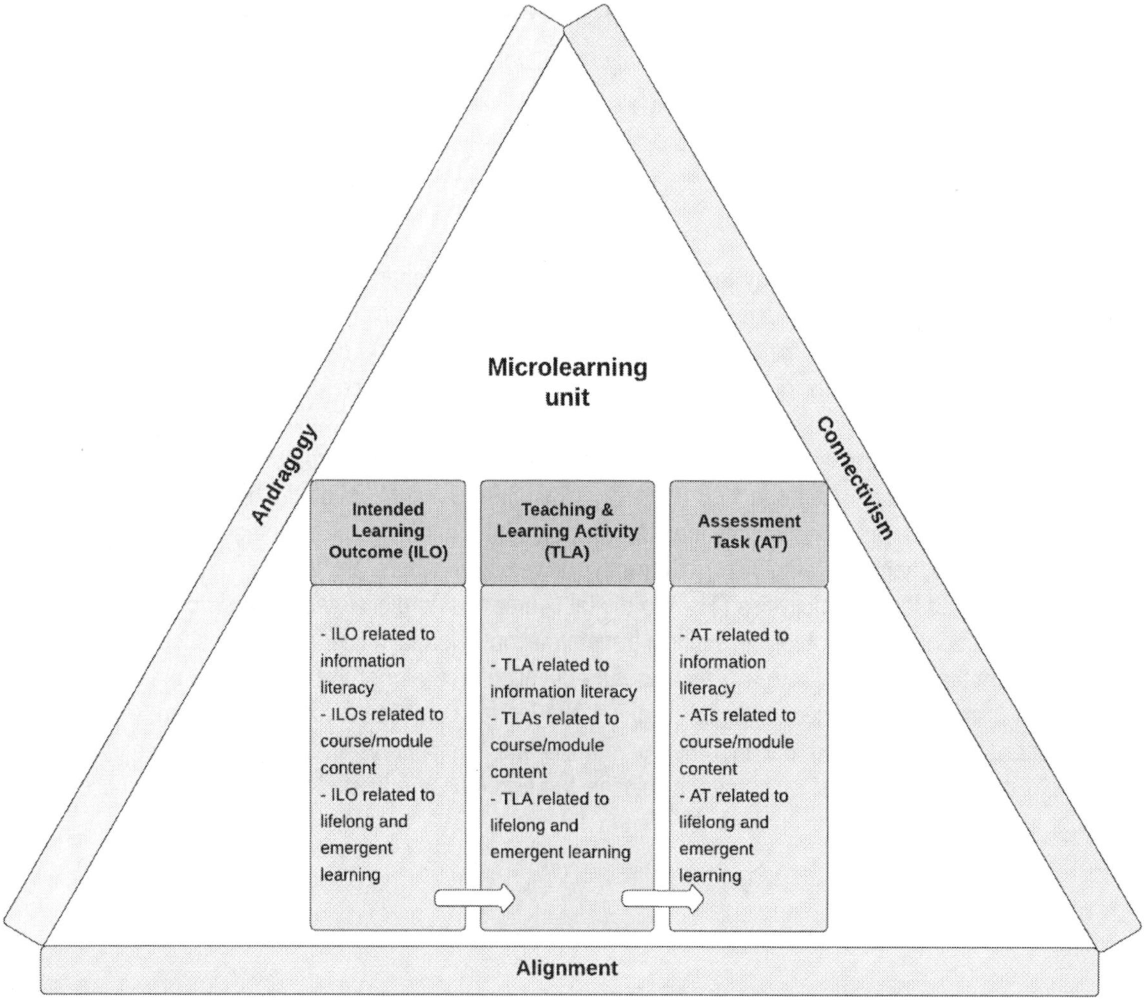

The following were identified as the main three design considerations of the proposed 'CAA model';

1. Connectivism
2. Alignment
3. Andragogy

Connectivism is a learning theory which explains how learning occurs in this digital age (Siemens, 2005). It was selected as the learning theory for the proposed framework because a scoping review we conducted showed that using connectivism to design T & L in higher education produces positive outcomes as; improve academic performance, foster creative thinking, enhance interactions with teachers and peers, promote collaborative learning, provide open and flexible learning environment, promote self-regulation of learning, facilitate action learning, improve problem solving and decision making skills, promote reflective practice and promote lifelong learning (Senadheera et al, 2022a). The integration of principles of connectivism in higher education has successfully incorporated informal learning into formal learning and enhanced skills required for emergent learning (Senadheera et al., 2022b). Therefore, in the 'CAA model', design of each microlearning object will be guided by principles of connectivism theory.

Alignment is a key principle in curriculum theory which states that assessment tasks should be aligned to what it is intended to be learned and with TLAs (Biggs and Tang, 2011). The principle of alignment was integrated in the proposed framework because the literature showed that alignment between intended learning objectives, T & L activities and assessment method produces effective T & L as it ensures maximum consistency throughout the process (Biggs and Tang, 2011). When defining the intended learning outcomes (ILOs), apart from the ILOs related to the content of the course, CAA model proposes to integrate the specific skills required for the success of digital learning. Accordingly, an ILO to enhance information literacy skills of students is proposed in order to assure that students have the competency to obtain, critically analyse, evaluate and effectively use information required for digital learning. Moreover, an ILO to enhance lifelong and emergent learning skills are proposed in the framework because the information in this digital age is rapidly evolving it should be assured that students are equipped with most updated information in their learning.

Andragogy explains how learning occurs in adults as learners (Knowles et al., 2005). Those principles are included in the framework as it was observed that, designing the microlearning lessons according to the adult learning principles can further enhance the positive impact of microlearning on students' academic performance in higher education (Major & Calandrino, 2018).

Keywords:

Connectivism, microlearning, andragogy, alignment, digital age.

Summary

The conceptual model presented in this paper provides an evidence-based outline to adapt microlearning to design digital T & L in higher education to achieve the best outcomes for the students in higher education in this digital age.

References

Allela, M. (2021). *Introduction to Microlearning.* https://oasis.col.org/colserver/api/core/bitstreams/07d80b84-b502-4ed4-8f9f-1504d4613084/content

Biggs, J. B., & Tang, C. (2011). *Teaching for quality learning at university* (4th ed.). Open University Press.

Hug, T. (2005). *Micro learning and narration. In fourth Media in Transition conference. 4048*, 6–8.

Knowles, M. S., Holton, E. F., & Swanson, R. A. (2005). The Adult Learner: The Definitive Classic in Adult Education and Human Resource Development. Oxfo. In *Industrial and Commercial Training* (Vol. 44, Issue 7).

Major, A., & Calandrino, T. (2018). Beyond chunking: Micro-learning secrets for effective online design. *FDLA Journal*, *3*(1), 13.

Senadheera, V., Muthukumarana, C., Rupasinghe, T., & Ediriweera, D. (2022a). Connectivism for improved learning outcomes in higher education in the digital age–A scoping review, 22nd International Postgraduate Research Conference, Faculty of Graduate Studies, University of Kelaniya Sri Lanka. 9.

Senadheera, V., Rupasinghe, T., & Ediriweera, D. (2022b). Connectivism for improved learning outcomes in higher education in the digital age–A scoping review [Manuscript submitted for publication]

Senadheera, V., Rupasinghe, T., & Ediriweera, D. (2022c). Impact of Microlearning on Academic Performance of Students in Higher Education: A Systematic Review and Meta-Analysis [Manuscript submitted for publication]

Siemens, G. (2005). Connectivism: A learning theory for the digital age, *International Journal of Instructional Technology and Distance Learning*, 2.

Wagner, E. (2002). Steps to creating a content strategy for your organization. *The ELearning Developers*, 103–117.

N-TUTORR – TRANSFORMING LEARNING & TEACHING ACROSS THE IRISH TECHNOLOGICAL HE SECTOR

Sharon Flynn, Seán O'Reilly, Technological Higher Education Association, Ireland

Abstract

This paper provides an overview of a transformative national programme across all technological HEIs in Ireland. The programme, financed by #NextGenerationEU funding, seeks to transform learning & teaching and the student experience by creating sustainable digital ecosystems that empower staff and students within a changing world. It will achieve this goal by: empowering students as active partners in transformation; by developing staff capabilities to support the transformation; and by investing in enabling digital infrastructure to increase flexibility and reduce barriers. A sector-wide partnership has developed, and is implementing, the programme in a unique collaboration of all technological institutions and the national representative association.

Keywords

Digital ecosystem, students, empowering learners, sustainable development goals, equality, diversity, inclusion, co-creation, student fellowship, champions, community of practice, academic integrity, universal design

Text

This paper outlines a major transformative national programme currently underway across the seven technological HEIs in Ireland. Ireland chose to invest €38m of #NextGenerationEU funding into the programme running from 2022 to 2024, designed to foster an inclusive digital education ecosystem for all learners in technological higher education. The programme explicitly acknowledges the intertwined nature of the digital ecosystem by focussing on multiple topics identified under this conference them of "Yes we can".

The N-TUTORR programme is focussed on transforming the student experience by empowering learners to become active partners in learning transformation; by developing the capabilities of all staff to address a sustainable pedagogical and learning environment; and by providing an enhanced digital ecosystem to enable these objectives. The programme is organised around three streams designed to enable the sector to achieve the goal of developing and implementing a major programme of work that demonstrates clear sectoral gains and digital transformation through collaborative engagement.

The programme builds on significant enhancements in learning, teaching and assessment capabilities which have been achieved within, and across, participating institutions over the past decade. Enhanced and 'future-proofed' digital ecosystems will act as enablers. They will support the technological sector to meet and address regional and national needs for digitisation, to cater for 21st-century learning and research, and to ensure that the sector is sufficiently equipped to deliver the returns on the national strategic policy for Higher Education.

The collaborative development and implementation of the programme is firmly based on evidence. The sector-wide evidence gathered as part of the "Next Steps for Teaching and Learning: Moving Forward Together" project coordinated by the Irish National Forum for the Enhancement of Teaching and Learning in Higher Education addressed key lessons learned during the pandemic. The national StudentSurvey.ie gathered specific data on students' experiences during the period of public health restrictions in addition to their overall experiences of higher education. The Technological Universities Research Network Report explicitly states the importance of state-of-the-art digital infrastructure and ICT provisions for the Technological sector.

The three work streams are:

- Transform the Student Experience through learner empowerment
- Transform Learning, Teaching and Assessment by Developing Staff Capabilities
- Enable Digital Ecosystems to transform Learning, Teaching and Assessment

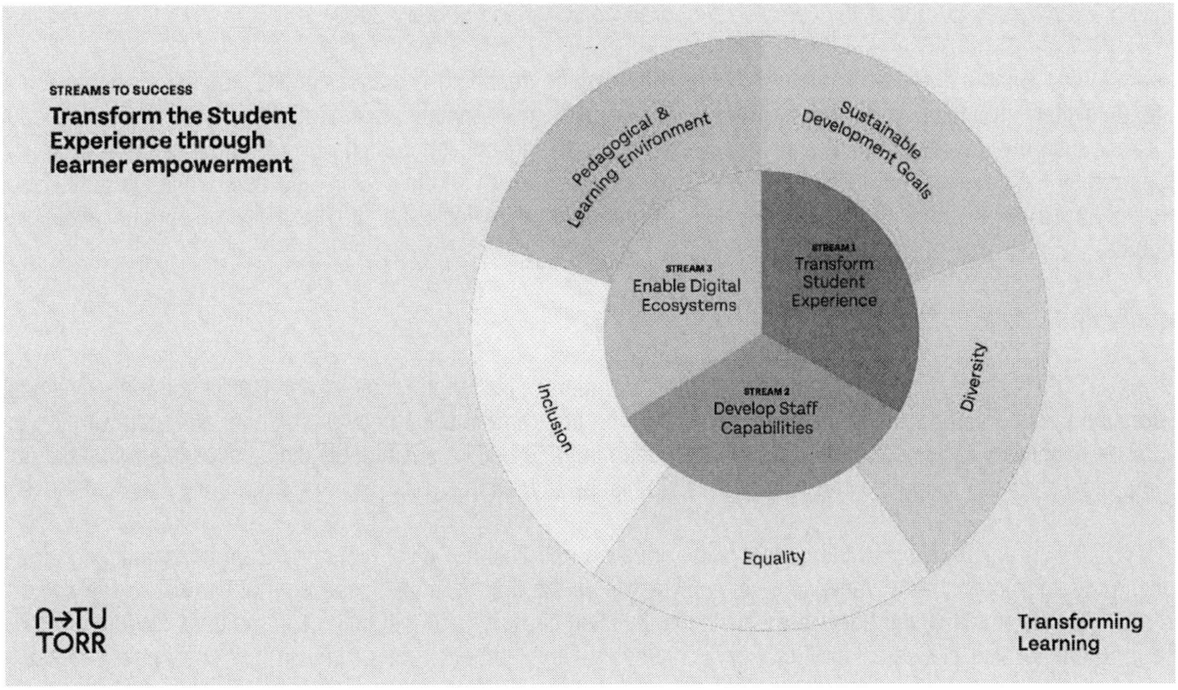

Figure 1: Overview of N-TUTORR programme

Structure of the overall programme

Stream one, "Transform the student experience though learner empowerment", addresses sustainable pathways to higher education, fostering a higher education ecosystem that is open to all. It includes design of a HyFlex foundation programme to empower prospective students with the digital capabilities, transferable skills and confidence to enter and succeed in higher education.

Two specific initiatives which aim to empower students and to demonstrate their as active partners are (i) student champions for promoting digital skills, education for sustainability, leadership & employability programme, and (ii) the Students as Partners in innovation and change fellowship programme. Under the student champions programme, one hundred Student Champions are being recruited to develop student engagement and empowerment in their local institution. Student champions are engaging with development of initiatives which address a specified list of thematic areas, namely: academic integrity, digital transformation in teaching and learning, education for sustainability, employability, equality diversity and inclusion (EDI), or universal design for learning (UDL).

Under the fellowship programme, 101 fellowships are being funded up to the value of €5000 each to enable students and staff to collaborate on small-scale enhancement projects that have an immediate impact on the student experience.

Stream two, "Transform learning, teaching and assessment by developing staff capabilities", is designed to support learners by the development of a sector-wide sustainable higher education curriculum framework. The main activities contained in this workstream relate to the establishment of sector-wide communities of practice to collaboratively build staff capacity, including the identification of academic champions for sustainable higher education futures; development of the curriculum framework and its integration into the curriculum of partner institutions; and formalisation of a consistent system to promote and recognise staff continuing professional development. A series of online masterclasses to support the community of practice began in February 2023.

Stream three, "Enable digital ecosystems to transform learning, teaching and assessment", focuses on provision of a suite of digital infrastructure enhancements to address: digitally-enabled examination / assessment embedding academic integrity; the embedding and mainstreaming of hybrid and on-campus digital enhancement approaches supported by the development of 'state of play ' and policy papers to inform sector-wide approaches to these issues; and enhanced deployment of institutional digital infrastructure to increase the flexibility of options available to students.

Conclusion

The N-TUTORR programme is an ambitious element of Ireland's National Recovery and Resilience Plan, which aims to transform learning and teaching for a digital world. The programme will empower students and staff with the tools and skills necessary to develop new ways of digital learning and build a sustainable digital ecosystem that caters for an improved student experience and equal access to higher education.

N-TUTORR is a unique sector-wide collaboration, involving all Technological higher education institutions in Ireland working together to ensure a whole sectoral approach. It is the first of many initiatives that will shape the sector for the next generation, changing how we do business, building capacity and fostering collaborations for future projects. The programme also places a key focus on Sustainable Development Goals, and on key challenges arising with respect to equality, access, community, and climate change.

References

National Forum for the Enhancement of Teaching and Learning, "Next Steps for Teaching and Learning: Moving Forward Together", https://www.teachingandlearning.ie/VITAL/nextsteps/#!/inav

Irish Survey of Student Engagement (Studentsurvey.ie) Interim Results Bulletin 2021, https://studentsurvey.ie/reports/studentsurveyie-interim-results-bulletin-2021

Technological Universities: Connectedness and Collaboration through Connectivity (October 2019). Report of the Technological Universities Research Network to the Department of Education and Skills. https://hea.ie/technological_universities/tu-research-network-turn/

COLLABORATION TO CREATE A MICRO-CREDENTIAL ECOSYSTEM

Jools O'Connor, Emma Francis, David Corscadden, Irish Universities Association, Ireland

Abstract

Collaboration is at the heart of the Irish Universities Association (IUA)-led MicroCreds project in Ireland. Our vision is to empower lifelong learning in Ireland by re-imagining the learner's relationship with education through agile, accessible and bite-sized qualifications. By working collaboratively with our university partners, our funders, enterprise, and external development agencies we are delivering on our four key strands through:

- Developing a National Framework for micro-credentials that recognises variance across the universities, enabling each to develop a portfolio consistent with its own strengths and missions and within its own enterprise eco-system and regional context.
- Setting up and delivering a sustainable model of data-informed university and enterprise collaboration through MicroCreds Innovate. We have developed a structured process for meaningful and ongoing collaboration with enterprise. Our Enterprise Advisory Group has a wide range of diverse enterprises, covering priority sectors and including SME representation, ensures enterprise-informed development, increasing the universities' capacity to anticipate, understand and respond to emerging skills needs. MicroCreds has been strengthened by harnessing local and regional university-enterprise links, including existing networks such as the Regional Skills Fora and Chambers of Commerce, as well as through targeted events.
- Creating a dedicated website featuring micro-credentials from our 7 partner universities to accelerate increased awareness, understanding and engagement with micro-credentials. The website will also have a promotion function to help grow the potential market regionally, nationally and beyond.
- Supporting partner universities to create an agilely developed and flexibly delivered suite of micro-credentials. Micro-credentials developed at partner IUA universities are setting the national standard for excellence in flexible and agile learning. Several partner universities are delivering cross-referenced linked projects under the Human Capital Initiative (HCI) Pillar 3 funding programme with ambitious plans for micro-credentials and flexible lifelong learning, MicroCreds is complimentary to such aligned lifelong learning-focused projects.

The HCI Pillar 3 state funding for MicroCreds has enabled significant developments to be made within our partner universities. Research from the OECD (2021) found that governments 'see the value of micro-credentials in upskilling and reskilling the labour force and widening access to higher education and that substantial investments have already been made by some governments across the OECD to increase the offering and uptake of micro-credentials'. The investment made in the development of systems, processes and procedures in our universities here in Ireland has been instrumental in the creation and delivery of hundreds of micro-credentials and has empowered our partner universities with the critical infrastructure needed for sustained success.

The creation of MicroCreds has enabled the sharing of best practice across our partner universities, who benefit from learning from each other in multiple cross-linked areas including teaching and learning, student recruitment and communications, and administrative systems and practices. MicroCreds centrally undertakes reviews and reporting on many aspects of the development, promotion and delivery of micro-credentials and our governance and working groups provide opportunities to disseminate findings and discuss successful impacts for shared best practice for the benefit of all our partner universities.

Keywords:

Micro-credentials, Lifelong Learning, Skills, Higher Education, Policy Development, Flexible learning, Short courses, Credentials

Introduction

Research into the Need for Micro-Credentials in Ireland

The labour market in Ireland is rapidly changing and the demand for upskilling and reskilling from both employers and employees is high. The National Skills Strategy 2025 aims to improve the relevance of skills provision to society and the economy and to secure more effective engagement with employers in skills development, improving the national rate of lifelong learning. To inform the MicroCreds project proposal, the IUA commissioned research on the provision of upskilling and reskilling opportunities in Ireland. The findings of this research showed that there was an opportunity to improve the capacity of Irish enterprise to better acquire the skills of the future.

As identified in the EUA's Trends 2018 report (Gaebel, 2018), there is a growing demand for flexible higher education across the European Higher Education Area. The OECD (2021) identified multiple providers of micro-credentials across both the higher education sector and private providers. The OECD also found multiple descriptions of micro-credentials, further complicating the marketplace for potential learners. This indicates that there is a strong need for a coherent national system of quality assured and accredited micro-credentials.

The MicroCreds project was created in response to multiple reports and frameworks calling for the development of future skills needs, including:

- The 2018-2020 HEA System Performance Framework: to provide a strong talent pipeline combining knowledge, skills & employability which responds effectively to the needs of our enterprise.
- Project Ireland 2040, National Strategic Outcome 5: A Strong Economy, supported by Enterprise, Innovation and Skills, facilitating re-skilling and reinvention of the existing workforce.
- Future Jobs Ireland 2019 deliverables including: doubling the participation in lifelong learning to 18% by 2025; promoting flexible training options; matching training to the skills needs of workers and enterprises.

The MicroCreds Project

MicroCreds is a 5-year €12.3 Million national project in Ireland, led by the IUA and delivered in partnership with each of the seven founding IUA universities (University College Dublin, Dublin City University, Trinity College Dublin, University of Limerick, Maynooth University, University of Galway and University College Cork). The project funding was awarded under HCI Pillar 3, with funding drawn from the National Training Fund. It was vital to receive this funding, which has empowered and enabled our partner universities to develop the systems, processes and procedures needed to deliver flexible courses which require a different set up to the traditional full-time undergraduate and postgraduate courses.

Main Findings

The MicroCreds project is currently at its mid-point and work to-date has provided insights in terms of funding, project outputs and the importance of collaboration.

Collaboration is at the heart of the micro-credentials project in Ireland. By working collaboratively with our university partners, our funders, enterprise, and external development agencies we are delivering on our four key project strands through:

- A National Framework for micro-credentials that recognises variance across the universities, enabling each to develop a programme consistent with its own strengths and missions and within its own enterprise eco-system and regional context.
- A sustainable model of data informed university and enterprise collaboration through MicroCreds Innovate. We have developed a structured process for meaningful and ongoing collaboration with enterprise.
- A website featuring micro-credentials from our partner universities to increase awareness, understanding and engagement with micro-credentials. The website also has a promotion function to help grow the potential market.
- Partner universities creating agilely developed and flexibly delivered micro-credentials.

The government funding received for the MicroCreds project enabled significant developments to be made within our partner universities. Research from the OECD (2021) found that governments 'see the value of micro-credentials in upskilling and reskilling the labour force and widening access to higher education and that substantial investments have already been made by some governments across the OECD to increase the offering and uptake of micro-credentials'. The investment made in the development of systems, processes, and procedures in partner universities in Ireland has been instrumental in the creation and delivery of hundreds of micro-credentials and has set up partner universities with the infrastructure needed for continued success.

The creation of MicroCreds has enabled the sharing of best practice across our partner universities who benefit from learning from each other in multiple areas including teaching and learning, student recruitment and communications, and administrative systems and practices. The project undertakes reviews and reporting on many aspects of the development, promotion and delivery of micro-credentials and our governance and working groups provide an opportunity to disseminate the findings and discuss successful impacts for shared best practice.

Conclusion

Our future vision for is for micro-credentials to be a recognised, accepted and invaluable part of lifelong learning in Ireland. The EU's Education and Training Strategic Framework sets out the strategic objective to make lifelong learning a reality and improve the quality and efficiency of education and training. One of the targets under this Framework is at least 47% of adults aged 25-64 should have participated in learning during the last 12 months by 2025. The continued expansion of micro-credentials can assist Ireland to meet its European and international benchmarks.

The impact of MicroCreds is transformative across our partner universities and is scalable across the entire national higher education system. The necessary innovative infrastructure created supports a step change in the rapid development and roll-out of flexible and agile education. The outcomes of the MicroCreds project will provide a basis for meaningful higher education system change to support skills development across enterprise and throughout the workforce in Ireland.

We also believe that there are policy implications that need to be addressed. One of the outcomes from the OECD (2021) research found that 'The actions of providers and governments will shape the extent to which micro-credentials are offered by higher education providers. It is crucial that micro-credentials are valued by the government and are supported through necessary policy developments and associated opportunities to fund future developments and access to courses.

References

The EU's Education and Training Strategic Framework https://education.ec.europa.eu/about-eea/strategic-framework

Future Jobs Ireland 2019 https://enterprise.gov.ie/en/publications/publication-files/future-jobs-ireland-2019.pdf

Gaebel, M. and Zhang, T., (2018) Trends 2018: Learning and teaching in the European Higher Education Area

The 2018-2020 HEA System Performance Framework https://hea.ie/assets/uploads/2018/01/higher-education-system-performance-framework-2018-2020.pdf

IBEC (July 2022) Future of the National Training Fund

Ireland's National Skills Strategy 2025 https://www.gov.ie/pdf/?file=https://assets.gov.ie/137349/3b66360a-64f4-45db-881f-eb326950051e.pdf#page=null

National Training Fund https://www.gov.ie/en/organisation-information/b3753-national-training-fund/

OECD (2021), "Micro-credential innovations in higher education: Who, What and Why?", OECD Education Policy Perspectives, No. 39, OECD Publishing, Paris, https://doi.org/10.1787/f14ef041-en.

OECD (2021), "Quality and value of micro-credentials in higher education: Preparing for the future", OECD Education Policy Perspectives, No. 40, OECD Publishing, Paris, https://doi.org/10.1787/9c4ad26d-en.

Project Ireland 2040 www.gov.ie/2040/

CAN A MOBILE APP HELP CREATE VIRTUAL LEARNING SPACES AND COMMUNITIES OF PRACTICE FOR STUDENTS AND TUTORS?

Irene O'Dowd, Hibernia College, Ireland; Janet Benson, Learnovate @ Trinity College Dublin, Ireland

Abstract

Engagement and collaboration can be challenging in the online learning space, a fact that was highlighted during the COVID-19 pandemic. As a leading provider of postgraduate blended-learning programmes, Hibernia College is cognisant of the challenges of creating authentic social-learning opportunities for online learners. In 2020 we launched a collaboration app for students and tutors, leveraging ubiquitous mobile technology to enhance the creation of virtual Communities of Practice (vCoPs) and virtual learning spaces. The platform, developed in partnership with a technology company, Moxo, provides workspaces and features to encourage online communication and collaboration.

The current research project, a collaboration between Hibernia College and Learnovate @ Trinity College, explores the impact of the app on students' and teachers' collaborative learning practices. Surveys and focus groups were conducted to investigate use of and attitude towards the app and explore whether use of the app had changed over time. Findings indicate that several factors influenced app use, including familiarity, perceived usefulness versus other platforms, and expectations for its use as part of the educational experience. Training on platform use was an important factor for teachers.

Further investigation continues, and we anticipate interesting outcomes from a comparative analysis of engagement by different groups over time.

Keywords:

Collaboration, engagement, learning technology, digital education, mobile app, virtual learning spaces, virtual communities of practice (vCoP)

References:

Dubé, L., Bourhis, A., Jacob, R., & Koohang, A. (2006). Towards a typology of virtual communities of practice. *Interdisciplinary Journal of Information, Knowledge & Management, 1.*

Johnson, C. M. (2001). A survey of current research on online communities of practice. *The internet and higher education, 4*(1), 45-60.

THE PURDUE REPOSITORY FOR ONLINE TEACHING AND LEARNING (PORTAL)

Jennifer Richardson, Wanju Huang, Purdue University, USA

Abstract

Online course enrollment has continued to grow steadily over the past decade (Seaman et al., 2018), mandating a need for ready-to-teach-online instructors. There is, however, a lack of professional development for faculty and graduate instructors in teaching. Taken together, this demonstrates a critical need to offer easy-access, on-the-job, and self-paced support to online instructors who want to enhance their online teaching skills. To fill this gap, *PoRTAL* (Purdue Repository for online Teaching and Learning) was created to offer support to instructors, graduate teaching assistants, and those new to online teaching and learning by providing evidence-based practices for online teaching and learning. The project scope was designed to transcend beyond the institutional level by implementing an Open Educational Resource (OER) approach so our digital repository of resources would be freely available to those outside of the institution, to serve practitioners interested in online teaching and learning globally.

The *PoRTAL* digital repository is a project that involves partners from across the campus: Teaching and Learning Technologies, Center for Instructional Excellence, Digital Education, and Purdue Libraries, spearheaded by faculty and students from the Learning Design and Technology program. The repository includes online teaching strategies, online learning resources, and tips for execution. The Tier 1 (just-in-time) resources on *PoRTAL*, provide 28 job aids that are categorized according to users' needs (e.g., instructor strategies, course design, course enhancement). Each Tier 1 resource is presented in a standardized format including the following information:

- What is it? – Definitions
- Why is it important? – Why is it important? - Background information and related research highlights
- How to do it? - With tips and tricks as a subsection
- Tools - Recommendations for tools that can be useful for applying the topic in online courses
- Additional Resources - Readings or websites that provide practical information
- References - Those cited in the document

Most of the tools, readings, and resources identified are free and openly available for anyone to use, allowing Tier 1 resources to be accessible to audiences beyond Purdue University. Since *PoRTAL* was launched in Spring 2019, it has generated more than 11,991 unique pageviews with users from the United States, South America, Europe, Asia, and Africa. Institutions worldwide (e.g., Cornell University) have recommended the *PoRTAL* page on their websites. The job aids available on *PoRTAL* have had more than 6,700 unique downloads. Numerous positive comments were shared by the users. For example, "A lot of general and in-depth information on teaching online. Helpful when I am also mentoring others who are teaching online courses with me." "[PoRTAL is] a resource to colleagues new to teaching, primer for designing online course activities, assessing student learning."

In this paper, we will discuss the *PoRTAL* resources, the design and development processes, as well as the review and evaluation procedure followed to ensure the quality of the repository.

Keywords:

Learning design, online teaching, open educational resource

Reference

Seaman, J. E., Allen, I. E., & Seaman, J. (2018). Grade increase: Tracking distance education in the United States. *Babson Survey Research Group*.

SPACE, HARDWARE, SOFTWARE; CONSIDERATIONS FOR DESIGNING AND BUILDING A ROOM FOR ONLINE TEACHING

Peter Windle, South East Technological University, Ireland

Abstract

This talk details the journey and decisions made on the path to creating four new media rooms, which we have called Pods, for delivering online classes in South East Technological University's (SETU) Department of Computing and Mathematics.

This Department has grown the number of fully online modules with over 50 online contact hours in any given week. This had place significant demand on existing resources in the Pods based in SETU's Centre for Technology Enhanced Learning (CTEL) for delivery of synchronous and asynchronous classes.

In 2021, SETU's Capital Projects Office initiated the project with the Department and requested the CTEL's assistance based on their experience in creating their own online pods.

This talk discusses the various considerations and solutions utilised on the project across several key areas including:

1. requirements gathering
2. physical requirements and constraints in the room selected for development
3. construction
4. selection of hardware used in the room
5. software used
6. booking
7. budget
8. fitout

This talk may be useful for anyone who may be considering creating or improving a space for delivering synchronous or asynchronous classes.

Keywords:

Online, synchronous, asynchronous, streaming, zoom, recording.

PREPARING DIGITAL MICRO-CREDENTIALS FOR THE UNIVERSITY

Elena Trepule, Giedre Tamoliune, Estela Dauksiene, Airina Volungeviciene, Vytautas Magnus University, Lithuania

Abstract

This paper is based on the research project supported by the Lithuanian Research Council. The aim of the project is to describe and create the process of issuing micro-credentials in higher education or to model processes that would allow learners to convey their new competencies from HE to employers through micro-credentials, and to link them to the Europass micro-credential infrastructure.

The project offers fourfold results: (1) theoretical research paper explaining the process of integration of digital micro-credentials into the study process revealing their potential to foster social, economic and higher education innovations and contribution to the sustainable post COVID - 19 pandemic recovery (Tamoliune et al, 2023). (2) Content and technical specification of the process of micro-credentialization, that includes: (a) a template model of the digital and micro-credential and its meta-data fields; (b) a template of open learning opportunity description that is harmonized with and meta-data fields. Both a template model of the digital and micro-credential and a template of an open learning opportunity are matched with the European union digital infrastructure for micro-credentialization. (3) Compilation of documents for the open learning environment ready for the process of micro-credentialization and technically adapted and prepared to issue micro-credentials that meet requirements of the technical specification (result No 2): adapting learning opportunity description form following content and technical specification and preparing a prototype of university micro-credential. (4) The piloting record of digital and micro-credentials issuing process. This last result of the project will maintain the records taken during the implementation of micro-credentialization (as the process) in VMU: registering the descriptions of learning opportunities in the Europass and piloting the issuing of micro-credential for at least 5 courses as open learning opportunities.

Keywords:

Digital micro-credentials, university, micro-credentialization

References

Tamoliune, G., Greenspon, R., Volungeviciene, A., Tereseviciene, M., Trepule, E., Dauksiene, E. (2023). Exploring the potential of micro-credentials: A systematic literature review. *Frontiers in Education.* https://doi.org/10.3389/feduc.2022.1006811

This project has received funding from European Regional Development Fund (project no 13.1.1-LMT-K-718-05-0003) under grant agreement with the Research Council of Lithuania (LMTLT). Funded as European Union's measure in response to COVID-19 pandemic.

BEYOND ALLOWING THE DISADVANTAGED IN: MIGRATORY BACKGROUND LEARNERS' EXPERIENCES WITH ONLINE HIGHER EDUCATION

Gemma Xarles-Jubany, UOC & Lancaster University, Spain & UK, Kyungmee Lee, Lancaster University, UK

Abstract

Around 272 million worldwide are international migrants, representing 3.5 per cent of the global population (IOM, 2019). The importance of resuming studies, particularly in higher education (HE), to gain knowledge and skills for employability, develop a voice and foster successful integration has been widely documented (Arar et al., 2019; UNESCO, 2019). Nevertheless, migrants have often been perceived as unskilled and HE has not been offered to them (Arar et al., 2019). Migrants who have tried to enrol have faced various barriers, effectively discouraging them from participating in HE (UNESCO IESALC, 2020).

In 2016, the United Nations General Assembly adopted the New York Declaration for Refugees and Migrants, committing Member States to protect the human right of all migrants (UN DESA, 2017) and urging universities to provide online HE opportunities to migrants worldwide (UNHCR, 2016). Since then, the number of online initiatives targeting this profile of students has been growing. Such rapid growth has mistakenly been considered evidence for the increased accessibility of HE. However, improving accessibility is a complex and multidimensional issue beyond providing university entrance (Lee, 2017). According to Levin (2007), providing authentic access to educational institutions means accommodating students by recognising their prior situations and needs, thus allowing them to benefit from their institutional experiences.

This qualitative inquiry aims to develop a more comprehensive understanding of the accessibility of online HE drawn from the lived experiences of migratory background learners' experiences with participating in a specific online HE setting. We conducted life history interviews with thirteen alumni with diverse migratory backgrounds who completed a fully online bachelor's degree between 2017 and July 2021 at the Open University of Catalonia (UOC). Our proposed presentation will focus on the experiences of one sub-group who arrived in Catalonia in their late childhood or adolesce, each from Africa (Morocco), Asia (India) and East and non-EU Europe (Ukraine). The presentation will share a range of factors that have influenced the three participants' academic journey, based on which the accessibility of online HE will be reconceptualised. Additionally, we will suggest strategies that could be put in place to better support this profile of students in the context of open universities.

Keywords:

Migrant students, online higher education, authentic accessibility, biographical narratives, Open University of Catalonia.

References

Arar, K., Haj-Yehia, K., Ross, D., & Kondakci, Y. (Eds.). (2019). Higher Education Challenges for Migrant and Refugee Students in a Global World. Peter Lang Publishing, Incorporated.

IOM. (2019). World Migration Report 2020. In European Journal of Political Research Political Data Yearbook (Issue 1, pp. 1–498). International Organization for Migration (IOM).

Lee. (2017). Rethinking the accessibility of online higher education: A historical review. Internet and Higher Education, 33, 15–23.

Levin, J. S. (2007). Nontraditional students and community. Palgrave Macmillan.

UN DESA. (2017). International Migration Report: 2017 (p. 38). United Nations Department of Economic and Social Affairs.

UNESCO. (2019). Migration, displacement and education: Building Bridges, Not Walls (Global Education Monitoring Report) (pp. 2–438). UNESCO Publishing.

UNESCO IESALC. (2020). Towards universal access to higher education: International trends. UNESCO IESALC.

UNHCR. (2016). Aiming Higher—The other one per cent. UNHCR Education Report 2016.

QUALITY ASSURANCE OF MICRO-CREDENTIALS: AN INTERNATIONAL REVIEW OF CURRENT PRACTICES

Mark Brown, Dublin City University, Ireland; Josep M. Duart, Universität Oberta de Catalunya, Spain

Abstract

This paper reports the findings of a worldwide analysis of quality assurance frameworks, processes and practices for micro-credentials. It is framed by last year's formal Council Recommendation to adopt a European approach to micro-credentials for lifelong learning and employability (European Commission, 2022). The research draws on a wider study on the quality assurance of digital higher education recently undertaken by the Organisation for Economic Co-operation and Development (OECD) (Staring, et al., 2022) and was designed to investigate whether micro-credentials raise specific quality assurance considerations. The methodology involved desk research and follow-up discussions with key actors to answer three main questions. Firstly, the study asks how national quality assurance agencies in OECD member countries are externally assuring the quality of micro-credentials. Secondly, it investigates what internal quality assurance practices have early adopter higher education institutions (HEIs) developed to implement micro-credentials. Lastly, the research seeks to find what institutional supports, resources, and infrastructures are available to develop micro-credentials.

The research findings reveal three categories of responses to micro-credentials by national quality assurance agencies:

- No specific quality assurance response
- Intentional adoption of existing frameworks and common standards
- Development of specific quality assurance indicators and processes for micro-credentials.

Based on this third category, the paper discusses several quality assurance considerations specific to micro-credentials, especially when offered through an online study mode. At the institutional level, the research found that publicly available information on internal quality assurance practices varies greatly across OECD member jurisdictions, with the most mature or explicit processes found in Australian universities. In the Irish and wider European context, an important weakness is identified in current publicly available information on internal institutional quality assurance practices. To help increase awareness of specific quality assurance considerations for micro-credentials, we highlight several additional issues as more HEIs look to plan, execute and implement their institutional strategies. These issues support the assumption that realising the full potential of micro-credentials will require important changes to quality assurance and academic recognition policies (Kato, Gyorfi & Weko, 2023). Finally, the paper shares several regional, national and European-wide efforts to support the development of resources, infrastructure and communities of practice to help HEIs develop and offer high-quality micro-credentials. These efforts highlight the value of nationally coordinated pilots and development projects, and the role European University Alliances are playing both directly and indirectly in maturing the understanding of quality assurance for micro-credentials.

Keywords:

OECD, micro-credentials, quality assurance, quality assurance agencies, online learning

References

European Commission. (2022). *Council recommendation of 16 June 2022 on a European approach to micro-credentials for lifelong learning and employability.* Brussels. https://eur-lex.europa.eu/legal-content/EN/TXT/?uri=uriserv:OJ.C_.2022.243.01.0010.01.ENG

Kato, S., Gyorfi, R., & Weko, T. (2023). *Micro-credentials for lifelong learning and employability: Uses and possibilities.* OECD, Paris. ISSN: 22260943 (online) https://doi.org/10.1787/5cc2d673-en

Staring, F., Brown, M., Bacsich, P., & Ifenthaler, D. (2022). Digital higher education: Emerging quality standards, practices and supports. OECD Education Working Papers, No. 281, OECD Publishing, Paris. https://doi.org/10.1787/f622f257-en.

BETWEEN THE ROCKS AND HARD PLACES: EXPLORING THE EXPERIENCES OF EDUCATIONAL TECHNOLOGY LEADERS

Gerry Gallagher, Dundalk Institute of Technology, Ireland; Mark Brown, Enda Donlon, Dublin City University, Ireland

Abstract

Leadership at many levels is required to more fully integrate educational technology into higher education practice. However, there is a dearth of empirical research in "educational technology leadership", located at the intersection of educational leadership and educational technology (Arnold & Sangrà, 2018; Jameson, 2013). In particular, little is known about the experiences of educational technology leaders, who work in the "middle" of their institutions and yet play a crucial role in leading change (Browne & Beetham, 2010).

This paper reports on a doctoral study which seeks to address this gap by examining the experiences of these leaders, including their perceptions of leadership, the approaches they find most effective, the challenges they encounter and the supports they identify to further enable their endeavours. Employing Narrative Inquiry (Smith et al., 2009) as the overarching methodology, the study consists of two phases, an online survey of educational technology leaders in Irish higher education and semi-structured interviews with ten middle educational technology leaders in the Irish Institute of Technology/Technological University sector.

Although seeing their roles more in terms of change agency than leadership, their practices clearly position them as leaders, relying primarily on influence rather than any formal positional authority. The leadership exemplified by these leaders embodies a congruence that encompasses a number of key dimensions. This congruence is central to their credibility and ability to influence. It is crucial, then, that this seldom acknowledged leadership be recognised, valued, and nurtured.

In addition, coherent institution-wide approaches where vision, strategy, policies, and actions are aligned can further enhance the efforts of these leaders so that institutions may move beyond small-scale incremental change to institution-wide integration.

The study provides insights into these educational technology roles for current and future educational technology leaders, senior higher education leaders, and the wider higher education community as they address the shared challenge of integrating technology into practice.

References

Arnold, D., & Sangrà, A. (2018). Dawn or dusk of the 5th age of research in educational technology? A literature review on (e-)leadership for technology-enhanced learning in higher education (2013-2017). *International Journal of Educational Technology in Higher Education, 15*(1), 15–44. https://doi.10.1186/s41239-018-0104-3

Browne, T., & Beetham, H. (2010). *The positioning of educational technologists in enhancing the student experience* (An ALT Occasional Publication). Association for Learning Technology (ALT).

Jameson, J. (2013). e-Leadership in higher education: The fifth "age" of educational technology research. *British Journal of Educational Technology, 44*(6), 889–915. https://doi.org/10.1111/bjet.12103

Smith, J. A., Flowers, P., & Larkin, M. (2009). *Interpretative phenomenological analysis: Theory, method and research.* Los Angeles : SAGE.

"SEX FROM MOLECULES TO ELEPHANTS" – LESSONS FROM PRODUCING AND TEACHING AN INNOVATIVE MOOC

Michael Brandeis, The Hebrew University of Jerusalem, Israel

Abstract

Engaging students in MOOCs (massive online open courses) has been a major challenge ever since their introduction more than a decade ago (Reich & Ruipérez-Valiente 2019). The completion rates of most MOOCs is unfortunately exceedingly low posing a big question mark over this promising novel teaching method. This talk will describe how we conceived and produced a highly innovative MOOC, teaching science to thousands of non-science university students while achieving a successful completion rate of above 90%. To engage learners intellectually and emotionally we combined carefully written narratives that "tell a story" with videos we shot in some of the wildest and most beautiful locations in the world. By learning about reproduction, students are taught cell biology, genetics, evolution, animal behavior and gain important insights into conservation and awareness to environmental issues. In this talk I will share the process of production from the initial ideas to final product and describe challenges faced and experiences gained. We collected detailed engagement data for all students for all 60 videos of the course, all 40 quizzes and all five assignments students had to post in a forum or social media. In addition, we have detailed feedback forms from more than 6000 students with numerical and free text feedback. Using this extensive amount of data we shed light on how to effectively teach online in a large university setting as well as in smaller high school classes.

Keywords:

Asynchronous online teaching, student engagement, MOOC, Environmental awareness

References

Reich, J. & Ruipérez-Valiente J.A. (2019). The MOOC pivot. *Science 363,130-131.DOI:10.1126/science.aav7958*

HARNESSING THE POTENTIAL OF LEARNING ANALYTICS: YES OF COURSE WE CAN!

Motasem Al Haj Ali, Rob Lowney, Mark Brown, Dublin City University, Ireland

Abstract

The field of learning analytics has matured considerably over the past decade (Khalil et al., 2022). However, significant challenges remain at an institution-wide level in translating the theoretical potential of harnessing meaningful data on teaching, learning and assessment into routine and systemic practices which inform and contribute to tangible actions and improvements for learners. For the purpose of this paper, 'learning analytics' is defined as a field that involves the measurement, collection, analysis, and reporting of data about learners, and their situated educational contexts, to understand and optimise learning and the environments in which it occurs (Siemens & Long, 2011).

The unique contribution of this paper is to demonstrate how one higher education institution (HEI) is responding to the above challenge by using and adapting existing analytics tools in Moodle to produce meaningful reports and useful dashboards for quality enhancement. It shares some of the built-in and customised reports that have been developed to help connect the dots and extract log data available through Moodle to illustrate how we have managed to make it work despite the limitations of functionality. More specifically, the paper describes how we have been able to waggle student feedback data collected through Moodle to successfully support faculties in meeting their high-stakes reporting and accreditation requirements. Effectively using student feedback data for quality enhancement is an established benefit of learning analytics (Mian et al., 2022). The initiative shared in this paper also has the potential to improve transparency, inform institutional strategies that engage more learners in providing constructive feedback on the quality of their learning experience, and, importantly, help to close the student evaluation loop.

We report future enhancement plans, including investing more in our existing capability and establishing a data warehouse to provide stronger technical infrastructure. Finally, the paper draws on the seven factors that Ferguson et al. (2019) claim must be taken into account when implementing learning analytics to help critically reflect on the challenges that still need to be addressed at an institutional level.

Keywords:

Learning analytics, Moodle, student evaluation, quality enhancement

References

Ferguson, R., Clow, D., Griffiths, D., & Brasher, A. (2019). Moving forward with learning analytics: Expert views. *Journal of Learning Analytics, 6(3),* 43–59. http://dx.doi.org/10.18608/jla.2019.63.8

Khalil, M., Prinsloo, P., & Slade, S. (2022). The use and application of learning theory in learning analytics: A scoping review. *Journal of Computing in Higher Education,* https://doi.org/10.1007/s12528-022-09340-3

Mian, Y., Khalid, F., Qun, A., & Ismail, S. (2022). Learning analytics in education, Advantages and issues: A systematic literature review. *Creative Education, 13,* 2913-2920. doi: 10.4236/ce.2022.139183.

Siemens, G., & Long, P. (2011). Penetrating the fog: Analytics in learning and education. *EDUCAUSE Review, 46,* 31-40.

WHAT CAN WE LEARN FROM A SPECIAL LEARNING EXPERIENCE?

Yuhong Lei, Jan McArthur, Lancaster University, UK

Abstract

Since the internationalisation of higher education is a fast-growing phenomenon, universities worldwide, especially in the USA and UK, account for a large portion of the international student population globally (Yu & Moskal, 2019). However, under the massive pressure of the COVID-19 pandemic, higher education institutions have moved most teaching activities online (Peimani & Kamalipour, 2021). Under such circumstances, it is hard to stimulate students' learning experiences to meet their expectations of higher education (Marinoni et al., 2020). During the pandemic, many international students, including international PGRs chose to remain in the UK due to reasons such as tightened border-security measures by many nation-states that closed their borders and curtailed international flights. Such a situation proved to be more difficult for international students who lack the support of their families (Cornelson & Miloucheva, 2020). Yet, there has been less attention paid to the learning experiences of international PGRs' in the UK, especially during the pandemic, even though they account for a significant portion of students in the UK.

Therefore, the authors believe it is important to explore the experiences of international postgraduate researchers and examine questions such as: were they isolated in their own accommodations or rented houses, how did they pursue and make the most of their learning, what social activities did they engage in during the lockdown, were they able to access study spaces on campus instead of the ones they otherwise used to study at, and how did they deal with their separation from the learning community and learning resources. Further, it is also important to inquire how the lockdown influenced their learning experiences and connections with others on campus, and what has been the quality of their education with the online learning environment.

To answer these questions, the author conducted a study during the lockdowns between June and July 2020 in the United Kingdoms. The author invited potential interested participants via social media and selected eight full-time international postgraduate researchers (four male and four female postgraduate researchers) who meet the criteria, of international PGRs who were students in the UK before 2019 and still living in the UK during the lockdown in 2020. Following this, semi-structured interviews were conducted through recorded voice calls, each lasting between forty-five to sixty minutes. The author found international PGRs had different learning experiences during the pandemic. While isolation impacted some international PGRs' learning experiences and their community connections negatively, others have not been badly affected by it. In fact, some have even benefited from it. These contrary learning experiences were mainly associated with different preferences for study spaces, different attitudes and usage of online learning environment, and personal ways of developing and maintaining social connections.

A first round of interviews was conducted in 2020. What have these students experienced after the interviews in 2020? After three years, some of our participants are approaching the end of their academic journey, with a few of them having already finished it. The authors believe it is important to have a follow-up interview with the same group of participants to know their learning experiences in the UK from the summer of 2020 to the summer of 2023. Specifically, the follow-up interview will enable knowing their later usage of physical spaces on campus, their online learning experiences, and their community connections. This round of interviews will bring an in-depth understanding of the learning experiences of international PGRs' in the UK, and thus improve the quality of learning experiences generally.

Keywords:

International students, learning experience, learning community, learning space, online learning.

References

Yu, Y., & Moskal, M. (2019). Missing intercultural engagements in the university experiences of Chinese international students in the UK. *Compare: A Journal of Comparative and International Education*, *49*(4), 654-671.

Marinoni, G., van't Land, H., & Jensen, T. (2020). The impact of COVID-19 on global higher education. *International higher education*, 102, 7-9.

Peimani, N., & Kamalipour, H. (2021). Online Education and the COVID-19 Outbreak: A Case Study of Online Teaching during Lockdown. *Education Sciences*, 11(2), 72.

Cornelson, Kirsten, and Boriana Miloucheva. 2020. *Political Polarization, Social Fragmentation, and Cooperation during a Pandemic. Volume 663 of Working paper*, University of Toronto Department of Economics.

DEVELOPING THE OPEN DIGITAL COMPETENCES FOR EDUCATORS WITH MICROCREDENTIALS

Diana Andone, Politehnica University Timisoara, Romania, Sandra Kucina Softic, University Computing Centre University of Zagreb, Croatia, Demetrios Sampson, University of Piraeus, Greece, Martin Dougiamas, Moodle, Australia, Jessica Gramp, Moodle, Australia, Anna Krassa, Moodle, Spain

Abstract

The concept of Digital Competences for Educators is very important within European educational policies. Recent definitions of DigCompEdu are provided in a scientifically sound framework describing what it means for educators to be digitally competent DigCompEdu: European Framework for the Digital Competence of Educators (Carretero Gomez et al., 2017) and in the EU DEAP (*Digital Education Action Plan 2021-2027 Resetting Education and Training for the Digital Age*, 2020) defined in Sep 2020. The JRC Science group have researched and published the Policy Approaches to Open Education, Case Studies from 28 EU States (OpenEdu Policies) (Inamorato et al., 2018) and the subsequent Policy recommendations on open education in Europe. Going open is a process for all involved: institutions, learners and teachers, as well as technological groups creating open education technologies (Open EdTech) (Brown, 2021) . It depends on creating both digital and non-digital opportunities to make education more collaborative, transparent, and inclusive. Open education needs support from policies, technological development, and pedagogical approaches, via a multi-stakeholder approach, that can act systemically to create the change to further advance it in schools and create an "open education ecosystem" (Giovannella et al., 2015).

This paper presents the partial results of the OpenDigCompEdu Erasmus+ project as to accelerate the digital competences of educators in school education from Spain, Romania, Croatia, Greece and Norway towards the sustainable adoption of more online and blended approaches in education through the use of open educational technologies and open education principles. This is built on the momentum created by the pandemic which showed the importance of both digital competences and existing OERs and OEP (Rako & Softic, 2020) that can create this vision with the support of Open EdTech.

To validate this the partners have developed 5 courses using the framework of the Moodle ABCtoLD method. ABC Learning Design is an engaging, fast workshop to help teaching teams co-develop module and programme designs for blended and online learning (Young & Perović, 2016). Individuals and teams can use the following six learning types to identify opportunities for online active learning and help prioritise changes and have been used an implemented in online course development, tested by several universities worldwide (Andone et al., 2020). The courses of: Open Digital Education ecosystem, Learn Moodle Basics, Teaching with Open Digital Tools, New Assessment models, OpenEdTech for Sustainability, Diversity & Inclusion and Climate Change in Education are small, online, multimedia rich courses developed with study cases from all partners, interactive online activities and using existing OERs – figure 1.

The courses are integrated in Moodle Academy and they are created following the European microcredential principles, as to be independent, stackable and certifies and validate the school educators digital competences. The courses are now developed in English and enter the pilot phase for the content evaluation, the courses framework and of their delivery in Moodle Academy. Further results of the evaluation performed in 5 countries will be presented.

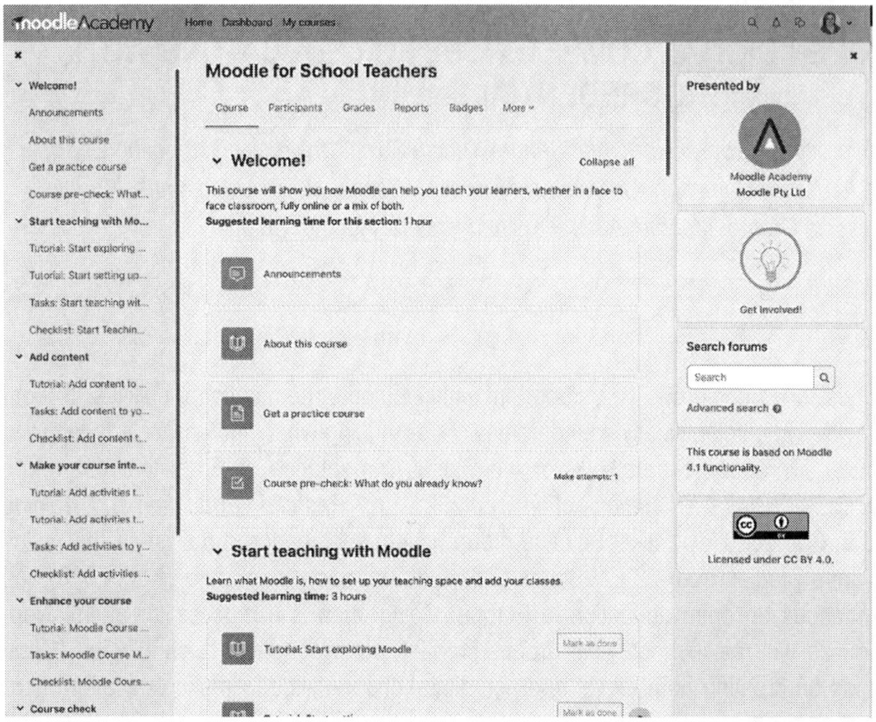

Figure 1: Caption from Moodle Academy of the Moodle for School Teachers course

Keywords:

Open Digital Competences, Moodle, school education, microcertificate

References

Andone, D., Mihaescu, V., & Vasiu, R. (2020). *ABCTOVLE - ABC-LD Course Design Experiences for Blended and Online Education. 3*, 142–149. https://doi.org/10.12753/2066-026X-20-188

Brown, M. (2021). What are the Main Trends in Online Learning? A Helicopter View of Possible Futures. *Asian Journal of Distance Education, 16*(2), Article 2. http://www.asianjde.com/ojs/index.php/AsianJDE/article/view/605

Carretero Gomez, S., Vuorikari, R., & Punie, Y. (2017). *DigComp 2.1: The Digital Competence Framework for Citizens with eight proficiency levels and examples of use* (JRC106281) [EUR - Scientific and Technical Research Reports]. Publications Office of the European Union. https://doi.org/10.2760/38842 (online)

Digital Education Action Plan 2021-2027 Resetting education and training for the digital age, (2020) (testimony of European Commission). https://eur-lex.europa.eu/legal-content/EN/TXT/?uri=CELEX:52020DC0624

Giovannella, C., Andone, D., Dascalu, M., Popescu, E., Rehm, M., & Roccasalva, G. (2015). Smartness of Learning Ecosystems and its bottom-up emergence in six European Campuses. *IxD&A, 27*, 79–92.

Inamorato, D. S. A., Nascimbeni, F., Bacsich, P., Atenas, J., Aceto, S., Burgos, D., & Punie, Y. (2018, January 4). *Policy Approaches to Open Education—Case Studies from 28 EU Member States (OpenEdu Policies)*. JRC Publications Repository. https://doi.org/10.2760/283135

Rako, S., & Softic, S. K. (2020). DEVELOPMENT AND USAGE OF OPEN EDUCATIONAL RESOURCES AMONG TEACHERS. *EDULEARN20 Proceedings*, 3849–3854. https://doi.org/10.21125/edulearn.2020.1053

Young, C., & Perović, N. (2016). Rapid and Creative Course Design: As Easy as ABC? *Procedia - Social and Behavioral Sciences, 228*, 390–395. https://doi.org/10.1016/j.sbspro.2016.07.058

CREATING HOPEFUL DIGITAL FUTURES IN UNIVERSITY SETTINGS: REFLECTIONS ON THE DEVELOPMENT OF AN INSTITUTIONAL DIGITAL EDUCATION POLICY

Sukaina Walji, University of Cape Town, South Africa,
Stephen Marquard, University of Cape Town, South Africa

Abstract

Digital education has become increasingly important in higher education, leading to a need for policy frameworks and strategies to guide blended and online learning implementation (Fűzi et al., 2022; Johnston et al., 2018; Veletsianos & Houlden, 2020). This paper examines the ongoing experiences and challenges of developing a consensus and understanding about the strategic role of digital education at a traditional South African research-intensive university and the concomitant development of an institutional digital education policy.

As leadership of a Teaching and Learning centre, we reflect on a two-year series of engagements that aimed to develop an institutional digital education strategy aligned with advancing various institutional imperatives, such as improving teaching quality, advancing curriculum change, and improving student throughput. We examine how a scaffolded co-creation process through dialogue and workshopping enabled different stakeholders to provide perspectives. During this process, academic teachers, who sometimes feel disempowered in the face of impending digital education, brought their experiences of crisis-informed online teaching into the conversations, while educational technologists and learning designers provided specialist inputs leveraging the opportunity of an institutional LMS migration to open new conversations. University senior leadership, often needing to consider competing imperatives towards social justice on the one hand and commercialisation on the other (Ivancheva et al., 2020), were another stakeholder group whose actions and decisions shaped the context in which discussions unfolded.

Through review and analysis of key documents, workshop notes and meetings recordings generated through this process, we explore how the development towards shared understandings amongst varied stakeholders required an iterative and sometimes seemingly slow process with the timeline punctuated and interrupted by periods of high stress and operational work. In developing the parameters and scope of a digital education strategy and policy, we found we had to work at multiple levels. We started from considering an ecosystem approach analysing the university's physical and digital infrastructure as well as the capacity development needed for staff and students to teach and learn in digital spaces. Another area was to develop clear definitions of what was meant by oft-used terms such as online and blended learning that made sense for a campus based residential university context.

A particular breakthrough came when the participants came together to establish a set of principles and values that created a bridge between the high-level purpose of digital education for the university and the nitty-gritty definitional and implementation aspects. The principles emanated from on-the-ground experiences, particularly in relation to the need to focus on students and staff coming together as a learning community in digital learning spaces and to foreground practices that supported inclusion and belonging.

We contend that traditional approaches to policy development may not be sufficient in complex university environments shaped by Covid-19 era teaching. Therefore, we share the experience of a values-based co-creation facilitation process that involved multiple stakeholders over a relatively long period of time to build trust and foster collaboration. We reflect on work-in-progress to consider the potential of co-creating hopeful digital futures in university settings.

Keywords:

Digital Education. Blended Learning. Online Learning. Policy. Leadership. Stakeholder Engagement.

References

Fűzi, B., Géring, Z., & Szendrei-Pál, E. (2022). Changing expectations related to digitalisation and socialisation in higher education. Horizon scanning of pre- and post-COVID-19 discourses. *Educational Review*, 74(3), 484-516. https://doi.org/10.1080/00131911.2021.2023101

Johnston, B., MacNeill, S., & Smyth, K. (2018). An Extended Conceptual Matrix for the Digital University. In J. E. Haythornthwaite, & R. Andrews (Eds.), *Conceptualising the Digital University* (pp. 151-169). Digital Education and Learning. Palgrave Macmillan. https://doi.org/10.1007/978-3-319-99160-3_9

Ivancheva, M. P., Swartz, R., Morris, N. P., Walji, S., Swinnerton, B. J., Coop, T., & Czerniewicz, L. (2020). Conflicting logics of online higher education. *British Journal of Sociology of Education*, 41(5), 608-625. https://doi.org/10.1080/01425692.2020.1784707

Veletsianos, G., & Houlden, S. (2020). Radical Flexibility and Relationality as Responses to Education in Times of Crisis. *Postdigital Science and Education*, 2(4), 849-862. https://doi.org/10.1007/s42438-020-00196-3

LIFELONG LEARNING STRATEGY FOR DELFT UNIVERSITY OF TECHNOLOGY

Willem Van Valkenburg, Sofia Dopper, TU Delft, Netherlands

Abstract

This LLL strategy provides the central strategy for Lifelong Learning based on TU Delft's mission, vision, and values. LLL is a core educational tasks of the university and this strategy is a starting document to address this.

Introduction

The Minister of Education has indicated in the Strategic Agenda Higher Education (2019) that education for (working) adults is one of the tasks pertaining to the social mission of public educational institutes.

Recently Delft University of Technology adopted their first university-wide Lifelong Learning strategy (Van Valkenburg, 2023). The strategy is based on the experience and expertise they have built in the last years with the Extension School programme and various faculty initiatives.

This LLL strategy provides the central strategy for Lifelong Learning based on TU Delft's mission, vision, and values. LLL is a core educational tasks of the university and this strategy is a starting document to address this. The LLL strategy will further be updated based on external and internal developments.

Defining Lifelong Learning

Lifelong Learning encompasses all learning activities undertaken throughout life with the aim of improving knowledge, skills, and competences, within personal, civic, social, or employment-related perspectives (European Commission, 2001).

Within this definition TU Delft focuses on formal learning. Formal learning refers to a type of learning programme in which the goals and objectives are defined by the training department, instructional designer, and/or instructor. This distinguishes it from informal, where the learner sets the goals and objectives.

Following in-depth discussions and an inventory of LLL activities within the faculties, the taskforce defined the scope of LLL at TU Delft based on eight criteria:

- TU Delft is responsible, and our academic staff is involved.
- It is a type of formal learning.
- It is a learning activity: unvalidated, validated, or accredited.
- The primary target audience is learners outside our university, not related to initial education, and we are mostly focused on alumni and working professionals.
- It is a recurring activity.
- Multiple modalities are included: classroom, blended, hybrid or online.
- There is market demand and business case.
- There is a form of quality assurance.

Ambition

TU Delft's ambition is summarized in Figure 1 below.

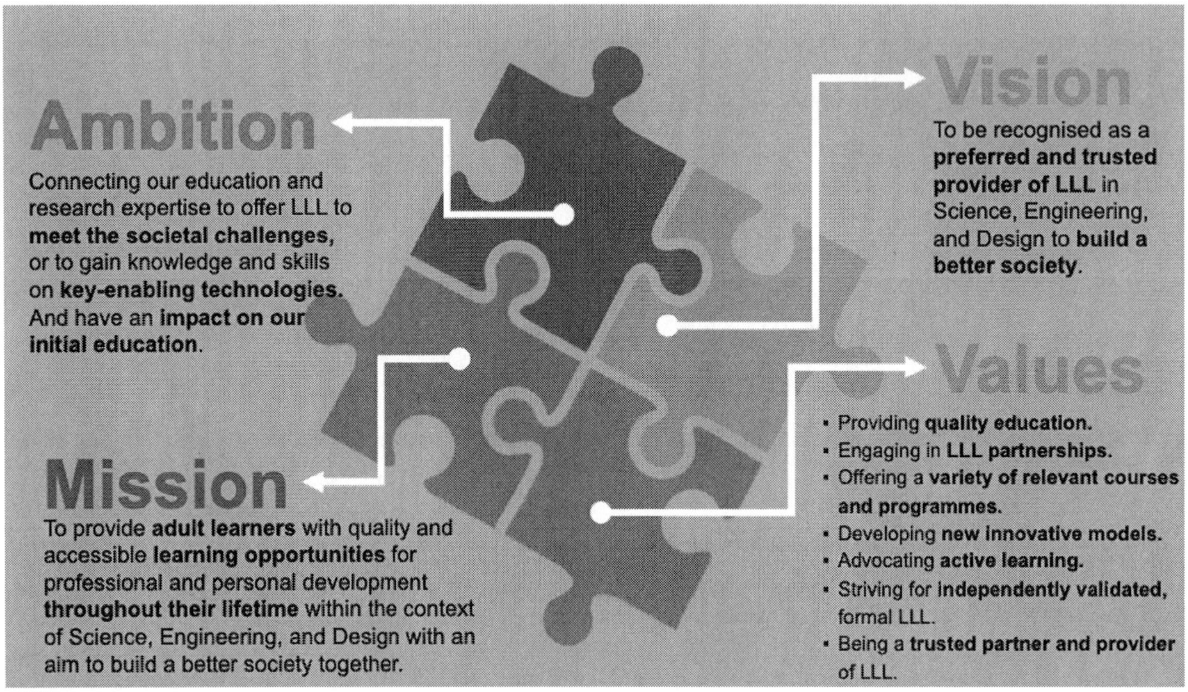

Figure 2: Ambition, vision, mission, and values

Metrics to success

An Important question is when this new strategy a success? As a public university, we are not a for-profit organisation. However, our aim is to offer LLL that has an increased impact on our education, on our lecturers and society at large. Some metrics of success that we could use for LLL activities are listed below. It is important that we embed the measurement of these metrics within our evaluation frameworks.

- Impact of offerings on the learners (worldwide audience, improve their skills)
- Impact on our relationship with our alumni (number of enrolments, involvement in course development)
- Impact of LLL on campus education and research (important for public-private financing)
- Impact on the reputation of the university (e.g., claiming a new field of research)
- Impact on the professional development of teaching staff.

Keywords:

Life long learning, impact, strategy, university, adult education.

References

European Commission (2001). *Making a European Area of Lifelong Learning a Reality.* https://www.europarl.europa.eu/meetdocs/committees/cult/20020122/com(2001)678_en.pdf

Ministry of Education (2019). *Strategische agenda hoger onderwijs en onderzoek.* https://www.rijksoverheid.nl/documenten/publicaties/2019/12/02/strategische-agenda-hoger-onderwijs-en-onderzoek (in Dutch)

Van Valkenburg, W.F. (2023); Hellendoorn, Hans; Saunders-Smits, G.N.; Groot Kormelink, J.B.J.; van Dam, A; van Leersum, N.K. *Lifelong Learning Strategy TU Delft.*

USING ONLINE LEARNING STANDARDS

Systematising Online Learning and Teaching Best Practice for Teaching Faculty

Geraldine Exton Grimes, Munster Technological University Kerry, Ireland

Abstract

Assisting teaching faculty in the most effective use of institutional learning platforms poses particular difficulties. Research prior to the pivot brought on by the pandemic in 2020 suggests that the use of templates and modelled baseline usage of Virtual Learning Environments (VLEs) was beginning to become more commonplace in Higher Education Institutions (HEIs) to address this problem (Masterman, 2017). However, when the teaching staff come from an industry background, with a non-pedagogical focus, it is appropriate to introduce methods which are more familiar from their industry experience.

In an innovative Engineering degree programme in a medium-sized University in Ireland, one such different approach is being trialled; mirroring more closely the experience of the Engineering industry and professional engineers. As part of this approach, we have created a set of online content standards. Standards covering broad issues around the education provided online, quality assurance, and policy development (ISO 2017; 2021; QQI 2018; National Forum 2021) provide an excellent foundation on which to base the specific standards needed for a small teaching team, for whom such high-level documents can successfully be adapted into the type of practical help they require (Skiba 2017; Martin et al 2017). The learning platform being used to host these standards, Realizeit, is an adaptive learning platform which includes a range of new and sometimes unfamiliar options for teachers, underscoring the dual need for standards that would present content in a consistent way across the programme, and a method to acquaint the teaching staff with the features that they may be unaccustomed to using.

These standards form part of a distributed approach to leadership on online teaching issues (Taylor 2020), which will lead to the formation of a community of practice around digital learning (Staring et al 2022) allowing this leadership to be one of influence, rather than authority (Outram & Parkin 2020). As there is a "cognitive load" on students when there is a lack of consistency in the resources that we provide, standards can help promote this consistency, thus providing "cognitive continuity" (Fresen et al 2014, p. 3). Through the standards we can also "provid(e) hints and tips to improve usage" (Bothma and Cant 2011, p. 382), and offer a pathway for those whose technology knowledge is less than they would like (Fresen et al, 2014). Most importantly, the standards are supportive in nature, promoting the use of best practice without being proscriptive, so there is no loss of academic autonomy (Masterman, 2017).

The standards are presented across a number of different documents: an informative text describing the rationale from across the literature; a style guide to aid in consistency; and a practical checklist to act as a reminder of the elements suggested in the literature yet still giving full autonomy over the final product to the teaching staff.

The online standards document covers best practice in a number of core areas: Accessibility issues covering alternative text, presentation of content, and discussion around expectations for learners; Key regulations and directives around copyright, and the benefits of using Open Educational Resources (OERs). Rationale for constructing thoughtful and well-designed learning outcomes is presented alongside strategies that can be used to develop learning communities among groups of online learners. The standards are designed to alert teaching staff to the existence of the body of research around online teaching and learning, and the main underpinning principles, as well as giving links to further information.

Conscious that teaching staff are often under time pressure, especially when teaching for the first time, we condensed the standards into a practical style guide, before creating a one-page checklist, adapted from the UCL Connected Learning Baseline (UCL Digital Education, 2020).

Feedback from the first iteration of the programme's initial modules, garnered from the analytics within the system itself, suggests there is further work to be done in developing the standards, and communication centring around why adhering to such standards is beneficial, to assist teaching staff to include more engaging, interactive lessons in the Realizeit platform, and therefore increase student motivation to access those lessons.

Utilising a heutagogical approach, further information, tailored to the teaching staff on this programme, has been organised into self-directed learning units in the Realizeit system, accessible to faculty as and when it is required. In conjunction with these online standards, the fundamental elements of successful online teaching and learning are becoming familiar to the teaching cohort and thus the learners will benefit in the longer term.

Keywords:

Online teaching and learning; Teacher CPD; Content standards; Industry teachers; Engineering; Online Engineering Degree

References

Bothma, C.H. & Cant, M.C. (2011). Adopting learning technologies: From belief to practice. *Educational Studies,37*(4), pp.375-389.

Fresen, J.W., Hill, R.K., & Geng, F. (2014). A collection of suggested electronic course templates for use in higher education. *Research in Learning Technology, 22*

ISO 29993:2017: Learning services outside formal education — Service requirements

ISO 29994:2021: Education and learning services — Requirements for distance learning

Masterman, E. (2017). Addressing inconsistency in use of the LMS: a collaborative approach. In H. Partridge, K. Davis & J. Thomas. (Eds.), *Me, Us, IT! Proceedings ASCILITE2017: 34th International Conference on Innovation, Practice and Research in the Use of Educational Technologies in Tertiary Education,* pp. 312-321.

Outram, S. and Parkin, D., 2020. A tailored undertaking: the challenge of context and culture for developing transformational leadership and change agency. In Delivering educational change in higher education (pp. 9-19). Routledge.

Staring, F., M. Brown, P. Bacsich and Ifenthaler, D., (2022), "Digital higher education: Emerging quality standards, practices and supports", OECD Education Working Papers, No. 281, OECD Publishing, Paris, https://doi.org/10.1787/f622f257-en.

Taylor, C., 2020. The distributed educational development team: a case study. In Delivering Educational Change in Higher Education (pp. 93-103). Routledge.

University College London Digital Education (2020). UCL Connected Learning Baseline. https://www.ucl.ac.uk/teaching-learning/publications/2020/may/ucl-connected-learning-baseline#Structure

AN EYE-TRACKER CAN LET US KNOW: DO THEY READ THE RESPONSE OF CHAT GPT?

Hayley Weigelt-Marom, Omri Kahana, Oren Ben-Aharon, Holon Institute of Technology, Israel

Abstract

In the last recent months, the use of artificial intelligence (AI) has entered our lives dramatically. The Chat GPT is one of the main AI text generators and is widely used among students. Using the Chat GPT requires reading the information received, but how do we read it?. Reading is a complex process, involving cognitive and mental aspects. This is the reason for reading different types of texts in different ways, using different reading strategies along the decoding and comprehension of a text. The goal of the current study is to examine how do we read the same informative texts presented in two different formats: as a Chat GPT answer versus a word document. The study (currently in progress) includes 60 participants studying at Holon Institute of Technology. In order to measure eye behaviours while reading, data will be collected using the eye-tracking device "Tobii Pro-Lab 120". Additionally, participants will fill out a questionnaire regarding comprehension and reading preferences of the two texts. Findings will be presented at the conference, yet the first results (10 participants) show a higher number of fixations while reading a text on Chat GPT in comparison to the number of fixation while reading a word document.

Keywords:

Chat GPT, Reading processes, Eye-tracking

Summary

"When students are presented with a prompt from ChatGPT, they typically read it carefully and analyze it to understand what is being asked of them. They may start by identifying the key phrases or keywords in the prompt and use them to generate ideas and organize their thoughts. Students may also consider the tone and style of the prompt to determine the appropriate tone and structure of their response. Additionally, they may draw on their prior knowledge and experiences to develop a thoughtful and well-reasoned answer. Overall, reading a prompt from ChatGPT requires a thoughtful and analytical approach in order to produce a coherent and effective response". This was the answer of Chat GPT to the prompt: how do students read a text on Chat GPT. **But is that correct?**

Reading alphabet writing involves decoding and comprehension (Li, Huang, Yao, & Hyönä, 2022). The decoding process involves transferring visual codes (into specific meaning for example: a letter to is phoneme, orthographic information to the word it means). Comprehension involves higher cognitive processes, and includes the integration of decoding information to meaning, as well as integration of previous knowledge and degree of language and cognitive abilities. Yet, as we all notice in our daily lives, the implementation of these two processes of reading tend to change due to additional variables, such as the purpose of reading, its importance, and it reliability. In fact, the readers state of mind while reading changes performances of these processes. The latter is mainly discussed in the literature in the context of reading strategies and metacognition processes (for example: Yapp, Graaff, & van den Bergh, 2021), emphasising its importance.

The current study examines eye behaviors and visual attention while reading two informative texts (equal in size and information): once as an expert's text document versus an answer of a Chat GPT prompt. Text subject will be new to students.

Method

Eye-tracking devices enable detecting eye movements while reading for better understanding the more objective behaviors while reading (for example: Carter, & Luke, 2020). At the User Experience Lab of the Faculty of Instructional Technologies, the Holon Institution of Technology, we are able to collect this data using the "Tobii Pro-Lab" with 120 Hz sampling frequency.

60 students (age 20-30), skilled readers will participate in this study. The texts are equal by subject matter and wording, and will be presented on the computer screen once as a word document and once as an answer on the Chat GPT. The order of texts will be counter balanced, to decrease the influence of first text exposure. Following the reading tasks, participants will fill out a questionnaire regarding comprehension and reading preferences of the two texts.

First Findings

This study arose hand in hand with the wake of the Chat GPT, in the last two months. Therefore, data is currently being collected. Data analyzed at this stage regards to Areas of Interest (AOI) purely of the texts and not of icons or images presented on the Chat GPT page. First results (10 participants) show a higher number of fixations while reading an answer to a prompt on the Chat GPT versus as an expert's text document. These again are very preliminary findings, and the full study will be presented in the near future.

References

Carter, B. T., & Luke, S. G. (2020). Best practices in eye tracking research. International Journal of Psychophysiology, 155, 49-62.

Li, X., Huang, L., Yao, P., & Hyönä, J. (2022). Universal and specific reading mechanisms across different writing systems. *Nature Reviews Psychology, 1*(3), 133-144.

Yapp, D., de Graaff, R., & van den Bergh, H. (2021). Effects of reading strategy instruction in English as a second language on students' academic reading comprehension. *Language Teaching Research*, 1362168820985236.

ARE FUTURE PEDAGOGIES LEAVING SOME TEACHERS BEHIND? PERCEIVED OBSTACLES TO BLENDED LEARNING

Ema Meden, Marko Radovan, Danijela Makovec Radovan, University of Ljubljana, Slovenia

Main findings

The findings in this paper are part of the work in an international BlendVET project supported by Iceland, Liechtenstein and Norway through EEA grants. The aim of the project is to improve teaching and learning practices in blended learning and to share knowledge and best practices with institutions from donor countries. A survey conducted in March 2022 among 214 teachers from vocational schools in Slovenia, Norway and Iceland found that 25.2% of the respondents used ICT more frequently after the pandemic. 80.9% of teachers said they already use a blended learning approach to some extent. This shows that schools and teachers are managing the transition quite successfully. However, 13.6% of teachers reported that they only used ICT for teaching during the pandemic when it was necessary. While the proportion of teachers having difficulty adapting is low, it raises the question of how to better support teachers in the digital transition. In this paper, we make some suggestions based on the barriers to blended learning cited by teachers. Of the 214 teachers surveyed, 29.4% felt that students did not have the appropriate equipment to participate in blended learning activities, and 15.4% of respondents said that their school did not have appropriate equipment. This could indicate that teachers perceive a certain level of digital divide. However, the perceived gap does not always stem from differences in access to technology, but also from differences in technology use and digital literacy (Guo & Wan, 2022). The issue of upgrading technology and infrastructure to support blended learning requires a deeper understanding of the causes of the digital divide. Another challenge reported by teachers was their lack of digital literacy. 21.5% of respondents felt that they lacked the necessary digital skills and knowledge to enable blended learning. There is also the question of how to effectively incorporate technology into their teaching methods. 16.4% of respondents said they lacked didactic skills related to blended learning. Another obstacle that could be related to teachers' pedagogical practices is the lack of motivation of students. 19.2% of the teachers surveyed stated that students were not fully engaged or motivated to participate in blended learning activities. As digital and pedagogical literacy overlap, it seems sensible to address them together. This has been highlighted in the Technological Pedagogical Content Knowledge - TPACK (Koehler et al., 2014) and a newer terminology with similar implications, e.g., hyphenated "digital pedagogical" competence (Hauck et al., 2020).

Summary

Blended learning has emerged as a promising educational approach that combines the advantages of traditional face-to-face teaching with the flexibility and interactivity of online learning. The use of ICT has increased during the pandemic COVID -19, making blended learning an even more important teaching approach. Hesitation to change is more pronounced with technological changes than with curricular changes, as technology changes very quickly (Ertmer & Ottenbreit-Leftwich, 2010). Blended learning combines classroom instruction with online learning and allows for more self-directed learning and student autonomy through the use of technology in the classroom or through distance learning. Blended learning has become a popular pedagogical approach, but a survey of 214 vocational teachers from Slovenia, Norway and Iceland found that some teachers still struggle to adapt to the digital shift. While the majority of teachers reported using a blended learning approach to some extent, 13.6% used ICT only when necessary during the pandemic. There were two findings on perceived barriers: (1) perceived lack of equipment and (2) perceived lack of competence. 29.4% of teachers felt that students lacked the necessary equipment for blended learning and 15.4% stated that their school did not have the appropriate equipment. Students and teachers should be made aware of the equipment available and its functions, but they should also be provided with the necessary tools if needed. The second finding was the perceived lack of competence of teachers. 21.5% of teachers stated that they lacked digital skills and 16.4% felt that they lacked didactic skills related to blended learning. Addressing digital and pedagogical skills simultaneously could help teachers with their digital transformation. The results of the survey provide a snapshot of the challenges vocational teachers face when implementing blended learning. Further research is needed to explore these challenges in more detail and to develop solutions and best practices that can help blended learning deliver the best possible outcomes for students.

Keywords:

Blended learning, vocational education, digital competencies, teacher training

References

Ertmer, P. A., & Ottenbreit-Leftwich, A. T. (2010). Teacher technology change: How knowledge, confidence, beliefs, and culture intersect. *Journal of research on Technology in Education*, *42*(3), 255-284. https://doi.org/10.1080/15391523.2010.10782551

Guo, C., & Wan, B. (2022). The digital divide in online learning in China during the COVID-19 pandemic. *Technology in society*, *71*, 102122. https://doi.org/10.1016/j.techsoc.2022.102122

Hauck, M., Müller-Hartmann, A., Rienties, B., & Rogaten, J. (2020). Approaches to researching digital-pedagogical competence development in VE-based teacher education. *Journal of Virtual Exchange, 3*(SI), 5-35. https://doi.org/10.21827/jve.3.36082

Koehler M. J., Mishra P., Kereluik K., Shin T. S., & Graham C. R. (2014). In M. Spector, D. Merrill, J. Elen & M.J. Bishop (Eds.), *Handbook of Research on Educational Communications and Technology* (pp. 101-111). Springer. https://doi.org/10.1007/978-1-4614-3185-5_9

RETHINKING LEARNING TECHNOLOGY AND LEARNING TRANSFER AS PREPAREDNESS FOR FUTURE LEARNING CHALLENGES

Gearoid O Suilleabhain, Munster Technological University, Ireland

Abstract

The phenomenon and concept of learning transfer has been a subject of sometimes-intense debate since the publication of a series of seminal articles on the subject by Thorndike and Woodworth (1901) over a hundred years ago. Over the intervening period, learning transfer has been researched extensively across studies incorporating a wide and ever-changing range of pedagogical and theoretical perspectives. Despite such attention, however, clear evidence even of the occurrence of learning transfer – beyond transfer between highly similar learning and target contexts – is actually a relative rarity in research literature. As Bereiter (1995) suggests at the end of his review: "Most research on transfer has been bad news for educators. It gives the impression that transfer usually doesn't happen..." (p. 26).

This paper returns to the often-overlooked empirical and theoretical issues associated with classical theories of learning transfer, suggesting ways in which some associated underlying assumptions may be seen to have influenced how we now think about the value and function of many well-known learning technology solutions and platforms including, most recently, those incorporating VR or other multimodal and immersive elements. Drawing on reconceptualisations of learning transfer as both "boundary crossing" (Tuomi-Grohn & Engestrom, 2003) and "preparedness" (Bransford & Schwartz, 1999), the paper goes on to suggest new ways in which to think about how technology facilitates and reveals learning processes and learning transfer. The paper concludes with some suggestions as to how adapting a more active and dynamic view of learning transfer can unconceal (Wrathall, 2010) the mechanisms by which various learning technologies prompt and support the interplay of prior learning and new learning efforts in a way that works to prepares learners for new future learning and performance challenges.

Keywords:

Learning Transfer, Learning Technology, Immersive Technology, Multimodal Learning, Virtual Reality, Preparation for Future Learning, Future Pedagogy

References

Bereiter, C., & Scardamalia, M. (1996). Rethinking learning. In D. Olson & N. Torrance (Eds.), The handbook of education and human development: New models of learning, teaching and schooling (pp. 485-513). Cambridge, MA: Blackwell.

Bransford, J., & Schwartz, D. L. (1999). Rethinking transfer: A simple proposal with multiple implications. *Review of research in education*, 24, 61-100.

Thorndike, E. L., & Woodworth, R. (1901). The influence of improvement in one mental function upon the efficiency of other functions. (I); II. The estimation of magnitudes; III. Functions involving attention, observation and discremination. *Psychological Review*, 8(4), 247-261, 384-395, 553-564.

Tuomi-Grohn, T., & Engestrom, Y. (2003). *Between school and work: New perspectives on transfer and boundary-crossing*. Amsterdam: Pergamon.

Wrathall, W. (2010). *Heidegger and Unconcealment: Truth, Language, and History*. Cambridge, MA: Cambridge University Press

UNGRADING ONLINE: CO-CREATING A SELF-ASSESSMENT RUBRIC WITH STUDENTS

Kaitlin A. Lucas, Irene (JC) Lubbe, Central European University, Austria

Abstract

The traditional grading system has been the norm in higher education for many years, but it has been increasingly criticized for its detrimental effect on student learning, motivation, and wellbeing (Knesek, 2022). Ungrading challenges the traditional grading system and encourages lecturers to adopt alternative assessment practices that focus on feedback, meta-cognition, and student agency (Blum, 2020). Co-creating a self-assessment rubric with students is an alternative practice that allows students to become an active participant in their own learning and in the assessment process. As such it encourages them to take ownership of their own learning and assessment (Fraile et al., 2017).

This short paper presents a narrative reflection on the experiences of two lecturers using this ungrading approach. In two iterations of an online elective in the Certificate in Teaching in Higher Education, we invited students to co-create a self-assessment rubric for their final project and use the rubric to assess their own learning. We do a step-by-step walkthrough of the six weeks of the course and share the activities, rational and results. Finally, we compare the two very different rubrics created by the two cohorts.

The approach is based on three main principles: (1) addressing classroom power dynamics through purposeful online course design, (2) valuing and incorporating students' knowledge and expertise in the development of assessment criteria, and (3) providing ongoing feedback and self-reflection opportunities. The approach also includes practical strategies for implementing these principles online, such as using Liberating Structures to elicit student perspectives (Lipmanowicz & McCandless, 2014), providing multiple opportunities for input and revision, and using technology to facilitate communication and collaboration. Consistent with the literature (Singer-Freeman & Robinson, 2020), the implementation results suggest that this self-assessment practice can have a positive impact on student learning, motivation, and engagement, and lead to course design improvements.

The report concludes with three main takeaways related to (1) the value of structured online synchronous discussions (2) the importance of transparency and clear expectations, and (3) quality improvements as a result of student input. It includes suggestions for future implementation and research in this area, recommending that ungrading and co-creating an assessment rubric with students can be applied across different educational contexts.

Keywords:

Ungrading; co-creation; self-assessment; rubric

References

Blum, S. (2020). *Ungrading: Why rating students undermines learning (and what to do instead).* West Virginia University Press.

Fraile, J., Panadero, E., & Pardo, R. (2017). Co-creating rubrics: The effects on self-regulated learning, self efficacy and performance of establishing assessment criteria with students. *Studies in Educational Evaluation, 53,* 69-76. https://doi.org/10.1016/j.stueduc.2017.03.003

Knesek, G.E. (2022, April 25). Why focusing on grades is a barrier to learning. *Harvard Business Publishing: Education.* [Blog post] https://hbsp.harvard.edu/inspiring-minds/why-focusing-on-grades-is-a-barrier-to-learning

Lipmanowicz, H. & McCandless, K. (2014). *The surprising power of liberating structures.* Liberating Structures Press.

Singer-Freeman, K., & Robinson, C. (2020, November). Grand challenges in assessment: Collective issues in need of solutions (Occasional Paper No. 47). National Institute for Learning Outcomes Assessment.

CHATGPT AND ME: THE STUDENT VOICE ON FUTURE LEARNING IN THE AGE OF ARTIFICIAL INTELLIGENCE

Louise Drumm, Cameron Graham, Stuart Taylor, Ingeborg Van Knippenberg, Sam Illingworth, Pamela Calabrese, Olumuyiwa Opaleye, Imi Dencer-Brown, Edinburgh Napier University, Scotland UK

Abstract

The pandemic accelerated the use of digital tools for teaching, learning and assessing in universities, but the future of digital education is being challenged by user-friendly large language models and generative artificial intelligence (AI) platforms such as ChatGPT. The progress in digital education practices is under threat from uncertainty, such as how to assess students' learning when materials can be, partially or wholly, generated by AI platform. There is little knowledge currently about students' attitudes and experiences of these emerging technologies. This paper concerns a research project conducted across a Scottish university in early 2023 which collected and analysed student attitudes to, and experiences of, ChatGPT and their own studies. Students were invited to contribute posts anonymously to an online 'Amnesty Padlet' on their experiences and thoughts about ChatGPT. The preliminary results are presented as emerging themes and framed against existing literature on learning, assessment and artificial intelligence. Key findings and recommendations from the research will be offered and this paper foregrounds the importance of listening to students at this time to ensure digital education is future-ready and students are equipped with skills for their own futures. This research project includes a student co-researcher who is also a co-author of this paper.

Keywords:

ChatGPT; Artificial Intelligence; AI; student voice; assessment; academic integrity

Paper:

The pandemic resulted in the accelerated use of digital tools for teaching, learning and assessing in universities, but the future of digital education is being challenged by the release of user-friendly large language models and artificial intelligence (AI) platforms such as ChatGPT. The progress made in digital education practices is under threat from uncertainty, such as how to validly assess students' learning when materials can be, partially or wholly, generated by AI platform. As professionals and educators in digital learning turn to redesigning assessments to circumnavigate ChatGPT (Cotton et al., 2023; Wallbank, 2023) or incorporate it as part of the process (McKnight, 2022), there is little knowledge currently about students' attitudes and experiences of these emerging technologies; the student voice is missing. It is not known, for example, whether students see them as legitimate aids for refining their own work, or a threat to the fairness of learning or value of their degrees.

This paper concerns a research project conducted across a Scottish university during an academic term in early 2023 which collected and analysed student attitudes to AI and their own studies. Students were invited, via digital and physical posters on campuses, to contribute posts anonymously to an online 'Amnesty Padlet' on their experiences and thoughts about ChatGPT. The students were offered the following prompts:

- Have you used it?
- Will you use it?
- What do you think of others using it?
- Should artificial intelligence play a role in learning and assessment at Edinburgh Napier?
- Vote other posts up or down if you agree/disagree with them.

The preliminary results are presented as emerging themes and framed against existing literature on learning, assessment and artificial intelligence (e.g. Swiecki et al., 2022). Key recommendations from the research are offered and this paper will foreground the importance of listening to students at this time to ensure digital education is future-ready and students are equipped with skills for their own futures. This research project includes a student co-researcher who is also a co-author of this paper.

References

Cotton, D. R., Cotton, P. A., & Shipway, J. R. (2023). *Chatting and Cheating. Ensuring academic integrity in the era of ChatGPT.* (Pre-print) Retrieved March 10, 2023, from https://edarxiv.org/mrz8h/download?format=pdf

McKnight, L. (2022, Oct 14). Eight ways to engage with AI writers in higher education, *Times Higher Education*, Retrieved March 10, 2023, from https://www.timeshighereducation.com/campus/eight-ways-engage-ai-writers-higher-education

Swiecki, Z., Khosravi, H., Chen, G., Martinez-Maldonado, R., Lodge, J. M., Milligan, S., Selwyn, N., & Gašević, D. (2022). Assessment in the age of artificial intelligence. *Computers and Education: Artificial Intelligence*, 3, 100075. https://doi.org/10.1016/j.caeai.2022.100075

Wallbank, A.J. (2023, Jan 18). ChatGPT and AI writers: a threat to student agency and free will? *Times Higher Education*, Retrieved March 10, 2023, from https://www.timeshighereducation.com/campus/chatgpt-and-ai-writers-threat-student-agency-and-free-will

TIME, SUPPORT, AND RELATIONSHIPS: EARLY FINDINGS FROM A 'LEARNER-CENTRED' TRANSITION TO BLENDED LEARNING

Hanorah Lyons, Cohen Ambrose, Limerick and Clare Education and Training Board, Ireland

Keywords:

Blended Learning; Further Education and Training; learner-centred; key considerations; buy-in; perceptions of blended learning; Rich Pictures

Context

Limerick and Clare Education and Training Board (ETB) is the state education and training authority for the Limerick and Clare region. The Further Education and Training (FET) Division is responsible for the management and operation of 37 College of FET Campuses in Limerick and Clare. Beginning in autumn 2021, the FET Division created a Blended and Online Learning Support Service as a sister branch to its existing Technology Enhanced Learning Support Service (TELSS) and charged its two new staff (the authors) with developing a Blended and Online Learning Strategy. This concise paper reveals some initial findings from the emerging areas of our research to date, focussing specifically on relevant literature and a recent workshop with FET provision coordinators which reviewed a draft of the ETB's strategy for implementing blended learning.

The ETB's vision for blended learning is to develop and provide quality blended and online learning courses that are learner-centred and built on existing good teaching practice. We define blended learning as the replacement of some, but not all, face-to-face teaching with designed, learner-centred, synchronous and asynchronous online content, activities, and assessments.

On the basis of these values of being learner-centred and wanting to provide quality blended learning, we set out to explore the key considerations to bear in mind when initiating an organisational transition to blended learning. In addition, we also wanted to examine the key stakeholders' (learning practitioners, learners, administrators, management and support staff) perceived ideas, understandings, and concerns as well as the opportunities for blended learning.

Literature Review

A review of projects, case studies and research papers (e.g., Murphy 2018, Graham et al, 2013, Visscher et al, 2009) for this research focused on how other educational institutions have implemented blended learning. What the review highlighted was the need to develop a clear institutional strategy and well-defined structures and procedures. It also revealed that it was essential to allocate time for professional learning and development and provide support and resources for all staff and learners. The information gathered as part of this research informed the development of a blended learning strategy, policy and procedure documents.

Primary Research Methods

We circulated a draft copy of the Blended and Online Learning Strategy to FET provision coordinators for comment and facilitated an interactive workshop with FET provision coordinators using Rich Pictures (Bell, Berg, and Morse, 2019). The implementation of blended learning into the ETB is a complex process and the Rich Pictures activity was selected as it provides participants with the opportunity to discuss their thoughts and ideas with their colleagues and to gather this data in one place, thereby building a clear picture of the situation. We specifically asked them to consider internal and external structures, processes, roles and relationships, issues and concerns.

Main Findings

Following analysis of the hand-drawn images three main themes emerged – Time, Support and Relationships and specifically how each of these main themes are interlinked and dependent on one another.

Time: Learning practitioners need to be given time (not on top of their existing timetable) to design and develop modules/courses for blended learning. If the learning practitioners are taken off timetable, then coordinators need replacement labour time for those learning practitioners taking part in professional development.

Support: Blended learning can present challenges in terms of infrastructure, technology resourcing and support, and the ETB must be committed and invest in support for learning practitioners, learners and provisions.

Relationships: Trusting relationships need to be developed between management, learning practitioners and learners. The importance of collaboration and the need to promote communities of practice among learning practitioners were identified by all groups.

Summary

Early findings from the initial stages of Limerick and Clare Education and Training Board's FET Division's transition to offering blended learning courses reflect the findings of the literature review, i.e. that the key stakeholders are primarily concerned with time (as both labour and as a resource), support (for both learners and teachers), and relationships (between all key stakeholders, both in the office and in the classroom). The next phase will be to take what we have learnt and build it into our existing practices and documentation.

References

Bell, S., Berg, T., & Morse, S. (2015). Rich Pictures: Sustainable Development and Stakeholders - The Benefits of Content Analysis. Sustainable Development, 24(2), 136–148. https://doi.org/10.1002/sd.1614

Blend4VET (2018) Exploring Blended Learning Approaches for VET Toolkit: Toolkits – Blend4VET Project

European Commission (2009) European Quality Assurance in Vocational Education and Training (EQAVET) Reference Framework: EQAVET - European Quality Assurance in Vocational Education and Training - Employment, Social Affairs & Inclusion - European Commission (europa.eu)

Graham, C., Woodfield, W., & Buckley Harrison, J. (2013) A Framework for institutional adoption and implementation of blended learning in higher education: (PDF) A framework for institutional adoption and implementation of blended learning in higher education (researchgate.net)

Limerick and Clare ETB (2022) FET Division Strategic Framework 2022-2025: (Framework | College of FET)

Ma'arop, A. H. & Embi M. A. (2016) Implementation of Blended Learning in Higher Education Institutions: A Review of the Literature. *International Education Studies.* ERIC - EJ1093338 - Implementation of Blended Learning in Higher Learning Institutions: A Review of the Literature, International Education Studies, 2016

Murphy, T. (2018) Guide to Developing Enabling Policies for Digital Teaching and Learning: (PDF) Guide to Developing Enabling Policies for Digital Teaching and Learning (researchgate.net)

QQI (2018) Statutory Quality Assurance Guidelines for Providers of Blended Learning Programmes. Statutory QA Guidelines for Blended Learning Programmes.pdf (qqi.ie)

QQI (2016) Core Statutory Quality Assurance Guidelines. Ireland: qg-1-core-statutory-quality-assurance-guidelines.pdf (qqi.ie)

Visscher, A., Hendriks, M., Andersen, O., Deitmer, L., Heinemann, L., Kesküla, E., Larsen, J., Pepper, D., & Tramontano, I. (2009). Guidelines for the Quality Assurance of Vocational Education and Training in EU Countries: (PDF) Guidelines for the Quality Assurance of Vocational Education and Training in EU Countries (researchgate.net)

INTERACTIVE ORAL ASSESSMENT: AN AUTHENTIC AND MEANINGFUL ASSESSMENT APPROACH

Fiona O'Riordan, Monica Ward, Dublin City University, Ireland

Abstract

An interactive oral assessment is a two-way conversation using an authentic work-based scenario to stimulate a free-flowing discussion. It is designed to be a curious type of conversation where the assessors' prompts or genuine natural questions allow students to showcase their learning in a professionally aligned environment. Thus, it facilitates exploration of students' deep and higher order understanding of a topic. Interactive oral assessments are designed within an evidence-based framework that was pioneered by Griffith University, Australia under the leadership of Danielle Logan-Fleming (Learning and Teaching Consultant at Griffith University). Griffith University has had much success using interactive oral assessment over the past seven years (Sotiriadou et al, 2020). Research shows us that interactive oral assessments have the potential to develop many transversal skills, such as critical and creative thinking, professional communication, and personal agility (Tan et al, 2021; Sotiriadou et al, 2020).

This concise paper presentation shares how educational technologies were leveraged to enhance interactive oral assessments in Dublin City University (DCU). A combination of tools and functions across the DCU technological ecosystem (Loop) were employed to streamline the assessment approach to make it more effective and efficient.

Educational Technologies

A key component of successful interactive oral assessment roll out in DCU is the weekly Interactive Oral Assessment (IO) Community of Practice (CoP) meetings. These meetings are facilitated through Zoom. An IO expert from Griffith University joins the weekly CoP from Gold Coast, Australia (AEST time zone). All meetings are recorded and made available as part of a YouTube playlist. International and national IO presentations and conferences are facilitated through Zoom. The recordings are then edited and made available via IO vignette YouTube playlist (https://youtu.be/yS3ustbYKew). During the weekly IO CoP meetings IO example recordings are created by the community as examples of IO for discussion with students. Again, Zoom and an editing piece of software are used to produce the short (10 mins) example recording. As part of the preparation support for students, the CoP work together to create detailed rubrics for each IO. These rubrics are entered in the Moodle (for summative grading purposes) and used with students to mock grade the recorded example (via Google forms). IO can be conducted in a physical or online environment. Many DCU academics give students a choice. For online IO assessments, Zoom is used and the sessions are recorded for quality review purposes. For both physical and blended IO assessments, the Moodle scheduler tool is used to allow students (or groups of students) select their time for the IO. All CoP meeting notes and documents are shared using Google Drive for IO. Some ambitious academics have used H5P to create an interactive learning resource, using the IO example recording, by adding tips, feedback, and suggested readings along the way.

Keywords:

Interactive Oral Assessment; Authentic Assessment; Educational Technologies

References

Tan, C. P., Howes, D., Tan, R.K.W. & Dancza, K.M. (2021) Developing interactive oral assessments to foster graduate attributes in higher education. *Assessment & Evaluation in Higher Education,* 47(8), 1183-1199. 10.1080/02602938.2021.2020722

Sotiriadou, P., Logan, D., Daly, A. & Guest, R. (2020) 'The role of authentic assessment to preserve academic integrity and promote skill development and employability', *Studies in Higher Education*, 45(11), 2132-2148. 10.1080/03075079.2019.1582015

REMOTE EXAMS AND ACADEMIC INTEGRITY

Henrietta Carbonel, Ambroise Baillifard, UniDistance Suisse, Switzerland

Abstract

Technology today appears to offer solutions to all our problems, and assessment in higher education is no exception. In the face of plagiarism, ChatGPT, collusion, or contractual cheating, educational technologies offer digital solutions, the most well-known of which are plagiarism detectors and remote proctoring. However, these technologies create a culture of surveillance, requiring students to be monitored 'for their own good' and that of higher education (Ross & Macleod, 2018). These technologies are not neutral and affect the trust between teachers and students. Moreover, in education, the means contribute qualitatively to the character of the results produced (Biesta, 2007; Carr, 1992). Finally, academic integrity cannot be limited to not being caught, it is a core value in the academic world and beyond, and therefore a fundamental pedagogical issue (Carless, 2009; Townley & Parsell, 2004).

New assessment paradigms aim at better preparing students for an increasingly complex world (Bearman et al., 2020). Quality assessment promotes learning, is sustainable, and ongoing, it gives students agency, may be authentic, allows for the questioning of assumptions and trying new paths, and the representation of knowledge in different ways (Bayne et al., 2020; Boud, 2000; Boud & Falchikov, 2007; Carless, 2009; Gough, 2013; Ibarra-Sáiz et al., 2021). Moreover, if the university is to, among other things, prepare for work, then it should offer, at least sometimes, conditions similar to those of professionals in the sector, including collaboration and technologies (Dawson, 2020).

Research on academic integrity is mainly focused on two areas: the measurement and causes of cheating, and the solutions (Gallant, 2022; Newton, 2018). A traditional scientific approach can inform our choices, but what worked yesterday will not necessarily work in the same way tomorrow (Biesta, 2010). Speculative design methods provide new approaches to researching the future, frequently applied to reimagining the future of higher education (Mitrović et al., 2021; Ross, 2023; Staley, 2019). They offer a means 'to explore and create possible futures under conditions of complexity and uncertainty' (Ross, 2018, p. 197, our translation).

The aim of this project is two-fold. We first characterise the different dimensions of quality assessment, including academic integrity. The second objective is to develop and test a speculative method to help teachers design quality remote assessments. We use a collaborative approach, bringing together international experts in assessment, speculative methods, institutional aspects, and AI researchers, as well as teachers, students, and instructional designers. This two-day scientific seminar took place at the end of May 2023 with 35 participants.

In the presentation, we will report on our method and findings: the characterisation of quality assessment, including academic integrity issues, and then on the method to support teachers in designing quality remote assessments.

Keywords:

Online exams. Remote Exams. Academic integrity. Cheating. ChatGPT. Large Language Models. Quality assessment.

References

Bayne, S., Evans, P., Ewins, R., Knox, J., Lamb, J., Macleod, H., O'Shea, C., Ross, J., Sheail, P., & Sinclair, C. (2020). *The manifesto for teaching online*. The MIT Press.

Bearman, M., Boud, D., & Ajjawi, R. (2020). New directions for assessment in a digital world. In M. Bearman, P. Dawson, R. Ajjawi, J. Tai, & D. Boud (Eds.), *Re-imagining university assessment in a digital world* (Vol. 7, p. 7-18). Springer International Publishing. https://doi.org/10.1007/978-3-030-41956-1_2

Biesta, G. (2007). Why « what works » won't work : Evidence-based practice and the democratic deficit in educational research. *Educational Theory, 57*(1), 1-22. http://dx.doi.org.ezproxy.is.ed.ac.uk/10.1111/j.1741-5446.2006.00241.x

Biesta, G. (2010). Why « what works » still won't work : From evidence-based education to value-based education. *Studies in Philosophy and Education, 29*(5), 491-503. http://dx.doi.org.ezproxy.is.ed.ac.uk/10.1007/s11217-010-9191-x

Boud, D. (2000). Sustainable assessment : Rethinking assessment for the learning society. *Studies in Continuing Education, 22*(2), 151-167. https://doi.org/10.1080/713695728

Boud, D., & Falchikov, N. (2007). *Rethinking assessment in higher education : Learning for the longer term.* Taylor & Francis Group. http://ebookcentral.proquest.com/lib/ed/detail.action?docID=292915

Carless, D. (2009). Trust, distrust and their impact on assessment reform. *Assessment & Evaluation in Higher Education, 34*(1), 79-89. https://doi.org/10.1080/02602930801895786

Carr, D. (1992). Practical enquiry, values and the problem of educational theory. *Oxford Review of Education, 18*(3), 241-251.

Dawson, P. (2020). Cognitive offloading and assessment. In M. Bearman, P. Dawson, R. Ajjawi, J. Tai, & D. Boud (Eds.), *Re-imagining university assessment in a digital world* (p. 37-48). Springer International Publishing. https://doi.org/10.1007/978-3-030-41956-1_4

Gallant, T. B. (2022). *The ICAI reader* (2nd ed): 44.

Gough, N. (2013). Towards deconstructive nonalignment : A complexivist view of curriculum, teaching and learning. *South African Journal of Higher Education, 27*(5), 1213-1233.

Ibarra-Sáiz, M. S., Rodríguez-Gómez, G., & Boud, D. (2021). The quality of assessment tasks as a determinant of learning. *Assessment & Evaluation in Higher Education, 46*(6), 943-955. https://doi.org/10.1080/02602938.2020.1828268

Mitrović, I., Auger, J., Hanna, J., & Helgason, I. (Eds.). (2021). *Beyond speculative design : Past - present - future.* Speculative Edu.

Newton, P. M. (2018). How common is commercial contract cheating in higher education and is it increasing? A systematic review. *Frontiers in Education, 3.* https://www.frontiersin.org/articles/10.3389/feduc.2018.00067

Ross, J. (2018). Speculative method as an approach to researching emerging educational issues and technologies. In L. Hamilton & J. Ravenscroft (Eds.), *Building research design in education* (1re éd., p. 197-210). Bloomsbury Academic.

Ross, J. (2023). *Digital futures for learning : Speculative methods and pedagogies.* Routledge.

Ross, J., & Macleod, H. (2018). Surveillance, (dis)trust and teaching with plagiarism detection technology. *Networked Learning, 8.*

Staley, D. J. (2019). *Alternative universities : Speculative design for innovation in higher education.* Johns Hopkins University Press.

Townley, C., & Parsell, M. (2004). Technology and academic virtue : Student plagiarism through the looking glass. *Ethics and Information Technology, 6*(4), 271-277. https://doi.org/10.1007/s10676-005-5606-8

NATIONAL QUALITY ASSURANCE GUIDELINES FOR DIGITAL EDUCATION: A MULITLAYERED BOX OF CHOCOLATES

Mark Brown, Eamon Costello, Prajakta Girme, Dublin City University, Ireland

Abstract

Quality is an elusive concept to define and is a bit like a box of chocolates with many different sizes, shapes and flavours. While not everyone has the same taste for chocolate, there has been a renewed focus on the quality of digital education since the COVID-19 crisis. Questions of quality and relevant quality assurance standards and processes have also come to the fore in response to concerns about contract cheating and recent developments in Artificial Intelligence, particularly following the launch of ChatGPT. This paper describes an initiative led by the authors in partnership with Quality and Qualifications Ireland (QQI) over the past 12 months to develop National Statutory Quality Assurance Guidelines for Providers of Programmes Supported by Digital Education. The Guidelines respond to some of the additional quality considerations arising from new digital education models. In describing the development of the National Guidelines, and the related methodology and public consultation process, the paper addresses the overarching question: What types of quality assurance standards, indicators and processes are required for new and emerging blended, hybrid and online learning approaches? In answering this question, we report key lessons and findings from a critical analysis of the international quality assurance literature in digital tertiary education. The term 'tertiary education' adopted by the OECD refers to all formal post-secondary education, including public and private providers. Key gaps and inherent tensions in the quality assurance literature are briefly identified by drawing on several contemporary publications in the area (Singh & Thurman, 2019; Staring, et al., 2022; Ubachs & Henderkx, 2023; Volungevičienė, et al., 2021). The main part of the paper then shares examples of the specific domains and quality considerations contained in the National Guidelines across three contexts: the organisational context, the programme context and the learner experience contest. A key feature of this discussion is to what extent online study modes give rise to additional quality considerations. Lastly, the paper reflects on the development of the National Guidelines and shares critical insights from the challenge of navigating a path between their legal and statutory requirements and a more enabling approach to quality assurance that seeks to build institutional and organisational cultures of continuous improvement. While evidence of the quality of the chocolate will highly depend on how institutions apply the guidelines, the paper concludes with several lessons for those responsible for leading and helping to enhance the quality of digital education.

Keywords:

Quality, quality assurance, digital education, online learning, hybrid learning, blended learning

References

Singh, V., & Thurman, A. (2019). How many ways can we define online learning? A systematic literature review of definitions of online learning (1988-2018). American Journal of Distance Education, 33(4), 289–306.

Staring, F., Brown, M., Bacsich, P., & Ifenthaler, D. (2022). Digital higher education: Emerging quality standards, practices and supports. OECD Education Working Papers, No. 281, OECD Publishing, Paris. https://doi.org/10.1787/f622f257-en.

Ubachs, G., & Henderikx, P. (2023). Quality assurance systems for digital higher education in Europe. In: Zawacki-Richter, O., Jung, I. (eds), Handbook of Open, Distance and Digital Education. Springer, Singapore. https://doi.org/10.1007/978-981-19-2080-6_41

Volungevičienė, A., Brown, M., Greenspon, R., Gaebel, M., & Morrisroe, A. (2021). *Developing a High-Performance Digital Education System: Institutional Self-Assessment Instruments.* European University Association, Brussels.

EMPLOYABILITY SKILLS ARTICULATION FOR MICRO-CREDENTIALING: EXTENDING GRADUATE CERTIFICATION TO ENHANCE EMPLOYMENT OPPORTUNITIES

Marcelo F. Maina, Lourdes Guàrdia, Universitat Oberta de Catalunya, Spain

Abstract

The issue of unemployment rates and market demands has been a major concern for international organisations in recent years (Jagannathan & Maclean, 2019). As a result, there has been a growing emphasis on enhancing graduates' employability skills, which are considered crucial for successful employment in today's continuously evolving job market (WEF, 2020). Studies have also shown that employers are increasingly requiring a skillful workforce, where not only specific but particularly soft skills (Abelha et al., 2020; Succi & Canovi, 2020) make a difference when hiring new personnel.

Micro-credentials offer an opportunity to bridge the skills gap offering new alternatives for lifelong learning (EC, 2021). They also add value to academic traditional transcripts and diplomas, making it possible to acknowledge skills developed throughout many different experiences and hence extending and complementing conventional academic awards, building personalised learning pathways and increasing opportunities for employment (Oliver, 2022).

We present an Employability Skills Micro-credentialing (ESMC) methodology (Maina et al., 2022) implemented as an ePortfolio of transition from academia to the labour market, consisting of a double articulation of students' skills (Goodwin et al. 2019) for teacher assessment and for employers' appraisal.

In the first articulation, students engage in a process of inquiry, reflection and integration. Students' reflect on their own experiences, explore and identify significant situations in which the development of employability skills have taken place, describe these situations, and select concrete evidence in support. During this process, teachers offer formative feedback until the students submit their work for final assessment and certification. A micro-credential per skill is issued as proof of the achievement.

In the second articulation, the students prepare their ePortfolio to exhibit their employability skills to prospective employers, for professional or job seeking purposes. Students revisit their ePortfolio, select the most relevant information to be displayed, including their earned micro-credentials, and record a three to five-minute video testimony using the STAR (situation, task, action and results) method for job interviewing, to demonstrate their readiness for work.

We illustrate the implementation of the methodology and results of a pilot in three African universities and one European involving 16 lecturers, 197 students, and 31 employers. Results show the methodology provides university recognition of employability skills on the basis of a transparent procedure and access to rich, concrete and multiple evidence, while increasing students' self-awareness, confidence, and external trust.

Keywords:

Employability skills, ePortfolio, Micro-credentials, Skills articulation, graduate students, extended recognition.

References

Abelha, M., Fernandes, S., Mesquita, D., Seabra, F., & Ferreira-Oliveira, A. T. (2020). Graduate employability and competence development in higher education—A systematic literature review using PRISMA. *Sustainability, 12*(15), 5900. https://doi.org/10.3390/su12155900

European Commission (2021). *Council Recommendation of a European approach to micro-credentials for lifelong learning and employability.* COM/2021/770 final. https://eur-lex.europa.eu/legal-content/EN/TXT/?uri=CELEX:52021DC0770

Goodwin, J. T., Goh, J., Verkoeyen, S., & Lithgow, K. (2019). Can students be taught to articulate employability skills?. *Education+ Training 61*(4), 445-460. https://doi.org/10.1108/ET-08-2018-0186

Jagannathan, S., Ra, S., & Maclean, R. (2019). Dominant recent trends impacting on jobs and labor markets-An Overview. *International Journal of Training Research, 17*(1), 1-11. https://doi.org/10.1080/14480220.2019.1641292

Maina, M.F., Guàrdia Ortiz, L., Mancini, F. et al. A micro-credentialing methodology for improved recognition of HE employability skills. *Int J Educ Technol High Educ 19*, 10 (2022). https://doi.org/10.1186/s41239-021-00315-5

Oliver, B. (2022). *Towards a Common Definition of Micro-credentials.* UNESCO. https://unesdoc.unesco.org/ark:/48223/pf0000381668

Succi, C., & Canovi, M. (2020). Soft skills to enhance graduate employability: comparing students and employers' perceptions. *Studies in higher education, 45*(9), 1834-1847. https://doi.org/10.1080/03075079.2019.1585420

WEF (World Economic Forum). *Future of Jobs.* https://www3.weforum.org/docs/WEF_Future_of_Jobs_2020.pdf

STUDENT AND STAFF EXPERIENCES OF PRACTISING PARTNERSHIP IN ASSESSMENT

Rob Lowney, Dublin City University, Ireland

Abstract

Student partnership is "a collaborative, reciprocal process" (Cook-Sather, Bovill, & Felten, 2014, p. 6–7) in which students contribute as best they can to educational processes. These processes can be in the domains of quality assurance, governance, student representation, or teaching, learning and assessment (National Student Engagement Programme, 2021). Assessment is an area of staff-student partnership area in Dublin City University (DCU) which has seen growth in recent years. Student partnership in assessment helps to develop students' assessment literacy (Ní Bheoláin et al, 2020), supports student engagement (National Forum for the Enhancement of Teaching and Learning in Higher Education, 2016), recognises students' agency in their learning (HEA, 2016), supports academic integrity (Egan, 2018) and supports universal design for learning (CAST, 2018). The DCU Teaching Enhancement Unit devised a framework for practising student partnership in assessment (2020). It places assessment partnership possibilities along a continuum, from simple to complex. Possibilities include student choice in assessment, self/peer assessment, directive feedback and co-creation of grading criteria. Several approaches have been piloted in DCU modules and the student/staff experiences captured through evaluations. Emerging findings show positive impacts on both parties. Students felt they understood assessment better and performed better because of the partnership approach. They also felt the partnership approaches they experienced would make it difficult for them to engage in academic misconduct. Staff similarly felt students were more engaged because of the partnership approach and they intend to continue practising such approaches in future. This paper at EDEN will share the experiences of students and staff who have practised assessment partnership over the past two years, and share the emerging findings from ongoing evaluations. Perspectives from conference attendees and other partnership practitioners are welcomed, to further refine the DCU framework.

Keywords:

Student partnership, assessment, co-creation, student engagement

References

CAST. (2018). *Universal Design for Learning Guidelines version 2.2.* http://udlguidelines.cast.org

Cook-Sather, A., Bovill, C., & Felten, P. (2014). *Engaging students as partners in learning and teaching: a guide for faculty.* San Francisco: Jossey Bass.

DCU Teaching Enhancement Unit. (2020). *Students as partners in assessment: partnership possibilities and perfecting partnerships.* Dublin: Dublin City University. https://bit.ly/sapia

Egan, A. (2018). *Improving Academic Integrity through Assessment Design.* Dublin: Dublin City University, National Institute for Digital Learning (NIDL).

HEA (Higher Education Authority) Working Group. (2016). *Enhancing Student Engagement in Decision-Making.* https://nstepsite.files.wordpress.com/2018/07/enhancing_student_engagement_in_decision_making_report.pdf

National Forum for the Enhancement of Teaching and Learning in Higher Education. (2016). *Students as Partners.* https://www.teachingandlearning.ie/publication/students-as-partners/

National Student Engagement Programme. (2021). *Steps to Partnership.* https://studentengagement.ie/about/framework/

Ní Bheoláin, R., Lowney, R. & O'Riordan, F. (2020). *Students as Partners in Assessment: A Literature Scoping Review.* Dublin: Dublin City University. https://doi.org/10.5281/zenodo.4270579

INCORPORATING COLLABORATIVE ANNOTATION INTO HYBRID LEARNING FOR MEANINGFUL LEARNING

Mark P. McCormack, Melat Tecle, John G. Keating, Maynooth University, Ireland

Abstract

During the COVID-19 pandemic, there was a coordinated push toward the development of resources and tools for educators in online learning and since then, educators and students found the learning techniques used during the pandemic complemented existing pedagogical strategies through hybrid-learning and improved the students' quality of learning [1] [2].

We believe it is valuable to observe students' discourse in order to improve our pedagogical approach. One such method of this is Collaborative Annotation, where students can make notes on their assignments with each other and discuss their ideas. There has been research exploring the integration of existing online learning approaches into the traditional classroom, such as those done by Singh [2] and Triyason [3]. However, there is no overall framework for integrating Collaborative Annotation into the classroom and this area of research is what we are pursuing.

Keywords:

Collaborative Annotation, Social Annotation, Online Learning, Hybrid Learning, Pedagogical Framework

Collaborative Annotation within Hybrid Learning

Collaboration is an active learning technique that allows students to develop novel ideas in isolation, bring them to a group context, and discuss these ideas with peers who may have different viewpoints. Collaborative Annotation (CA) enhances this approach by allowing for ideas to be discussed directly within the material, keeping track of all ideas made as annotations, and discussing which annotation may be considered as more correct.

The key factor here is that Collaborative Annotation is used for assessment, both as an assessment for learning and assessment as learning. When students engage in a dialogue using this technique, they will critique and comment on each other's work to come to some new understanding of the material in question. In this regard, we see the assessment as learning, and when a teacher reviews the comments, the students made on each other's work and gives them each their own feedback, this is the assessment for learning.

Razon's [4] findings suggest CA results in increased learning comprehension amongst students, meaning they do not just memorize the material but internalize and understand its concepts. Research also reveals that students' soft skills significantly increase with this methodology, which can lead to improved future job prospects [3].

However, this is only one metric to analyse this approach. There is little existing research regarding the pedagogical strategies to integrate this methodology into traditional or hybrid learning contexts. Kalir [5] believes that a read, remark, remix (RRR) approach should be taken to integration. We believe RRR to be promising, though it requires further development to articulate the precise practical steps needed for integration. This research actively works to improve this approach, defining the methodology to integrate with other learning contexts and analysing different tools' impacts in each stage of this process.

We believe that Hybrid Learning is the perfect environment for Collaborative Annotation, as students may conduct their dialogic discussions online or at home while attending their classes and receiving teacher feedback in person. Our software builds upon this by integrating pedagogical tools into the tool such as the assignment of students to modules, teacher/student assessment, and module organization similar to existing MOOC's such as Moodle.

Meaningful Learning with Collaborative Annotation

For our purposes, we consider meaningful learning as students being able to identify what they are doing well, what they can improve on, and how they can then learn from their mistakes [8]. We also believe meaningful learning involves discourse amongst students so they can explore different views on some material and perhaps come to new conclusions they would not have been able to discover by just themselves. I believe meaningful hybrid learning holds the same philosophies, but to achieve this, there must be a rigorous assessment framework, this way both educators and students can be sure that they are achieving the learning outcomes set for them.

Collaborative Annotation is useful particularly to students as it allows for their discourse to be tracked and used as a form of assessment as/for learning. While students chat with each other about what the correct answer/different meanings of some material are, they result in critically analyse each other's viewpoints and in turn their own. Over a set time, this has been shown to result in both better material retention and more importantly an improved quality of learning, comprising both enjoyment of the process and knowledge of the material [9].

From this discourse, educators can understand how their students engage with and understand their material. From this, they can reflect on their teaching approach and improve their methodologies such that students reach the educators desired learning outcomes [10]. For example, if a teacher notices much of the discussion on a material revolves around the non-desired area, they can place more focus in their next lesson in the future on the more important area of work.

Regarding best practices, Collaborative Annotation can be integrated into existing pedagogical practices by use of homework. Given the prevalence of the internet, most students are likely to have some form of discourse regarding their materials outside the classroom, so it may be valuable for us as educators to integrate this directly into our pedagogical strategy such that the analysis and modification of our teaching approach seen above can be used.

Summary

Collaborative Annotation is a pedagogical assessment strategy whereby students engage in discourse regarding their assignment and can learn from each other's viewpoints by comparing them with their own. Teachers can then analyse this to improve their teaching strategy. The process of Collaborative Annotation leads to more meaningful learning in hybrid learning as it forces students to compare their thoughts on materials with others, find what gaps they have in their own knowledge, and learn from their peers in the process.

References

Pokhrel, S., & Chhetri, R. (2021). A literature review on impact of COVID-19 pandemic on teaching and learning. *Higher education for the future*, *8*(1), 133-141.

Singh, J., Steele, K., & Singh, L. (2021). Combining the best of online and face-to-face learning: Hybrid and blended learning approach for COVID-19, post vaccine, & post-pandemic world. *Journal of Educational Technology Systems*, *50*(2), 140-171.

Triyason, T., Tassanaviboon, A., & Kanthamanon, P. (2020, July). Hybrid classroom: Designing for the new normal after COVID-19 pandemic. In *Proceedings of the 11th International Conference on Advances in Information Technology* (pp. 1-8).

Razon, S., Turner, J., Johnson, T. E., Arsal, G., & Tenenbaum, G. (2012). Effects of a collaborative annotation method on students' learning and learning-related motivation and affect. *Computers in human behavior*, *28*(2), 350-359.

Kalir, J., Cantrill, C., Dean, J., & Dillon, J. (2020). Iterating the marginal syllabus: Social reading and annotation while social distancing. *Journal of Technology and Teacher Education*, *28*(2), 463-471.

Novak, E., Razzouk, R., & Johnson, T. E. (2012). The educational use of social annotation tools in higher education: A literature review. *The Internet and Higher Education*, *15*(1), 39-49.

Wiggins, B. L., Eddy, S. L., Wener-Fligner, L., Freisem, K., Grunspan, D. Z., Theobald, E. J., ... & Crowe, A. J. (2017). ASPECT: A survey to assess student perspective of engagement in an active-learning classroom. *CBE—Life Sciences Education, 16*(2), ar32.

Taniguchi, S. T., Freeman, P. A., & Richards, A. L. (2005). Attributes of meaningful learning experiences in an outdoor education program. *Journal of Adventure Education & Outdoor Learning, 5*(2), 131-144.

Krouska, A., Troussas, C., & Virvou, M. (2018, July). Social annotation tools in digital learning: A literature review. In *2018 9th international conference on information, intelligence, systems and applications (IISA)* (pp. 1-4). IEEE.

Singh, S., & Meyer, B. (2019, July). Using social annotations to augment the learning space and learner experience. In *Proceedings of the 2019 ACM Conference on Innovation and Technology in Computer Science Education* (pp. 527-533).

HOW ONTARIO EVOLVED AS A MAJOR HUB OF ONLINE LEARNING IN NORTH AMERICA

Maxim Jean-Louis, Contact North, Canada

Abstract

In colleges, universities, and Indigenous institutes, online learning is in part a response to the growing student demand for flexibility in learning and to the regional and rural nature of large parts of the province. Ontario has 4,900 publicly funded elementary and secondary schools, 23 publicly assisted universities, 24 colleges of applied arts and technology, nine Indigenous institutes, over 500 private career colleges and other private institutions such as faith-based institutions. All have students engaged in online learning. In the school system, completing two credits online is now required for high school graduation. Online learning has grown faster in Ontario than in other parts of Canada and across Canada. Registrations in online courses in higher education are growing faster than registration in face-to-face learning. This presentation will explore how Ontario became a hub for online learning.

Keywords:

Virtual learning strategy, policy-driven development, collaboration, support infrastructure.

Summary

Ontario has emerged as a major hub of online learning, thanks to a combination of policy leadership, investment in infrastructure, and support for collaborative program and course development. Ontario has invested significantly in online learning, with the Ontario Virtual Learning Strategy alone backed by an investment of over $70 million since 2020. Ontario is home to a range of virtual learning offerings, including K-12 online courses, which will see 230,000 course registrations in 2023-24, certificates, diplomas, and degrees from universities, colleges, and Indigenous institutes, and micro-credentials from various organizations. In all, there are over 42,000 college and university courses, 3,850 micro-credentials and 2,000 other qualifications available online.

Online registrations in Ontario have grown faster than the rest of Canada, with the college sector leading the way. Ontario's success in online learning is a system-wide activity, and other jurisdictions would benefit from emulating its policy leadership, investment, and support infrastructure. Recently, Ontario has announced new investments in online learning, including additional funds for micro-credentials and other student supports.

The key elements of the strategy pursued by the Government of Ontario, working in partnership with institutions and digital learning partners like eCampusOntario and Contact North | Contact Nord involves these elements:

- **Digital content** - development and/or adaptation of virtual learning content.
- **Digital capacity** - deployment of targeted supports for institutions in need of digital capacity to enable high-quality online learning and supports to expand. institutional access to broader and more sustainable markets, both domestically and globally.
- **Digital fluency** - deployment of supports to equip faculty and students with the skills and resources required to effectively teach and learn online.
- **Digital delivery** - identification, procurement and deployment of educational technologies to support fully-online program and course offerings.
- **Digital infrastructure – Ontario has the most substantial digital infrastructure in Canada (including 5G networks) and is investing $4 billion to ensure that all citizens have access to broadband by 2025.**

The aim of these activities is to support three key outcomes:

1. **Be the Future: Ensure learners have high-quality education**: anytime, from anywhere. This requires quality and innovation, better data, and digital access to enable lifelong learning and fuel Ontario's global competitiveness.

2. **Be Lifelong Learners: Enable learners to meet the needs of the rapidly evolving labour market** at any stage of their careers by providing digital support and infrastructure for new short-duration training.

3. **Be a Global Leader: Strengthen Ontario's leadership domestically and globally**, by expanding access for Ontario's institutions to the global marketplace for virtual learning. With this, the ministry aims to position Ontario as a global leader for virtual innovation in teaching and learning.

Backed by a $70 million investment (€48 million) and supported by a significant infrastructure, the Virtual Learning Strategy is also seen as a way of encouraging the growth and development of Ontario's burgeoning EdTech sector. Experimentation and collaboration between public institutions and between public institutions and these companies is explicitly encouraged.

IMPLEMENTING CHALLENGE-BASED LEARNING: WHAT THE EMERGING LITERATURE SAYS

Clare Gormley, Dublin City University, Ireland

Abstract

No doubt many of us have heard the calls for Higher Education Institutions (HEIs) to develop future-focused curricula that will prepare students to tackle the urgent societal issues of our time. In times like these, it might be said that the time has come for pedagogies of a particular persuasion - those that will help students engage in a process of problem-solving that can be applied in the many unpredictable contexts they are likely to face.

Challenge-Based Learning (CBL) has been suggested as one such pedagogy, one that might form part of a 'pedagogical toolkit to meet future trends in HE' (Gallagher & Savage, 2022, p.391). CBL has previously been described in numerous ways. One of the most commonly cited definitions is that by Apple Inc. who describe CBL as:

> *an engaging multidisciplinary approach to teaching and learning that encourages students to leverage the technology they use in their daily lives to solve real-world problems. Challenge Based Learning is collaborative and handson, asking students to work with peers, teachers, and experts in their communities and around the world to ask good questions, develop deeper subject area knowledge, accept and solve challenges, take action, and share their experience. (Nichols & Cator, 2008, p.1)*

However various other definitions of CBL exist, some of which put more of an emphasis on the sustainability and/or societal impact of this approach (Malmqvist et al., 2015). Indeed, one of the challenges of research, according to previous literature reviews, has been the lack of a common definition on what exactly CBL is (Gallagher & Savage, 2020; Leijon et al., 2021).

The current paper is based on a systematized literature review - a review informed by systematic approaches (Grant & Booth, 2009) - that aims to further inform the CBL evidence base. Exploring an identified gap, it has a specific focus on CBL implementation and will share a number of emerging themes:

Firstly, it is clear that a 'definitional muddying' issue persists. However, rather than focusing on a fixed definition, recent literature is recognising variety in CBL implementations and suggesting more flexible frameworks (van den Beemt et al., 2022, p.2).

Secondly, there are challenges with putting CBL into practice in higher education, which could be described as an implementation gap. Barriers are becoming more commonly reported, indicating tensions that need to be addressed for successful implementation (Rosén et al., 2022). These include a need for professional learning that helps teachers new to CBL adjust to their role and strategies/policies to reduce institutional barriers to working across disciplines.

Thirdly, there seems to be a weakness in the literature on the significance of the leadership component of CBL initiatives. While leadership is recognised as important to the success of teaching and learning in general, little has yet been written from the perspective of those leading CBL implementations.

This paper will explore these and other literature-driven themes in the hopes of generating fruitful discussion on both the theory and practice of CBL.

Keywords:

Challenge-Based Learning, CBL, Futures, Curriculum, Innovation

References

Gallagher, S.E. & Savage, T. (2020). Challenge-based learning in higher education: an exploratory literature review. *Teaching in Higher Education, 0*(0), pp. 1–23.

Gallagher, S.E. & Savage, T. (2022). Challenge Based Learning: Recommendations for the Future of Higher Education. In E. Vilalta-Perdomo et al. (Eds.), *The Emerald Handbook of Challenge Based Learning* (pp. 391–411). Emerald Publishing Limited.

Grant, M.J. & Booth, A. (2009). A typology of reviews: an analysis of 14 review types and associated methodologies, *Health Information & Libraries Journal, 26*(2), pp. 91–108.

Leijon, M., Gudmundsson, P., Staaf, P., & Christersson, C. (2021). Challenge based learning in higher education– A systematic literature review, *Innovations in Education and Teaching International, 0*(0), pp. 1–10.

Malmqvist, J., Rådberg, K.K. & Lundqvist, U. (2015). Comparative Analysis of Challenge-based Learning Experiences, in 11th International CDIO Conference, Chengdu University of Information Technology, China.

Nichols & Cator (2008) Challenge Based Learning White Paper. Cupertino, California: Apple, Inc.

Rosén, A., Peters, A.K., Daniels, M., Danielsson, M., Hemphala, J., Hakansson, M., & Sandstrom, G.O. (2022). Transformation-Driving Education: Perspectives Emerging in a Dialogue between Teachers with Experiences from Challenge-Driven Education, in 2022 IEEE Frontiers in Education Conference (FIE), Uppsala, Sweden.

van den Beemt, A., van de Watering, G. and Bots, M. (2022). Conceptualising variety in challenge-based learning in higher education: the CBL-compass, *European Journal of Engineering Education,* pp. 1–18.

ENHANCING THE QUALITY OF FORMAL ONLINE LEARNING SPACES: A TOOL FOR SELF-POSITIONING AND DEVELOPMENT

Hiba Asri, Cadi Ayyad University, Morocco; Mélanie Bonvin, UniDistance, Switzerland; Christophe Borne, Université Lyon 1, France; Natalie Bornet, UniDistance, Switzerland; Henrietta Carbonel, UniDistance, Switzerland; Jean-Michel Jullien, UniDistance, Switzerland, Eric Panassier, Université Lyon 1, France; Abdelali Rochdi, Cadi Ayyad University, Morocco

Abstract

Learning spaces have become much more diverse with the increase in accessibility of digital technologies. Whether in traditional or online universities, one essential part of the learning space is the learning management system (LMS). LMSs are ubiquitous and an important component of learning experience nowadays. They offer access to resources without time or geographical constraints, allowing the interactions to continue beyond the scheduled class time (Lamb et al., 2022). However, the quality of formal online learning spaces is still very heterogenous in our institutions. Consequently, there is a need for a tool that can assist educators in developing quality and engaging formal online learning spaces.

This concise paper presents an international project including researchers and practitioners from Cadi Ayyad University, Morocco, University of Lyon 1, France, and UniDistance, Switzerland, as well as a reviewer from the University of Edinburgh, UK. We aim to create a quality matrix for formal online learning spaces, allowing educators to position themselves with regard to their current online teaching practices, and suggesting improvement paths based on their instructional goals, objectives and strategies. Through this international collaboration, we cover a broad range of types of universities, both traditional and online, from 2'500 to over 100'000 students, from 20 to over 400 years old, with different access to technologies, fields of research, pedagogical practices, and thus uses of formal online learning spaces.

We conducted a literature review to define the main criteria for a quality learning management system (Anand and Eswaran, 2018; Damnjanovic et al. 2015; Kurilovas, 2009; Shchedrina et al., 2021), compared these criteria to models in our own universities, and discussed with experts to develop a matrix which includes pedagogical and technological criteria of quality for the design of an LMS, across four levels of sophistication. Currently, we are conducting semi-structured interviews with teaching teams of the three universities to evaluate the matrix and its use. This feedback will allow us to adjust our matrix according to the actual practices of teachers. During the conference, we will share the latest version of the matrix, as well as the results of the interviews regarding its use.

Overall, this project aims to contribute to the improvement of the quality of formal online learning spaces by defining criteria, creating a positioning tool, and suggesting improvement paths based on teaching strategies and objectives.

Keywords:

Learning Spaces. Learning Management System. Online teaching practices. Quality of learning spaces

References

Anand, A., & Eswaran, S. (2018). CASE STUDY MOODLE Approach to learning and content management system (LCMS). *International Journal of Computer Sciences and Engineering*, 6(7), 1147-1152.

Damnjanovic, V., Jednak, S., & Mijatovic, I. (2015). Factors affecting the effectiveness and use of Moodle: students' perception. *Interactive learning environments*, 23(4), 496-514.

Kurilovas, E. (2009). Methods of multiple criteria evaluation of the quality of learning management systems for personalised learners needs. In EC-TEL'2009 Workshop" Learning Management Systems meet Adaptive Learning Environments.

Lamb, J., Carvalho, L., Gallagher, M., & Knox, J. (2022). The Postdigital Learning Spaces of Higher Education. *Postdigital Science and Education*, *4*(1), 1–12. https://doi.org/10.1007/s42438-021-00279-9

Shchedrina, E., Valiev, I., Sabirova, F., & Babaskin, D. (2021). Providing adaptivity in Moodle LMS courses. *International Journal of Emerging Technologies in Learning* (iJET), 16(2), 95-107.

USING YESTERDAY'S EXPERIENCES TO OVERCOME TOMMORROW'S CHALLENGES - REFLECTION-BASED COMPTENCE DEVELOPMENT IN THEORY-PRACTICE STUDIES

Nicole Geier, Laura Eigbrecht, Ulf-Daniel Ehlers, Cooperative State University Baden-Wuerttemberg, Karlsruhe, Germany

Abstract

Higher education increasingly faces the challenge of educating students in their respective subject area and supporting them in developing future skills. At Cooperative State University Baden-Wuerttemberg (DHBW), where students spend half of a term in theory and the other half in practice learning settings, we develop a future skills teaching/learning concept and an associated digital reflection tool for skills development for skills acquisition in dual studies. The respective project (DIRK Dual – Digital reflection tool for competence development in dual studies) aims to support students at the interface between theory and practice learning, guide them in becoming self-responsible learning experts and become aware of the future skills development that takes place when working at the practice partner organisations (dual partners).

Currently, students need to hand in a report on tasks and competence reflection regarding their practice phases once a year. This instrument aims to interlock students' experiences from both theory and practice phases and trigger reflection-based learning. However, the report is perceived as too static and not serving the student's needs when it comes to self-reflection and competence development. Accordingly, DIRK Dual aims at (1) digitalising the report instrument, (2) designing a more continuous reflection and feedback process including coachings on these two topics and peer learning activities, and (3) building an accompanying future skills module, resulting in a badgified future skills certificate at the end of the undergraduate programme.

Goals (1) and (2) are to be rolled out across the university and accredited as mandatory in the curricula. To integrate the future skills certificate into the curriculum, however, will be of choice of the study programme leaders. Students whose programme leaders do not integrate the modules in the curriculum will be given the chance to acquire the certificate on their own, as an elective.

We therefore refer to the concept of the reflective practitioner (Schön, 1983) and the 17 future skills profiles according to Ehlers (2020). Learning units are developed for each future skills profile, which consist of three parts: 1) learning nuggets including a short introduction to the content of the corresponding skill, what the skill comprises and application examples; 2) a pool of activities from which students choose two and which they are asked to conduct during their following practice phase in order to further develop their chosen future skill and to reflect on it; 3) a reflection task that is intended to help students understand where they stand in their skill development and how they can further develop their future skills in the future on their individual learning path. Another integral part is peer learning and peer exchange which will sharpen both reflection and feedback competence.

Both pathways, the refined report on tasks and competence reflection and the future skills certificate, will use an e-portfolio tool for reflection practices. This will enable students to collect significant reflective moments and to put them in a portfolio for presentation purposes in the end. Besides reflection artefacts, the tool will also incorporate feedback on artefacts and students' training schedules. In both cases, whether students complete the project's modules or not, they will use the e-portfolio tool to create the process and reflection report at the end of each study year. Either way, this project aims to help students become reflective practitioners (Schön 1984) and wants to set them off to a life-long learning path, enabling them to build skills along the way as needed in their private and working life.

Keywords:

Reflective learning; life-long learning; e-portfolio; future skills

References

Ehlers, U.-D. (2020). Future Skills. Lernen der Zukunft – Hochschule der Zukunft. Wiesbaden, Heideberg: Springer VS (Zukunft der Hochschulbildung – Future Higher Education).

Schön, D. (1984). The Reflective Practitioner: How Professionals Think in Action. New York: Basic Books Inc.

USING TUTORSTACK TO FACILITATE ONLINE SOCIAL INTERACTIONS, SOCIAL PRESENCE & MINGLING IN FUTURE ONLINE LEARNING COMMUNITIES

Colm Dunphy, Eamonn de Leastar, Peter Windle, SETU, Ireland

Abstract

Learner communities foster a sense of belonging, personal relatedness, connection, (Osterman, 2000), identity, and better learning experiences. They help prevent isolation and loneliness (Rovai, 2005; Rosell, 2018). This is especially important in online education Garrison et al. (2000).

Anderson's (2003) 'equivalency theorem' highlights three 'modes of interaction'. These must be facilitated by a framework for blended online and digital (BOLD). 'Emergency remote teaching' resulted in many student-content interactions as teachers struggled to be live in online virtual classrooms (Power et al., 2022; Wetzlmair et al, 2021; Sy et al, 2022). A vital element was absent - social presence.

So how do we facilitate social presence online? What are the indicators (Lowenthal, 2014), behaviours (Short, et al.,1976) and measures (Kreijns, Xu and Weidlich, 2021) of social presence?

This paper presents a solution in the form of a defined framework for blended, online, and digital teaching success, delivered in synchronous or asynchronous modes, using open, free, effectively free, or low-cost technology solutions. TutorStack is a pedagogical framework supported by a technology stack (combination of technologies). The framework highlights four key layers of a technological solution to deliver high quality online synchronous and asynchronous programmes, for blended, online and digital and is ideally suited to small private online course (SPOCs).

In this paper, we highlight specific examples from an ongoing case study of online mature learners. Examples include hangback sessions, huddles, homework threads, collaborative posts, themes, connections, and the use of Slack, Zoom, and Gather.Town. A prototype of how online mingling features from Gather.Town might be incorporated into the open source tutors.dev system is outlined.

TutorStack

TutorStack (Dunphy et al., 2019) is an integrated technology solution that unbundles the Learning Management System (LMS) identifying four key features/layers: 1) Learning Materials & Resources; 2) Communications/Community Building; 3) Assessment & Feedback; 4) Media. This paper is concerned with Layer 2 but with references to the other layers as the solutions become integrated.

Slack is the tool of choice for all communications. Originally a text-based work chat system. We create a workspace for each programme cohort. Slack facilitates private messages (DMs) between two and eight people. Channels facilitate broader/larger discussion. These can be public or private. Sharing of files is facilitated through drag and drop. Unlike text messaging and WhatsApp tools, Slack has threads so responses to questions are organised, and context is maintained. Audio and video communication, and screen sharing (and previously remote control) make it an ideal choice for supporting students online. Integrations allow other tools to be seamlessly integrated within Slack. For example, the recommended Zoom integration can transparently replace the Slack audio-visual calls, screen share and remote-control features for even higher quality.

Examples

#watercooler channel for non-academic chat where students can chat as they would at break times around the water cooler or kettle.

#connections channel pre-induction, where students follow posts by staff who introduce themselves (as might happen at icebreakers in first classes in a traditional classroom)

Lecturers create initial posts for homework questions/challenges. Students reply with the output of their solutions (e.g., the graphical output of a computer program that they are asked to write). This prompts other students to do their homework and leads to follow on conversations, peer learning and community building as students ask, "how did you do that?"

Emoj Surveys for quick visual responses without needing detailed analysis.

Slack collaborative posts are posts in which the authors enable others to modify/collaborate on their post. So consider a post to summarize a class. The lecturer posts a basic entry for example "Week 3 class 1 – Loops." Students are asked to collaborate on the post and add all the different types of loops covered in class, the elements of the loops and so on.

Themes are part of Tutors (2021) utilised in TutorStack Layer 1. Traditionally, themes were used for dark mode, light mode, compact mode, and switching the formatting between different schemes of colours and fonts, for the learning management system. Two common themes are the Tutors standard theme and the Dyslexia theme. Additional themes for Christmas, Valentines and Halloween were developed to enhance social presence – creating a "smile moment" when experienced unexpectedly.

At the end of each online class, one click access to Zoom hangback sessions (a predefined recurring Zoom meeting) hyperlinked from the tutors cards or companion app icons, mimic the situation in traditional classrooms, where students wait until others leave the room to speak to the lecturer at the end of class.

Slack huddles are initiated by flipping a button in Slack. The context is the current text chat conversation you are in. Initiating a huddle effectively calls all parties in the discussion. The idea of a huddle is that it is less formal, ad-hoc without an agenda, and may only need voice. A huddle starts as a voice call but video and screen sharing / whiteboarding can be switched on if necessary. An unexpected use case was during recorded live online streamed classes using TutorStack with YouTube (7 sec delay). Students start one or more huddles and talk between themselves (facilitating the rumble from f2f classes but without the teacher being distracted, or the rumble being recorded on video. A rapporteur for each huddle can type any questions into the channel if verbal questions can't be answered by the group. These are monitored by the lecturer leading to a cleaner higher quality recording for those that can't make the live classes.

Gather.Town attempts to address the ability to mingle. It has a two-dimensional gaming interface in which environments can be built. Each user has an avatar (character) that can be walk around the environment. When you bump into another character, a video call is immediately initiated. Consider how you might mingle in the lobby area at a traditional conference. Smiling and saying hello to complete strangers. In the virtual online world Gather.Town affords this type of interaction. There is no scheduled predefined meeting. Video calls start and end effortlessly. You can bump into someone and decide not to interact just as you would in real life. You may also decide to have a chat with someone. One downside of the technology is the gaming interface. We hope to leverage similar ideas in Tutors, without the gaming interface, specifically within the TutorsLive component. Students online now, will be dynamically grouped into what they are working on, with call and chat buttons available for each group. This could leverage a Slack Huddle, or be implemented natively. For now, we are exploring Gather.Town further through a funded N-TUTTORS project with other colleagues and students.

Summary

Examples outlined show how Slack can facilitate online social interactions and social presence in online communities. The new Huddle feature promotes less formal, ad-hoc interactions without an agenda. Hangback Sessions leverage Zoom and Tutors to make it easier to have informal online interactions. However, Gather.Town looks to be the most immediate form of mingling online especially with people you don't know. Work continues on the TutorsLive components to bring the immediacy of Gather.Town video calls to Tutors and TutorStack without requiring additional licenses for Gather.Town.

Keywords:

TutorStack, tutors.dev, social presence, mingling online, slack, Gather.Town.

References

Anderson, T. (2003). Getting the mix right again: An updated and theoretical rationale for interaction. *The International Review of Research in Open and Distributed Learning*, *4*(1), 2. https://doi.org/10.19173/irrodl.v4i2.149

Dunphy, C., Windle, P., DeLeastar, E., & Widger, L. (2019). *TutorStack - A multi-layer technology stack providing a modular, free and/or open solution for Blended and Online Digital (BOLD) without product or vendor lock-in.* Tutor Stack Links; Colm Dunphy. http://www.colmdunphy.com/tutorstack/TutorStack.html

Garrison, D. Randy., Anderson, T., & Archer, W. (2000). Critical Inquiry in a Text-Based Environment: Computer Conferencing in Higher Education. *The Internet and Higher Education*, *2*(2-3), 87–105. https://auspace.athabascau.ca/bitstream/handle/2149/739/?sequence=1

Kreijns, K., Xu, K., & Weidlich, J. (2021). Social Presence: Conceptualization and Measurement. *Educational Psychology Review*, *2022*(34), 139–170. https://doi.org/10.1007/s10648-021-09623-8

Osterman, K. F. (2000). Students' Need for Belonging in the School Community. *Review of Educational Research*, *70*(3), 323–367. https://doi.org/10.2307/1170786

Power, A., Park, V., Owens, M., & Palapal Sy, M. (2022). Academics' Experiences of Online Interprofessional Education in Response to COVID-19. *British Journal of Midwifery*, *30*(4), 222–228. https://doi.org/10.12968/bjom.2022.30.4.222

Rosell, C. (2018). Offline or Online Learning Communities, Which are More Effective? - CAE Computer Aided Elearning. [online] CAE Computer Aided E-learning. Available at: https://www.cae.net/offline-or-online-learning-communities/ [Accessed 21 Oct. 2020].

Short, J., Williams, E., & Christie, B. (1976). *The social psychology of telecommunications.* J. Wiley

Sy, M. P., Park, V., Nagraj, S., Power, A., & Herath, C. (2022). Emergency Remote Teaching for Interprofessional Education during COVID-19: Student Experiences. *British Journal of Midwifery*, *30*(1), 47–55. https://doi.org/10.12968/bjom.2022.30.1.47

Tutors. (2021). *Tutors Open Source Project* (E. de Leastar, Ed.). Tutors.dev. https://tutors.dev/

Wetzlmair, L.-C., Kitema, G. F., O'Carroll, V., El-Awaisi, A., Power, A., Owens, M., Park, V., McKinley, M., Anderson, E. S., & Loder-Fink, B. (2021). The Impact of COVID-19 on the Delivery of Interprofessional education: it's Not All Bad News. *British Journal of Midwifery*, *29*(12), 699–705. https://doi.org/10.12968/bjom.2021.29.12.699

IMPLEMENTATION OF SCAFFOLDING IN ONLINE HIGHER EDUCATION COURSES

Jennifer C. Richardson, Daniela Castellanos Reyes, Holly Fiock, Mohammad Shams Ud Duha, Yishi Long, Purdue University, United States; Secil Caskurlu, Florida State University, United States

Abstract

Attrition in online courses occurs as students face multiple challenges from familiarizing themselves with the online environment to lack of just-in-time instructor support or social support from their peers (Darby & Lang, 2019). Therefore, providing scaffolding is crucial in online courses to sustain students' interest and overcome the challenges, which will in turn help students achieve their learning objectives. Scaffolding in education happens when a more knowledgeable other helps a learner to perform certain tasks until the learner can do it independently (Brush & Saye, 2002; Vygotsky, 1978; Wood, et al., 1976). Using a multiple case study design, we identified scaffolding strategies in online courses from four participants through semi-structured interviews and course observations.

Five types of scaffolding from the literature: conceptual, metacognitive, procedural, strategic, (Hannafin et al., 1999) and motivational (Belland et al., 2013) and we then further broke those out by hard (fixed, pre-planned) and soft (personalized, just-in-time feedback) scaffolds (Brush & Saye, 2002). The use of both hard and soft scaffolds for all five types of scaffolding were observed in each course, yet implementation of those scaffolds varied. Hard scaffolds included detailed assignment descriptions with probing questions (procedural and metacognitive), while others were unique to the online environment including a case walk-through to understand how case-based learning is applied (strategic), course overview videos (procedural, motivation), and peer review groups or rooms (metacognitive). Soft scaffolds provided learners with personalized, just-in-time feedback.

While our participants utilized all types of scaffolding their mechanisms for implementation varied depending on task intention (discussion forums, announcements). Participants utilized specific technology tools depending on their contexts and preferences (videos, audio feedback, VoiceThread, discussions). Participants also shared their approaches to measuring the success of scaffolds, which is an area lacking in literature. Finally, participants identified an additional type of scaffold that we had not anticipated and found little research on – scaffolds for the affective domain in higher education courses.

Our results showed that instructors' implementation of scaffolding differed based on their discipline and teaching philosophy, and the unique features of online courses. Implications for practice and research are discussed. We will share scaffolding strategy examples from across the types and mechanisms we observed.

Keywords:

Online learning, scaffolding, learning design, course design.

References

Belland, B. R., Kim, C., & Hannafin, M. (2013). A framework for designing scaffolds that improve motivation and cognition. *Educational Psychologist, 48*(4), 243–270. https://doi.org/10.1080/ 00461520.2013.838920

Brush, T. A. & Saye, J. W. (2002). A summary of research exploring hard and soft scaffolding for teachers and learners

using a multimedia supported learning environment. *The Journal of Interactive Online Learning, 1*(2), 1–12.

http://www.ncolr.org/ jiol/ issues/pdf/1.23.pdf

Darby, F., & Lang, J. M. (2019). *Small teaching online: Applying learning science in online classes*. Jossey-Bass.

Hannafin, M., Land, S., & Oliver, K. (1999). Open learning environments: Foundations, methods, and models. In C. M,

Reigeluth (Ed.), *Instructional-Design theories and models: A new paradigm of instructional theory* (Vol. 2, pp. 115–140). Lawrence Erlbaum Associates.

Vygotsky, L. S. (1978). *Mind in society: The development of higher psychological processes.* Cambridge: Harvard University Press.

Wood, D., Bruner, J., & Ross, G. (1976). The role of tutoring in problem solving. *Journal of Child Psychology and Child Psychiatry, 17,* 89–100. https://doi.org/10.1111/j.1469-7610.1976.tb00381.x

"YES WE CAN" – MENTORSHIP OF ONLINE LEARNERS TO FOSTER STUDENT SUCCESS

Daniel Farr, Kennesaw State University, USA

Abstract

This concise paper explores a few brief ideas for online courses and pedagogical transformations that may improve student success.

The long-term impact of COVID on our higher-education students remains uncertain. Still, in the short-term, this concise paper offers insight into the experience and shifts observed among undergrad college students at a large public university in the U.S. South. Teaching at one of the largest public universities in our state, with a high acceptance rate (~83.1%), we attract a diverse student population (~50% non-white) with a high proportion of first-generation college attendance (38%), with the majority working part- or full-time, my students face unique challenges from traditional non-working full-time students. Informed by significant experience teaching entirely in-person, fully online, and in hybrid formats, I will explore the pedagogical transformations I have made to support student engagement and successful outcomes. Having completed my undergrad and graduate training via entirely in-person classrooms, I needed to be trained about the needs of online learners and how to approach my classes in a distinct manner. I have spent the last decade developing skills and pedagogies to support the success of my online learners. While one might expect strong online learning skills among today's college students, many who experienced significant portions of their high school or early college career fully online/distanced due to COVID, this has anecdotally appeared to have negatively impacted my students' study and work skills, necessitating a transformation of my pedagogy and online course designs.

Scheduling and Time Management

While in the past many instructors could design a course with broad sweeps of dates and flexibility about when assessments and deadlines may occur, today's students—especially those who are balancing school with work—need precise and specific dates and weekly timelines to support their success. With my online and hybrid courses, I must enforce clear and rigid scheduling/teaching progress for my students and myself to pace assessments and maintain regular and successful engagement. I find this clear schedule is particularly needed within the larger courses I teach (90+ seats). Typically, for example, I plan the full semester and schedule all quizzes, discussions, and exams scheduled from the first day to allow students to make specific and detailed plans. Often, I employ a clear weekly structure, such as: Monday I post weekly reminders and update announcements via the learning management system (LMS), Thursday has the first discussion boards posts due with quizzes opening, and on Sunday discussion response posts and quizzes due. I intentionally schedule multiple deadlines every week (for example, Thursday and Sunday) to encourage students' engagement with the online class at least twice weekly. I purposely schedule major deadlines on Sundays for most courses to support flexibility among my students – for example, online quizzes are available over a 4-day period, so students can complete the assessment at their discretion in that time span – working either on weekdays or weekends. I strive to have a clear schedule of deadlines but embed flexibility within the week to accommodate individual student needs and planning.

In course evaluations, students often comment upon the multiple ways I have provided deadlines and reminders across the course, including: (1) traditional date list format at the end of the course syllabus, (2) detailed visual monthly calendar document (students seem to especially appreciate this), (3) weekly announcement reminders of deadlines, and (4) through use of LMS platform tools to have all deadlines digitally integrated into their schedule. Ultimately, I am finding today's students need more frequent reminders of deadlines and activities to stay focused and on top of course expectations.

Long Syllabi Require Additional Concise Documents

While in the past students relied heavily upon a course syllabus for key information, many are less engaged with this document today. In part, I understand why students struggle to stay informed by the course syllabus, given the sheer volume of information. When I began teaching over twenty years ago, many of my syllabi were 4-6 pages in length. In contrast, my syllabi of today are often 15+ pages long. This length is in part consequence of adding policies to resolve past student issues or detail assignments but have also been impacted by increased university demands to include extensive institutional information that is also found in other sources, such as the Student Catalog. As syllabi have become more "contractual" and lengthier, I find additional "concise" documents, such as separate calendar documents or assignment lists and grade weights, are more frequently visited by students and lead to better outcomes.

Discussion Engagement

Traditional classroom discussions have transformed to online discussion boards – often a singular prompt is used initially, but this poses challenges – the more frequently you teach the same course and use the same prompts the more often students will then seek out online resources from which to plagiarize. Ideally, I recommend changing prompts every semester, however, annually is likely effective.

Real-world connections

Historically, students often seem to regard their classes as distinct and singular. Today's learners are increasingly recognizing the intersectional connections across their coursework and asking how their class relates to their trajectory in the "real world" (for example, jobs after graduation). Often, we are trained to focus on measurable learning outcomes for our students. However, students do not typically relate to these measures in the way that administrators and colleagues do. Working to embed how topics and course skills translate to future goals can be integral to improving learning outcomes and "connection" to a class – for example, one can embed this within class discussions (i.e., prompt: Thinking about your career goals, or a specific job of your preference, how does knowing about/understanding ____ impact your ability to succeed?). Another path that can be useful, contingent on the field of study, is to ask students to bring in real-world examples – creating concrete connections between course concepts and their lives (i.e., prompt: select a music video/lyrics, provide a link to a video, and discuss how <concept> emerges, etc.). Other examples that can be useful to deploy in online discussions include other media examples, TikTok, television commercials, and even photos from their own daily lives. You might then draw from those discussion board examples to support writing a course paper or include some in an exam/quiz. To share an example from Families course, I have a discussion board wherein students post and discuss television commercials linked to a specific theme, such as racial-ethnic diversity and the family. Subsequently, students will select three commercials from among those brought by their classmates to the discussion to then write a separate paper about. This encourages more engagement with the discussions and higher-level critical thinking skills.

Announcements

As noted, regular use of announcement tools or weekly email updates will help distinguish your online class from other courses that are less "mentoring" in orientation and show you are engaged with their success. This can raise the pedagogical issue of weighing "student mentoring" and expectations of student "responsibility." How many announcements do you wish to post? How often is too often? In a typical 15-week semester, I find students are most comfortable with a once-per-week announcement of what is going on. I may also post an "extra" reminder announcement if a high-weight paper or assignment is due. In shorter semesters of 4- or 8-week the pacing can make it challenging and may result in more announcements. Anecdotally, it seems if I post more than two announcements per week students start to feel overwhelmed or annoyed by too many reminders. If it is available in your LMS, I highly recommend the scheduling of announcements in advance to simplify your own time management. This also an opportunity for successful impression management—if you appear to be posting an announcement every Monday morning with a slightly varied specific time students will believe you are highly organized and right on the computer first thing every week.

Instructor videos

One of the most impactful changes an instructor may integrate to increase student connection and affinity is using mini-videos and shorter "skills" videos to support student success across multiple arenas of their academic pursuits. Some examples: (1) time management and schedule building, (2) building faculty/mentor relationships, (3) leaving a positive impression as a student, (4) other field-specific skills – for example, citation and reference practices, how to use relevant library databases, how to adjust settings in their campus email or LMS, etc., (5) thinking about their college career in bigger terms than the semester (what's the long term goal – how will you create a record of distinction?), among others. Ironically, I find a number of students skip over chapter/topical videos and lectures yet will engage with "bigger picture" skills videos about college life and success, as long as they are short.

Digital tools

Undoubtedly, students today are using additional means beyond the classroom and LMS to be in touch with each other, for example, GroupMe or WhatsApp. Given the potential of these tools to support cheating and inappropriate student dynamics it is important to speak to your perspective on these technologies. One cannot pretend these activities are not occurring. In the last two years I have piloted the use of GroupMe as a classroom tool to share reminders and clarifications to the class as the instructor – this can be especially useful and low-level obligation if you work with a Teaching Assistant who can take lead on the postings and preliminary responses. Students also appreciate that they can ask peers questions with the knowledge that there will not be suspicion of nefarious behavior. This also can give the instructor the opportunity to offer immediate response or clarifications when feasible in their schedule.

It is my hope that from this concise paper you will draw some ideas that can help inform your online teaching and improve student learning outcomes.

Keywords:

Online teaching, online learning, online pedagogy, student success, time management

PREPARING STUDENT-TEACHERS FOR ICT ADOPTION IN UNDER-RESOURCED SCHOOLS: AN ANALYSIS OF TEACHER EDUCATORS' STORYLINES AND CLAIMED POSITIONS

Felix Kwihangana, University of Manchester, UK

Abstract

This paper reports on a study that explored how preservice language teachers in the Rwandan under-resourced context negotiate a digital teacher identity (i.e. an identity as technology-using teachers). The study used an identity lens because the changing technological landscape means "teachers and teacher educators have little choice but to redefine roles and identities" (Nunan, 2016, p. 168). It was partly motivated by the observed lack of research-based understanding of the impact teachers' digital identity has on their practice (Nykvist & Mukherjee, 2016), especially in under-resourced contexts where fast-changing technological transformations and limited ICT resources are coupled with a lack of research to understand the outcomes of investments in educational ICTs (Kozma & Vota, 2014; Tolani-Brown, McCormac, & Zimmermann, 2009). The study also responds to the growing realisation that teachers' digital competences hardly ever have a prominent position in the teacher education curriculum (Instefjord & Munthe 2017, p. 44).

Data generation used qualitative semi-structured interviews with five language teacher educators. The interviews were designed based on the teacher educator technology competencies (Foulger, Graziano, Schmidt-Crawford, & Slykhuis, 2017) while the study design and data analysis followed positioning theory and its positioning triangle as an analytical framework (Harré and Moghaddam 2003, p. 9). Two main questions guided the analysis: (1) How do teacher educators position themselves and their student-teachers in relation to technology integration and (2) How does this positioning affect teacher educators' technology use on the language teacher education?

The analysis identified teacher-educators' self-interested disengagement in their student-teachers' development of ICT competences. It revealed often contradictory positions and digital teacher identities assigned to student-teachers through ICT-related storylines. These positions show that the language teacher educators in the study shaped their student-teachers' digital teacher identities by claiming different positions that allowed them to reject responsibilities towards their student-teachers' development of ICT competencies.

Thus, findings lead to the conclusion that the moulding of student-teachers' digital teacher identities in this under-resourced context were heavily influenced by teacher educators' drive for self-preservation. This self-preservation entailed teacher educators developing ICT storylines in which they claimed favourable and often unfavourable ICT user positions in order to reinforce an overall identity of a pro-ICT or ICT-using teacher educator whose duty precluded (or was agnostic to) a need to support student-teachers to acquire ICT skills for use in their future language classrooms. The self-preservation drive fed off teacher educators' contextual understanding of the gains of being recognised as competent ICT using educator, the contextual meaning of what it means to be a technology-using teacher, and the teacher educators' perception of their own technology competencies.

These findings of the study will especially interest scholars, practitioners and policy makers working on teacher education, teacher training ICT in education in general, but especially those with interest in the ICT policies and practices around teacher training in resource-constrained contexts.

Keywords:

ICT in teacher education, digital teacher identity, under-resourced contexts, positioning theory, teacher educator technology competences.

References

Foulger, T. S., Graziano, K. J., Schmidt-Crawford, D., & Slykhuis, D. A. (2017). Teacher educator technology competencies. *Journal of technology and teacher education*, *25*(4), 413-448.

Harré, R., & Moghaddam, F. (2003). Introduction: The Self and Others in Traditional Psychology and in Positioning Theory. In R. Harré & F. M. Moghaddam (Eds.), *The self and others: Positioning individuals and groups in personal, political, and cultural contexts* (pp. 1–12). Westport: Praeger Publishers.

Instefjord, E., & Munthe, E. (2017). Educating digitally competent teachers: A study of integration of professional digital competence in teacher education. *Teaching and Teacher Education*, *67*, 37–45. https://doi.org/10.1016/j.tate.2017.05.016

Kozma, R. B., & Vota, W. S. (2014). ICT in Developing Countries: Policies, Implementation, and Impact. In J. M. Spector, M. D. Merrill, J. Elen, & M. J. Bishop (Eds.), *Handbook of Research on Educational Communications and Technology* (4th ed., pp. 885–895). https://doi.org/10.1007/978-1-4614-3185-5_72

MINEDUC. (2003). *Education Sector Policy*. Retrieved from http://mineduc.gov.rw/fileadmin/user_upload/EDUCATION_POLICY.pdf

Nunan, D. (2016). Language Teacher Identity in Teacher Education. In G. Barkhuizen (Ed.), *Reflections on Language Teacher Identity Research* (pp. 164–169). London: Routledge.

Nykvist, S., & Mukherjee, M. (2016). Who am I? Developing Pre-service Teacher Identity in a Digital World. *Procedia - Social and Behavioral Sciences, 217*. https://doi.org/10.1016/j.sbspro.2016.02.012

Tolani-Brown, N., McCormac, M., & Zimmermann, R. (2009). An Analysis of the Research and Impact of ICT in Education in Developing Country Contexts. *Journal of Education for International Development*, *4*(2), 1–12.

MAKING VIDEO-DRIVEN LEARNING EASY FOR EVERYONE: A PILOT PROJECT

Patricia Mangeol, Sandbox Inc., Canada

Abstract

Video is emerging as a tool to support quality, engaging teaching and learning in online academic environments. Students routinely seek out videos in news media, social media, and documentary-style entertainment to learn new knowledge or skills (Krämer & Böhrs, 2017). But many educators have yet to leverage the educational potential of this development. Making good video-driven learning takes time, multi-faceted skills, and collaboration. As it stands, it is often the prerogative of a minority of technologically and media savvy educators.

Through a partnership with the Leadership Lab at Toronto Metropolitan University, we piloted a video-driven online learning solution called *Dive: Student Aid* (*Dive*). The product is an interactive public affairs case study on the topic of student financial aid reform in Ontario, Canada. It includes sixteen short, Netflix-style video episodes combining live interviews and animation. Multimedia resources emerge in the progress bar during the episodes and allow students to more deeply explore ideas from the videos.

Toronto Metropolitan University conducted an evaluation of *Dive* in 2021 involving the participation of more than four hundred students and ten faculty members across eight universities and colleges in Ontario (Côté & Khela, 2022). Participants tried *Dive* in graduate and undergraduate programs across public policy, public administration, government relations, management, law, business, and health sciences. Both students and faculty pointed to three key themes to consider in moving forward with video-driven learning:

1. **Engagement can complement rigour**: Students and faculty noted that the narrative-based episodes and visuals supported learning objectives and were engaging for students. Specifically, they noted that Dive helped them to teach and learn the course content. This suggests that there does not have to be a tradeoff between engagement and academic rigour in video-driven learning.
2. **We can combine personalization with standardised curriculum**: The episodes were customizable such that the learning experience could be broad or deep, depending on the learning context and students' knowledge levels. This suggests the *Dive* model could be suitable for a range of disciplines, levels of study, and pedagogical approaches. It could allow learners to engage in a flexible and personalised learning experience based on their knowledge, learning goals, and preferences, while being structured around a core curriculum.
3. **Video-driven learning has potential to support accessibility**: Some students with learning disabilities highlighted the value of the video medium as an option for accessing complex content without substantial reading requirements.

Dive inspired enthusiasm for digitally enabled teaching and learning at a time when students and educators were feeling the burden of widespread shifts to online learning in higher education (Shlenskaya et al., 2020). It opened a path for educators to actively shape the role of the "teacher of the future" through individualised, video-based teaching material that is amenable to wide variations in teaching and learning approaches. There are many ways to move forward with these insights: the key appears to be collaboration between media creators and educators, making both more actively involved in shaping the trajectory of online learning.

Keywords

Video, multimedia, digital learning, virtual learning environments, technology-enabled learning, EdTech, online learning models, online teaching, accessibility, personalised learning, self-directed learning, self-paced learning, student engagement, student behaviours

References

Belt, E. S., & Lowenthal, P. R. (2021). Video use in online and blended courses: a qualitative synthesis. *Distance Education, 42*(3), 410-440. https://doi.org/10.1080/01587919.2021.1954882

Côté, A. & Khela, S. (2022). Dive: Student aid digital learning tool evaluation: Final report of the VLS digital delivery demonstration project. Submitted to the Government of Ontario's Virtual Learning Strategy.

Evans, J. (2022). *Free agent learning: Leveraging students' self-directed learning to transform K-12 education.* John Wiley & Sons.

Grajek, S. & 2022–2023 EDUCAUSE IT Issues Panel (2022). 2023 Top 10 IT Issues: Foundation Models. https://er.educause.edu/articles/2022/10/top-10-it-issues-2023-foundation-models

Ibrahim, M. (2012). Implications of designing instructional video using cognitive theory of multimedia learning. *Critical Questions in Education, 3*(2). https://eric.ed.gov/?id=EJ1047003

Krämer, A., & Böhrs, S. (2017). How do consumers evaluate explainer videos? An empirical study on the effectiveness and efficiency of different explainer video formats. *Journal of Education and Learning, 6*(1), 254-266. https://eric.ed.gov
/?id=EJ1125234

Kosterelioglu, I. (2016). Student views on learning environments enriched by video clips. *Universal Journal of Educational Research, 4*(2), 359-369. https://eric.ed.gov/?id=EJ1089708

Lorenceau, A., Marec, C., & Mostafa, T. (2019). Upgrading the ICT questionnaire items in PISA 2021. *OECD Education Working Papers, OECD Publishing, No. 202.* https://www.oecd-ilibrary.org/education/upgrading-the-ict-questionnaire-items-in-pisa-2021_d0f94dc7-en

Noetel, M., Griffith, S., Delaney, O., Sanders, T., Parker, P., del Pozo Cruz, B., & Lonsdale, C. (2021). Video improves learning in higher education: A systematic review. *Review of Educational Research, 91*(2), 204-236. https://journals
.sagepub.com/doi/abs/10.3102/0034654321990713?journalCode=rera

Poquet, O., Lim, L., Mirriahi, N., & Dawson, S. (2018). Video and learning: a systematic review (2007–2017). *Proceedings of the 8th International Conference on Learning Analytics and Knowledge, Australia,* 151-160. https://dl.acm.org/doi
/abs/10.1145/3170358.3170376

Sandbox Labs (2023). Dive: Creating an interactive storytelling platform to push the boundaries of digital learning. https://
www.sandboxinc.ca/case-studies/dive

Shlenskaya, N., Karnaukhova, A., Son, L., & Lapteva, E. (2020). Teachers' burnout in online university courses in the time of pandemic. *Proceedings of the 4th International Conference on Education and Multimedia Technology, Japan,* pp. 95-99. https://dl.acm.org/doi/abs/10.1145/3416797.3416841

Turan, Z., & Cetintas, H. B. (2020). Investigating university students' adoption of video lessons. *Open Learning: The Journal of Open, Distance and e-Learning, 35*(2), 122-139. https://www.tandfonline.com/doi/abs/10.1080/02680513.2019.
1691518

Yousef, A. M. F., Chatti, M. A., & Schroeder, U. (2014). Video-based learning: A critical analysis of the research published in 2003-2013 and future visions. *Proceedings of eLmL 2014, The Sixth International Conference on Mobile, Hybrid, and On-line Learning, Spain,* 112-119. https://www.researchgate.net/profile/Ahmed-Mohamed-Fahmy-Yousef/
publication/278707623

MICRO-CREDENTIALING ROADMAP OF MOOCS THROUGH TEST EQUATING METHOD

Murat Akyildiz, Damla Mustu Yaldiz, Anadolu University, Turkey

Abstract

Higher education institutions are increasingly turning to MOOCs in response to concerns that traditional forms of education may not adequately prepare individuals for the demands of the modern era. Leading universities have taken significant steps to establish the legitimacy of MOOCs in higher education (Brown et al., 2015). Efforts have been made to ensure that MOOCs can be recognized as a credible tool for learning and skill acquisition in higher education, including the implementation of microcredit programs (UNESCO, 2018).

The Council of the European Union's Recommendation outlines key aspects of micro-credentialing practices, such as the quality of learning, assessment methods, and the platform used for delivery, to guide the recognition and utilization of informal and non-formal learning in higher education (Council of the European Union, 2022).

Recognition of non-formally acquired learning experiences at the formal education level requires equivalence in measurement and evaluation. However, neither the European Commission's recommendation nor the related literature provides a clear roadmap for translating non-formally acquired skills into formal education credits. The primary question addressed in this research is: Can micro-credential scores be utilized in formal distance education processes through the test equating method?

The study will divide students receiving distance education into two groups: formal education and MOOCs. Test equating will be used to compare the scores of students who learn the same subject through formal education and MOOCs. This will yield insight into how much micro-credential scores can be considered equivalent to scores earned in formal education environments. Test equating is a statistical process used to adjust scores obtained from different test forms, allowing for their interchangeability (Kolen and Brennan, 2004). This study will employ the circle-arc test equating method (Livingston and Kim, 2009), which is suitable for small sample sizes.

The participants will be divided into three experimental groups and one control group. The experimental groups will receive different MOOCs, while the control group will receive formal education. The study will involve 61 students who are enrolled in a data analysis course offered through formal distance education by the sociology department at a university. The participants will learn about regression through the assigned MOOCs on Edx, Udemy, and Coursera. Each experimental group will have 15 participants who will take a certification exam containing questions specific to the platform and unit they studied.

Four different measurement tools will be used in the study. The first tool will be an exam containing questions specifically prepared for the regression subject in the formal education environment. Other tools consist of questions on regression that the MOOCs will present.

The circle-arc method will be used to analyze the data collected from the experimental and control groups. The method allows the construction of test equations with a relatively small number of participants, typically between 10-15 per group. The researchers will develop equation formulas and test score linking tables to compare the scores obtained from MOOCs and formal education methods. The main aim is to transfer the assessment scores of MOOCs to formal education assessment scores.

Keywords:

Microcredits, MOOCs, test equating, assessment

References

Brown, M., Costello, E., Donlon, E., & Giolla-Mhichil, M. N. (2015). A strategic response to MOOCs: How one European university is approaching the challenge. The International Review of Research in Open and Distributed Learning, 16(6), 177-198. https://doi.org/10.19173/irrodl.v16i6.2157

Council of the European Union. (2022). Council Recommendation on a European approach to micro-credentials for lifelong learning and employability. https://eur-lex.europa.eu/legal-content/EN/TXT/PDF/?uri=CELEX:52022XG0317(01)&from=EN

EDUCAUSE. https://library.educause.edu/resources/2022/2/2022-educause-horizon-report-teaching-and-learning-edition

Kolen, M. J., & Brennan, R. L. (2004). Test equating, scaling, and linking: Method and practice (2nd ed.). Springer-Verlag. https://doi.org/10.1007/978-1-4757-4312-0

Livingston, S. A., & Kim, S. (2009). The circle-arc method for equating in small samples. Journal of Educational Measurement, 46(3), 330–343. https://doi.org/10.1111/j.1745-3984.2009.00087.x

UNESCO. (2018). Digital credentialing: Implications for the recognition of learning across borders. UNESCO Education Sector. https://unesdoc.unesco.org/ark:/48223/pf0000264428

World Economic Forum. (2020). The future of jobs report 2020. https://www.weforum.org/reports/the-future-of-jobs-report-2020

HOW TO SUPPORT DIGITAL COMPETENCIES FOR A CROSS-UNIVERSITY TEACHING MODEL

Christina Suchi, Bavarian Virtual University (BVU), Germany

Abstract

"Lederhosen & Dirndl", "beer" and "Oktoberfest": These terms are often associated with the German federal state of Bavaria. However, Bavaria also has a unique model in Europe for cross–university funding, development and sharing of digital teaching – the Bavarian Virtual University (BVU). The BVU was established in 2000 as a network organization of the universities and universities of applied sciences in Bavaria. Our primary goal is to improve studying conditions for the growing number of students who require flexibility in terms of time and place. Secondly, we are making university knowledge freely accessible to an interested public.

During the last years, however, the BVU has increasingly evolved from a funding institution to a service institution for the teaching staff of its member universities. Especially because the forced digitization by the COVID19 pandemic was rather not the catalyst everyone thought: Although ad hoc qualification on systems such as Zoom took place to a huge amount, long-term digital competencies weren't built that often.

With a wide variety of workshops, individual consulting, and an anchored quality management system, the BVU therefore pursues the goal of building teachers' long-term skills for cross-university teaching. Nevertheless, we also have to consider the individual offerings of our member universities in this area.

In our presentation we would like to give an insight into how the network institution BVU has become a stable partner by supporting Bavarian university teachers to build the needed competencies to teach students in the digital era.

Keywords:

Bavarian Virtual University (BVU), cross-university teaching, digital competencies, service institution

EXPLORING THE BARRIERS AND FACILITATORS OF MICRO-CREDENTIALS FROM A STAFF AND STAKEHOLDER PERSPECTIVE.

Niamh OMahoney, University College Cork, Ireland

Abstract

The world of work is changing fast. A revolution in the skillset required for societal and industrial growth has begun. A transformative approach to education is essential to creating a diverse talent pool. Micro-Credentials offer an accessible and inclusive approach to filling the knowledge gaps associated with this skill reform.

Micro-Credentials are short, accredited learning experiences that facilitate flexible, innovative professional development and lifelong learning (IUA, 2020). This qualitative research study explores the barriers and facilitators of micro-credentials in Ireland from a staff and stakeholder perspective. There is ample literature available on the theoretical value of micro-credentials. However, the number of qualitative research studies completed on the topic is limited.

This study employs constructivist grounded theory (Bryant, A. and Charmaz, 2007) as a methodology and uses a two-phase method process to gain insight and collect original data via focus groups and semi-structured interviews.

Key themes are explored during the focus group phase of research, including the benefits and challenges of micro-credentials, the accessibility of micro-credentialing and the micro-credential learner profile. The interview phase of the research enables a more in-depth conversation around the personal experience of participants on micro-credentials, including the implementation process, developing a culture of lifelong learning and the outlook for micro-credentialling.

The goal of this study is to compile a database of knowledge from staff, and stakeholder perspectives on Micro-credentials, enabling informed micro-credential creation in the future that aligns with the public's needs.

Keywords:

Education, Transformative Education, Next generation teachers and learners, Tertiary education, Micro-Credentials, Accessibility, Inclusivity.

References

Bryant, A. and Charmaz, K. eds., 2007. The Sage handbook of grounded theory. Sage.

Irish University Association, MicroCreds, https://www.iua.ie/ourwork/learning-teaching/microcreds/. Date accessed: 09/06/2023.

CREATING ONLINE LEARNING EXPERIENCES REQUIRES MORE THAN DIGITAL SKILLS

Bettina Schwenger, University of Auckland, Aotearoa, New Zealand

Abstract

With growing student participation and diversity, online qualities can provide new learning and teaching opportunities. Tertiary institutions have changed expectations, by, for example, asking educators to use more digital technologies, and reconsider the course environment. Educators can feel unsure though how to purposeful redesign and facilitate activities online, including for students with varying knowledge (Ako & Synapsys, 2018; Boelens, de Wever & Voet, 2017).

Being digitally competent requires more than technical skills, as a collaboration with educators in a first-semester course in Education confirmed. Their wish for a more flexible design approach to support students' digital information literacy for the ePortfolio assessment led to this study. Data were collected from students and teachers utilizing open-ended questionnaires, focus groups, and individual interviews.

Recommendations for sustainable educator development for digital teaching and learning will be discussed. These include underpinning skills and pedagogical practices such as fostering active and independent learning by using online qualities.

Keywords:

Educator digital competencies; Digital information literacy; Academic development.

Summary

This research investigated how literacy development can be integrated to enhance students' experience by including active learning online. Digital information literacy (DIL) comprises the need to interpret and evaluate sources to produce new information. Students must be aware of key information sources, identify the need for information, plan and search for appropriate sources, critically evaluate, organise, produce and present information (Gosling & Nix, 2011). Although specific literacies development is essential for all tertiary students (Gunn, 2013), it is surprising how little research exists about the connections between undergraduate course demands, design for online and face-to-face learning, teachers' capabilities, and the development of appropriate student literacies. The study responded to the research gap. Designing blended learning with digital information literacy can offer students opportunities to actively create new information and is likely to enhance their experiences.

As Aotearoa New Zealand (Aotearoa) tertiary and higher education institutions increasingly offer online learning as part of face-to-face courses (blended learning), one of the aims of this study was to identify how to harness the digital qualities for a design that develops digital information literacy. The capabilities of educators to understand and integrate online qualities into the course, to design for the learning to be achieved, were central to the study. A second aim was therefore to identify the required educator capabilities and how to support their development.

The capabilities required by educators for digital learning and teaching include the ability to

- Understand online affordances of available tools (for example in the Learning Management System) and use these to integrate formative feedback to scaffold independent learning, self-assessment, foster relationships, make blended learning stronger, facilitate active learning online and face-to-face
- Identify course demands (including assessment) of digital literacies and practices
- Understand the type of learning that students are to develop

- Design the course aligned for learning and
- Integrate the development of digital literacies aligned with the assessment demands.

To develop the above capabilities, educators need access to academic development with the following qualities:

- Offer opportunities for thinking and reflection, experience and activity, conversation, and interaction (Dyke, Consley, Ravenscroft & de Freitas, 2007)
- These opportunities need to be sustained over time to support transfer from theory to applied pedagogical practices (Green et al., 2010)
- Support teachers to consider their epistemology, underpinning beliefs and understanding of teaching and learning
- Opportunities to question how the teaching team conceptualises learning and knowledge. Are these seen as a way for students to acquire through transmission or for students to participate and learn through contribution (Hong & Sullivan, 2009). How are these views reflected in the courses?

References

Ako Aotearoa & Synapsys (2018). *Technology in leaming: Benchmarking and developing sector capability.* Wellington, New Zealand: Ako Aotearoa.

Boelens, R., De Wever, B., & Voet, M. (2017). Four key challenges to the design of blended learning: A systematic literature review. *Educational Research Review, 22*, 1-18. doi: 10.1016/j.edurev.2017.06.001

Dyke, M., Conole, G., Ravenscroft, A., & de Freitas, S. (2007). Learning theory and its application to e-learning. In G. Conole & M. Oliver (Eds.), *Contemporary perspectives in e-learning research: Themes, methods and impact on practice* (pp. 82–97). New York, NY: Routledge.

Green, N. C., Edwards, H., Wolodko, B., Stewart, C., Brooks, M., & Littledyke, R. (2010). Reconceptualising higher education pedagogy in online learning. *Distance Education, 31*, 257–273. doi:10.1080/01587919.2010.513951

Gosling, C., & Nix, I. (2011). Supported open learning: Developing an integrated information literacy strategy online. In T. Mackey & T. Jacobson (Eds.), *Teaching information literacy online* (pp. 91–108). New York, NY: Neal-Schuman.

Gunn, C. (Ed.). (2013). *Promoting learner engagement and academic literacies through blended course design.* Hershey, PA: Emerald.

Hong, H. -Y., & Sullivan, F. R. (2009). Towards an idea-centered, principle-based design approach to support learning as knowledge creation. *Educational Technology Research and Development, 57*, 613–627. doi:10.1007/s11423-009-9122-0

A "THRESHOLD" SELF-PACED ONLINE TRAINING FOR TEACHING STAFF: WHAT'S NEW?

Jue Wang Szilas, Patrizia Birchler Emery, University of Geneva, Switzerland

Abstract

In our latest publication (Wang Szilas & Birchler Emery, 2022), we have presented the development of a three-level approach to train the digital skills of the continuing education teaching staff, in particular those related to the use of the Moodle platform: namely, the Threshold level, the Standard level and the Advanced level. We adopted a design-based research (DBR) method to develop this project and have gone through two design circles, the main findings of which have been discussed as follows:

- 1st DBR circle (2019-2020): identify the essential skills for each level and organize the workshops
- 2nd DBR circle (2021-2022): implement a Threshold level self-paced online training course on Moodle for all teaching staff

We are now at the end of the second design circle and the beginning of the third design circle with the following objectives:

- 3rd DBR circle (2023-2024): refine the design and find out more general design principles that can be adopted by other similar projects

What we want to share in this paper are the latest discoveries and especially the reflections made during the analysis of the data collected, including course participation, evaluation of learning outcomes, and feedback from participants through a questionnaire.

Based on our analysis of the data we have collected so far, some preliminary results have already started to prompt us to reflect on the following points:

- Design principles to be drawn from this project
- Future training courses to develop the skills for the standard and personalized level
- Best way to engage more learners, as participation is not mandatory and role of the institution in promoting the engagement
- Encourage and ensure that our teachers do use their new competences in designing their courses

There are three key findings in this paper. Firstly, because teaching teams are very diverse and each profession has its own characteristics, we believe it is necessary to develop specific training for specific groups of teachers; secondly, it is necessary to give the possibility of not using advanced digital tools or methods for teaching exclusively but staying at the first level, because people have different attitudes to digital tools. It is not necessary to use very high-level and complex digital technologies in some teaching. Finally, there is a need to provide a progressive training that guarantees the acquisition of an adequate level of competence in a very short period of time to cope with distance learning in emergency situations.

Keywords:

Digital Transformation, Digitalization of Higher Education, Digital Competence, Teacher Training, Design-Based Research, Lifelong Learning, University Continuing Education

References

Amhag, L., Hellström L., & Stigmar, M. (2019). Teacher educators' use of digital tools and needs for digital competence in higher education. *J. Dig. Learn. Teach. Educ.* *35*(4), 203–220. DOI: 10.1080/21532974.2019.1646169https://doi.org/10.1080/21532974.2019.1646169

Kopp, M., Gröblinger, O., & Adams, S. (2019). Five common assumptions that prevent digital transformation at higher education institutions. In: L. Gómez Chova, A.López Martínez, & I. Candel Torres (Eds.), *INTED2019 Proceedings* (Vol. 1, pp. 1448–1457). IATED. DOI: 10.21125/inted.2019.0445

Pool, J., & Laubscher, D. (2016). Design-based research: Is this a suitable methodology for short-term projects? *Educational Media International*, 53(1), 42-52.

Rodrigues, L. S (2017). Challenges of digital transformation in higher education institutions: A brief discussion. *Proceedings of the 30th International Business Information Management Association Conference, IBIMA 2017 - Vision 2020: Sustainable Economic development, Innovation Management, and Global Growth, Madrid,* 2017, pp. 4490–4493.

Scott, E. E., Wenderoth, M. P., & Doherty, J. H. (2020). Design-based research: A methodology to extend and enrich biology education research. *CBE—Life Sciences Education*, *19*(2), es11. DOI:10.1187/cbe.19-11-0245

Wang Szilas, J., & Birchler Emery, P. (2022). Training digital competences of educators in continuinge: A three-level approach. In: T. Väljataga, M. Laanpere, M. (Eds.), *Shaping the digital transformation of the education ecosystem in Europe. EDEN 2022. Communications in Computer and Information Science* (Vol. 1639, pp.127-136). Springer, Cham. DOI: 10.1007/978-3-031-20518-7_10

PERCEPTION AND COLLABORATION: EARLY FINDINGS FROM A BLENDED LEARNING DESIGN PILOT PROGRAMME FOR FET TEACHERS

Cohen Ambrose and Hanorah Lyons, Limerick and Clare Education and Training Board, Ireland

Keywords:

Online & Blended Learning; Further Education and Training; Teacher Professional Development; Collaborative Learning; Teacher Perceptions

Context

Limerick and Clare Education and Training Board (ETB) is the state education and training authority for the Limerick and Clare region. Beginning in Autumn 2021, the Further Education and Training (FET) Division created a Blended and Online Learning Support Service as a sister branch to its existing Technology Enhanced Learning Support Service (TELSS) and charged its two new staff (the authors) with developing a Blended and Online Learning Strategy. With Teacher Professional Development (TPD) as a central component of that strategy, this concise paper reveals some initial findings from a pilot of the Blended Learning Design Programme (BLDP), a 30-week blended TPD programme piloted during academic year 2022-23, in which teachers design a course for blended learning. This pilot programme sought to learn whether and the extent to which teachers experience changes in their previously held perceptions about teaching and learning design as a result of learning to design blended courses.

The BLDP a TPD programme spread across two 15-week semesters, consisting of face-to-face workshops and synchronous online virtual class sessions; one-to-one learning design support sessions; and self-paced, online multimedia eLearning toolkits, each including one or two collaborative 'e-tivities', which Salmon (2013) defines as pre-designed, web-based, asynchronous learning activities that encourage and support two or more participants to work together to complete a task. Participating teachers also maintain Learning Design ePorfolios on which they receive regular feedback from their colleagues and the facilitators, often co-designing and developing learning resources in pairs or teams.

Literature Review

In a systematic review of 15 publications about PD for OBL, Phillipsen, et al. (2019) look for the most important components of successful PD and present six recommendations for PD programmes, two of which include 1) considering the effects of a transition to OBL on teachers' "professional identity and educational beliefs" and 2) to ensure teachers have a first-hand OBL experience that includes collegial collaboration. In a 2012 study exploring the extent to which learning to teach online courses might be a catalyst for third level faculty to review their perspectives on teaching, McQuiggan found that learning to teach online can potentially change faculty beliefs about teaching, both online as well as face-to-face. In a 2011 study examining teachers' and support staff's conceptions of eLearning PD, Stein, et al., found that transitioning to eLearning has the potential to offer teachers a new approach to their thinking and practice. The findings of these studies highlight the importance of placing teachers' perceptions of teaching and learning at the heart of TPD for OBL programme design.

In their 2012 study that investigated the impact of 'teacher design teams' and collaborative course design on instructors' professional learning, Nihuka and Voogt found that, on the whole, the collaborative aspects of the PD helped bolster instructors' confidence in course design and promoted their awareness of the potential of eLearning technologies and how to use them. In their 2012 case study examining approaches to faculty development of online learning resources, Macdonald and Campbell illustrate "the power of a peer community in the development of these resources, not only in the identification of appropriate areas for intervention but in the collaborative design of activities and the authentic use of tools (p. 890)." This selection of the literature clearly shows the importance of collegial collaboration in OBL course design processes.

Primary Research Methods

We conducted semi-structured interviews with the pilot cohort of eight teachers and an initial thematic analysis of the interview transcripts.

Main Findings

When it came to some ways in which the BLDP had influenced the teachers' approaches to teaching and learning design generally, there were statements suggesting teachers had begun making changes in their practices (see Table 1).

Teacher 2	Teacher 5	Teacher 7
"I'm a bit more experimental. You can get set in your ways and you have your ways of doing things, and now it's saying, 'well, I know that this works, so I'm going to try it and bring it in', you know. I'm a bit more experimental, I think, in my approach. The [BLDP] has helped me with new approaches and new ideas."	"I was curious about what I could learn to improve my own practice."	"What I was doing was actually good practice but I didn't know that. I just knew it was working. I didn't know, for example, that I was creating cognitive presence by making my work engaging for the learners."

Table 1

One of the most impactful components of blended learning design that the teachers acknowledged challenged them significantly was asynchronous learning design. Asynchronous online learning is any type of learning that learners undertake on their own schedule, and which does not require synchronous (or real-time) interactions with their peers or the teacher. Collaborative constructivist asynchronous online learning design proved to be a novel and significant challenge for the participants (see Table 2).

Teacher 2	Teacher 4	Teacher 8
"I suppose it gave me the courage [that] we can do this so that they work completely independently. This doesn't have to be done through a virtual classroom. It's got me thinking."	"The asynchronous element is very challenging [...] because it requires that engagement [and] in order to get that engagement, you have to put a lot of work into it from different perspectives."	"What I'm finding tricky, is to get [learners] to do [asynchronous tasks]. It's challenging to figure out how to do that and how to design that. Everybody is struggling to see if they can crack that nut."

Table 2

The theme that received the most references was "valuing collegial collaborative learning" (see Table 3).

Teacher 3	Teacher 4	Teacher 7	Teacher 8
"There was an awful lot of [peer-review] encouraged. It can be sometimes very difficult to get people to comment on other people's work. It went a long way towards [maintaining] engagement."	"Collaboration is a very emotional thing. You have to establish trust. With trust comes everything else. [...] You can learn from everybody and I am learning from everybody. And I love this."	I have valued "learning collaboratively, sharing feedback to each other all the time."	"I suppose it can be a little bit intimidating because [the other teachers are] all very strong individually, and they come from very different areas subject wise."

Table 3

The findings emerging from this research show that TPD for OBL should 1) consider the possibility that teachers will experience changes in their previously held assumptions and beliefs about teaching and learning design; and 2) include a major emphasis on collegial collaboration, challenging teachers to work together in a community of inquiry to co-design and develop courses and online learning resources. Based on these emergent findings, the presence of collegial collaboration and social belonging is key to successfully progressing pedagogical changes in Irish further education and training.

Summary

Early findings from the pilot of the Blended Learning Design Programme for FET teachers show that TPD in blended learning design has the potential to change teachers' approach to learning design and teaching more broadly.

References

Macdonald, J., & Campbell, A. (2011). Demonstrating online teaching in the disciplines: A systematic approach to activity design for online synchronous tuition. Innovations in Education and Teaching International, 48(4), 383-391.

McQuiggan, C. A. (2007). Faculty development for online teaching as a catalyst for change. Online Journal of Distance Learning Administration, 10(4).

Nihuka, K. A., & Voogt, J. (2016). Collaborative e-learning course design: Impacts on instructors in the Open University of Tanzania. International Journal of Education and Development using Information and Communication Technology (IJEDICT), 12(1), 90-106.

Philipsen, B., Tondeur, J., Pareja Roblin, N., Vanslambrouck, S., & Zhu, C. (2019). Improving teacher professional development for online and blended learning: A systematic meta-aggregative review. Educational Technology Research and Development, 67(5), 1145-1171.

Salmon, G. (2013). E-tivities: The Key to Active Online Learning (2nd Edition). Routledge.

Stein, S. J., Shephard, K., & Harris, I. (2010). Conceptions of e-learning and professional development for e-learning held by tertiary educators in New Zealand. British Journal of Educational Technology, 41(1), 145-165.

'CONNECTIVE ALIGNMENT' INSTEAD OF 'CONSTRUCTIVE ALIGNMENT' AS THE EDUCATIONAL APPROACH FOR HIGHER EDUCATION IN THE DIGITAL AGE

Vindya Senadheera, University of Kelaniya, Sri Lanka/ University of Peradeniya, Sri Lanka; Thilini Rupasinghe, Dileepa Ediriweera, University of Kelaniya, Sri Lanka

Abstract

The students in current higher education are 'digital natives.' They have grown up in a digital world and are highly competent in adopting the rapid advancements of technology. They use technology in every aspect of their life, including their education (Turner, 2015). They learn from formally organized courses as well as from informal learning (Decius et al., 2022). Hence, informal learning has been identified as crucial for the sustainability of higher education in the current global context (Gramatakos & Lavau, 2019). Technology facilitates informal learning and has made a substantial change in how learning occurs in current learners. Therefore, there is a need for updated educational approaches used in higher education to cater to current learning needs. In contemporary higher education, 'constructive alignment' is the most widely adopted educational approach (Biggs and Tang, 2011). There are two aspects of 'constructive alignment'; constructive and alignment. The 'constructive' aspect comes from the 'constructivism' learning theory which states that students construct meaning through relevant, specifically designed meaning-making learning activities. It should be noted that 'constructivism' learning theory was developed at a time when learning was not influenced by technology. Therefore, 'constructivism' cannot explain how learning occurs in learners in this digital age even in the absence of specific meaning-making learning activities such as in informal learning.

'Connectivism' on the other hand, is a learning theory that explains how learning occurs in the digital age (Siemens, 2005). Connectivism identifies informal learning as a significant aspect of learning (Siemens, 2005). In connectivism, the individual is the starting point of the learning process. Personal knowledge exists in a network (Siemens, 2005). Learning is the process of connecting, growing and navigating through the networks which consist of nodes (Siemens & Tittenberger, 2009). Learning occurs on three levels: neural, conceptual, and external. A new node of information in these three levels results in new connections, which results in new knowledge and increased understanding in the learner. Connectivism is guided by the understanding that learner's decisions are based on rapidly changing foundations, because new information is constantly being acquired (Siemens, 2005). Therefore, the learner should engage in continuous learning/lifelong learning to make valid decisions in their learning. This continuous amplification of knowledge and learning by the extension of a personal network is the essence of connectivism (Siemens, 2005). Connectivism has offered positive outcomes for higher education students such as improve academic performance, foster creative thinking, enhance interactions with teachers and peers, promote collaborative learning, provide open and flexible learning environment, promote self-regulation of learning, facilitate action learning, improve problem solving and decision making skills, promote reflective practice and promote lifelong learning. Connectivism has been shown to be effective in delivering functioning knowledge. The integration of principles of connectivism in higher education has successfully incorporated informal learning into formal learning and has enhanced skills required for emergent learning (Senadheera et al, 2022).

Alignment is a key principle in curriculum theory which states that assessment tasks should be aligned to what it is intended to be learned and with T & L activities (Biggs and Tang, 2011).The 'alignment' denotes to what the teacher does, which is to set up teaching and learning activities (TLA) and assessment tasks (AT) appropriate to achieving the intended learning outcomes (ILO) (Biggs and Tang, 2011). The principle of alignment was integrated in the proposed approach because the literature showed that alignment between ILO, TLA and AT produces effective teaching and learning, ensuring maximum consistency throughout the process (Biggs and Tang, 2011). Therefore, in order to design the proposed educational approach, 'connective alignment' (Figure 1), 'connectivism' is joined with the alignment component instead of the 'constructivism' used by Biggs & Tang (2011).

Figure 1: Connective Alignment

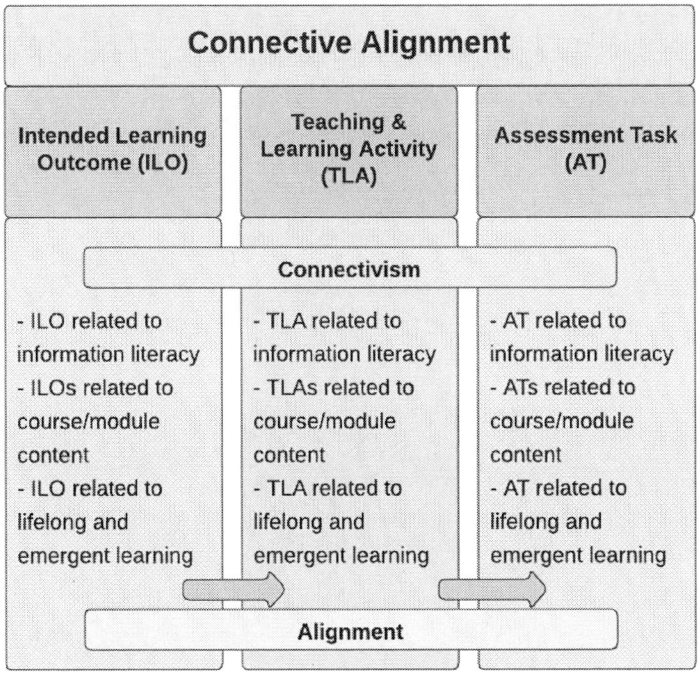

In 'connective alignment', connectivism is used as the theoretical framework to design teaching and learning the ILOs, TLAs and ATs. Moreover, when defining the (ILOs, apart from the ILOs related to the content of the course, connective alignment proposes integrating the specific skills required for the success of learning in this digital age. Accordingly, an ILO to enhance the information literacy skills of students is proposed in order to assure that students have the competency to obtain, critically analyse, evaluate and effectively use the information required for learning. Moreover, an ILO to enhance lifelong and emergent learning skills is proposed because the information in this digital age is rapidly evolving it should be assured that students are equipped with the most updated information in their learning.

Keywords:

Connectivism, alignment, constructivism, outcome-based education, digital age

Summary

In a context where there is a huge need for an educational approach in higher education to cater to the learning needs of current learners, this paper provides the educational approach; 'connective alignment', which can fulfill that need.

References

Biggs, J. B., & Tang, C. (2011). *Teaching for quality learning at university* (4th ed.). Open University Press.

Decius, J., Dannowsky, J., & Schaper, N. (2022). The casual within the formal: A model and measure of informal learning in higher education. *Active Learning in Higher Education*, 0(0).

Gramatakos, A.L. and Lavau, S. (2019), Informal learning for sustainability in higher education institutions, *International Journal of Sustainability in Higher Education*, Vol. 20 No. 2, pp. 378-392.

Senadheera, V., Rupasinghe, T., & Ediriweera, D. (2022). Connectivism for improved learning outcomes in higher education in the digital age–A scoping review [Manuscript submitted for publication]

Siemens, G. (2005). Connectivism: A learning theory for the digital age, *International Journal of Instructional Technology and Distance Learning*, 2.

Siemens, G., & Tittenberger, P. (2009). *Handbook of emerging technologies for learning*. Manitoba, Canada: University of Manitoba.

Turner, A. (2015). Generation Z: Technology and social interest. *The Journal of Individual Psychology*, 71, 103-113.

FROM EDUCATION TO MEDICINE: A REFLECTION ON PRACTICE ON TRANSFER OF LEARNING IN SCENARIO-BASED ELEARNING

John P Egan, University of Auckland, Aotearoa, New Zealand

Abstract

This paper is a reflection on practice (Schön, 1983), as I endeavour to design a research study related to scenario-based learning (SBL) as used in a new, wholly online clinical education advanced elearning course. For students, transfer of learning (Caffarella, 2002) usually focuses on learning transfer from the course context to their own lives, often in their profession. As an academic, transfer of learning also occurs within my own practice. Lessons learnt through this experience, and a proposed study design are explored.

Keywords: elearning, scenario-based learning, medical education

Scenario-based learning (SBL) includes problem-based, case-based, and inquiry-based learning and is an effective tool for teaching postgraduate students in professional programmes (Iverson and Colkey, 2004). In particular, SBL can bridge the gap between academic or theoretical study of a subject and the realm of practice (Zhao, 1996), including medical education (Norton et al, 2012).

In a previous elearning course, I used SBL to significant effect, which was confirmed via a scholarship of teaching and learning study (Egan, 2020). Asynchronous scenario discussions served as an effective threading mechanism, enabling students to integrate what could be learnt from their readings, assessments, and the discussions themselves. The scenarios fomented student-content, student-staff and student-student interactions (Anderson, 2008).

Context shift

A new role meant a shift to leading an online elearning methods course in clinical (medical) education. Unlike many of my colleagues I am not clinically qualified: my work experience, practice contexts, and research have all been calibrated to adult and higher education.

The course I inherited was largely theoretical course and overly ambitious in terms of student workload. Over the next several years, we redesigned the course twice to make it more manageable. What these redesigns revealed was an appetite among clinical education postgraduate students to learn theoretical aspects of clinical elearning, as well as how to create effective elearning materials for their own contexts. Our challenge has been achieving this within a single course with an equitable workload. Thus we proposed offering a second, advanced clinical elearning course. It is this new course where scenario-based learning would feature prominently.

Why Online

Clinicians must integrate ongoing professional learning and development in a career that features excessive workload and challenging and variable timetabling. Thus, in clinical postgraduate medical education, online learning is ascendant—a trajectory further accelerated thanks to COVID19. Online learning is viewed by many clinicians as easier to integrated into their busy lives.

Our postgraduate clinical education programme needs to concomitantly offer substantive impact on practice (leading to improved outcomes for patients and the health sector more broadly) and meet the rigourous requirements of university postgraduate study. Many of these students either hold leadership roles or aspire to do so. All of them are involved in some aspects of clinical site supervision of trainees, delivery of university-based teaching, or delivering continuing medical education workshops and short courses.

Advanced elearning in clinical education

This new advanced elearning course could reflect my academic and subject matter expertise and my professional experience in higher education, academic development, learning design and learning technologies. But I am not a clinician, nor have I completed a clinical credential of any sort. I am, however, an academic leader: both as a unit director and an associate dean of teaching for our health sciences faculty. As an academic leader—and in particular, as a leader tasked with shepherding our programmes, students and staff during disruptions related to COVID19—I a, involved in a spectrum of issues related to clinical education and the rapid "pivot to remote learning". These experiences proved a rich source of inspiration for this new course's SBL activities.

The principles for developing our SBLs were as follows:

- Positionality: Each scenario was written so students could not readily argue "this would never happen in my work". A key strategy for this is collegial queries of the sort that occur frequently in professional contexts.
- Deceptive brevity: The scenarios each must be one to two paragraphs, but they also must integrate key concepts from the week's materials. Once students start connecting these three things (discussion scenario, reading, assessment) they begin to interpolate rich discussion responses.
- Transferability: Each scenario is specific, but also written in ways that allow learners to identify commonalities with their own working contexts. It is not unusual for a student to say, "I am going to try this".
- Comprehensiveness: Across all the scenarios, we integrate IBL, PBL, and CBL across allied health professions. We cover hospital, social and long-term care, and community acute care. Some scenarios feature Indigenous or other communities of colour; urban, rural and international settings are integrated too.

Any single scenario might not reflect an individual student's lived experiences, but we aspire for every student to see aspects of themselves in multiple scenarios.

Lessons Learnt

Having delivered the first cohort of the course, the overall approach to SBL seems to have transferred well, in terms of my own practice. With regards to the students, they anecdotally describe effective short-term learning transfer. Some of our first scenarios worked much better than others, so we will refresh a few of these for the next iteration of the course in July 2023.

Study Design

Based on the design of a previous scholarship of learning and teaching study, we will adapt that research protocol to this course. That study design required at least 3 years of course cohorts, to ascertain if any temporal changes occur, in terms of learning transfer. That means our data collection won't commence until late 2024.

References

Anderson, T. (2008). "Towards a Theory of Online Learning" in (T. Anderson, Ed.) *The Theory and Practice of Online Learning,* (pp. 45- 74). Edmonton: Athabasca University Press. https://www.aupress.ca/app/uploads/120146_99Z_Anderson_2008-Theory_and_Practice_of_Online_Learning.pdf

Brookfield, S. (2005). Transfer of learning. In L. English (Ed.), *International encyclopedia of adult education* (pp. 627-630). New York: Palgrave MacMillan.

Egan, J. P. (2020). Beyond the Afterglow: Effective Transfer of Learning Through Purposeful Instructional Design. *Teaching & Learning Inquiry,* 8(1), 173-186. https://doi.org/10.20343/teachlearninqu.8.1.12

Caffarella, R. S. (2002). *Planning programs for adult learners: A practical guide for educators, trainers, and staff developers* (2nd ed.). San Francisco: Jossey-Bass.

Iverson, K., & Colky, D. (2004). Scenario based e-learning Design. *Performance Improvement, 43*(1), 16-22. https://doi.org/10.1002/pfi.4140430105

Norton, G., Taylor, M., Stewart, T., Blackburn, G., Jinks, A., Razdar, B., Holmes, P. & Marastoni, E. (2012). Designing, developing and implementing a software tool for scenario based learning. *Australasian Journal of Educational Technology* *28*(7):1083-1102 DOI: 10.14742/ajet.790

Schön, D. A. (1983). *The Reflective Practitioner: How Professionals Think In Action*. New York, NY: Basic Books.

Zhao, J. J. (1996). Using case studies for international business communication training. *Business Communication Quarterly, 59*(4), 11–24. doi:10.1177/108056999605900402

ACTIVE PARTICIPATION IN SYNCHRONOUS ONLINE LEARNING

Karen Kear, Jon Rosewell and Helen Donelan, The Open University, UK

Abstract

Active learning has been a tenet of the Open University's (OU) distance learning methods for 50 years. Tutorials have always been an important component of OU distance learning; these have moved online, initially to improve access and then as a consequence of the pandemic.

The benefits of active participation in synchronous online sessions have been highlighted in several studies. Interacting with other students and their teachers can enable students to feel part of a learning community, to hear other people's views, and to clarify their understanding of a topic (Rogers *et al.*, 2021; Wang *et al.*, 2022). However, educators designing tutorial events face the challenge of overcoming students' reluctance to participate actively (Butler *et al.*, 2018).

This paper reports results from a study that investigated current practice and student and tutor perceptions of tutorials by means of two large scale surveys and fourteen focus groups, conducted across all faculties of the university. Over 600 students and 200 tutors responded to the surveys which gathered both quantitative and rich qualitative data.

Tutors can design tutorials that encourage active participation by including activities such as questioning and discussion, and by making use of tools offered by the online environment such as polls, shared whiteboard and chat channel. However, this assumes that students will be willing to participate in this way. Tutors report that most students are unwilling to use the microphone or webcam, although they are more likely to use text chat or anonymous tools such as a shared whiteboard.

The survey data showed that students' anxiety and lack of confidence are major factors restricting their willingness to engage actively. Over one third of students indicated they were stressed when expected to take part actively. Some students appear happier to listen passively. They often feel they have little to contribute and are worried about what other students and their tutor will think about their contribution.

The surveys provided insights into differences in perception between tutors and students. When surveyed, tutors suggest students may not use the microphone or webcam due to technical issues or unsuitable home environment. However, in the student survey data other reasons are given more frequently, including 'being happy to listen', lack of confidence, anxiety and being behind in their studies.

Work continues to understand how to encourage and support students and teachers in these environments. This may include persuading students of the value of participating and building their confidence to do so. Tutors need to accommodate a wide range of student preferences and to reduce the stress, for example by providing material in advance and making greater use of anonymous low-stakes activities, such as polls and whiteboards.

Keywords:

synchronous learning; social learning; active learning; engagement; participation; confidence; anxiety

References

Butler, D., Cook, L., Haley-Mirnar, V., Halliwell, C., & MacBrayne, L. (2018). Achieving student centred facilitation in online synchronous sessions. *Proceedings of 10th EDEN Research Workshop, Barcelona*, pp. 76–82. http://www.eden-online.org/wp-content/uploads/2018/11/RW10_2018_Barcelona_Proceedings_ISSN.pdf

Rogers, K., Thomas, C. & Holmes, H. (2021). Encouraging student participation in mathematical activities in synchronous online tuition. *Open Learning: The Journal of Open, Distance and e-Learning*, DOI: 10.1080/02680513.2021.1938523

Wang, Q., Wen, Y. & Quek, C.L. (2022). Engaging learners in synchronous online learning. *Education and Information Technologies*. https://doi.org/10.1007/s10639-022-11393-x

CHINESE INTERNATIONAL STUDENTS' ONLINE LEARNING EXPERIENCE IN HIGHER EDUCATION

Yiyi Mao and Kyungmee Lee, Lancaster University, UK

Abstract

During the COVID-19 pandemic, the Chinese government opened a small window for Chinese international students, allowing them to stay in China to attend online courses offered by their foreign universities. This was not authorised before the pandemic (Ministry of Education, 2020). For this reason, little research focused on international Chinese students' distance learning experiences before the pandemic (e.g., Kung, 2017). These have been criticised for their overuse of monolithic approaches and the underuse of theories, which has resulted in stereotypes and misunderstandings about Chinese students (Lee & Bligh, 2019). Those studies done during the pandemic have also largely been affected by the peculiar situation (e.g., Yong, 2021). Therefore, this is the right time to examine Chinese overseas students' distance learning experiences in the post-pandemic.

Drawing on Moore's transactional distance theory and Berry's acculturation, this qualitative study conducted semi-structured interviews to investigate Chinese international students' online distance learning journey, aiming to provide a holistic and in-depth understanding of online international students and to offer implications for online distance higher education. The research will present the diversity of online international students and Chinese students' perceptions of online distance learning in a cross-cultural context. Meanwhile, the research will also identify potential challenges in online distance learning and will help online course designers understand the demands of international students and better support them in online classrooms.

Keywords:

Online distance learning; higher education; Moore's transactional distance theory; Berry's acculturation; qualitative study; international students

References

Kung, M. (2017). Methods and Strategies for Working with International Students Learning Online in the U.S. *TechTrends*, 61(5), 479-485. doi: 10.1007/s11528-017-0209-x

Lee, K., & Bligh, B. (2019). Four narratives about online international students: A critical literature review. *Distance Education*, 40(2), 153-169.

Ministry of Education of the People's Republic of China (2020). New policy for Chinese students studying abroad during the COVID-19 pandemic.http://www.moe.gov.cn/fbh/live/2020/52834/mtbd/202012/t20201223_507111.html. Accessed 10 Apr 2022.

Yong, S. (2021). A reflective commentary about teaching international non-accounting postgraduates amid COVID-19. *Pacific Accounting Review*, 33(5), 616-624. doi: 10.1108/PAR-09-2020-0156

SHIFTING IRISH POSTGRADUATE CERTIFICATES IN TEACHING AND LEARNING ONLINE

Fiona Concannon, University of Galway, Ireland

Abstract

Supporting educators continuing professional development (CPD) through accredited postgraduate programmes in teaching and learning has been a feature of Irish higher education for over two decades. As part of a wider trend within professional postgraduate education, these courses have seen a shift towards online and blended modes, accelerated by events of the last three years. This research details the findings of a qualitative investigation to elicit the experiences of educators teaching on these programmes, during the rapid shift to emergency remote teaching and beyond. The aim was to examine the Irish context, with a defined group of educators - those who teach the teachers - who are well versed in educational theory and good practice, working in units, often as third space professionals, under intense pressure to support their colleagues throughout their institutions in a time of crisis. Using methods of purposive sampling, and thematic analysis of semi-structured interviews with seven educators, the findings revealed a diverse spectrum of cultures and institutional contexts of continuing professional development programmes for staff who teach. This response of these postgraduate programmes to the pandemic was explored with respect to five key areas: their approach to participant engagement and online teaching presence, content development, course evaluation, assessment, technology, and overall course management. A picture emerged of a committed group of educators who served to bolster and support participants of their programmes at a critical time, by focusing on relationship building, whilst maintaining core values and beliefs of supporting and enabling professional learning, translating these into online spaces, through varying approaches and levels of accompanying institutional supports. Key themes emerged, highlighting the importance of protected time for educators to engage in these programmes, the need for adequate long-term support for the growing demand for ongoing flexibility and online modality, retaining community building and peer learning opportunities that provide space for practice, exchange, and deeper critical reflections. These findings echo the work of Pilkington (2016) and King (2022) around building cultures where teaching is valued and supported in higher education, along with giving insights into the role of third space professionals (Whitchurch, 2012) within Centres of Teaching and Learning who contribute to these programmes, and considerations of a post-digital understanding of modality (Fawns et al., 2021). Inter-institutional networking opportunities between these programmes were also identified as an area for growth, to enhance teaching across the sector, as programmes move to more mature blended or online learning designs.

Keywords:

Continuing Professional Development, Online Postgraduate Education, Developing Educators' Competencies, Higher Education.

References

Fawns, T., Aitken, G., & Jones, D. (2021). Online Postgraduate Education in a Postdigital World : Beyond Technology. Springer International Publishing AG.

King, H. (Ed.). (2022). Developing Expertise for Teaching in Higher Education: Practical Ideas for Professional Learning and Development. Routledge. 10.4324/9781003198772-1

Pilkington, R. (2016). Supporting continuing professional development (CPD) for lecturers. In D. Baume & C. Popovic (Eds.), Academic Practice in Academic Development (pp. 17). Routledge. 10.4324/9781315720890

Whitchurch, C. (2012). Reconstructing Identities in Higher Education: The rise of third space professionals. Routledge. 10.4324/9780203098301

SHAPING THE FUTURE OF HIGHER EDUCATION: WHAT IS THE ROLE OF THE CENTRE FOR ACADEMIC DEVELOPMENT?

Mark Brown, Clare Gormley, Rob Lowney, Suzanne Stone, Dublin City University, Ireland

Abstract

Few educators would dispute that teachers need support to harness the transformative potential of new digital tools for teaching, learning and assessment. With the ever-changing nature of the digital learning landscape, and the impact this has on staff workload (EUA, 2022), teachers and those who support teaching cannot be expected to learn how to successfully incorporate the pedagogical affordances of these tools into their virtual and physical classrooms on their own. Put simply, no teacher is an island. In theory, Academic Development, and a strategic emphasis on teaching enhancement with a strong digital focus, is a long-term investment in developing individual and institutional capacity and the quality of the student learning experience. Arguably, an investment in staff development for teaching and learning also pays for itself in longer-term indirect benefits such as increased job satisfaction, employee retention, and extended careers within academia, to name a few.

While Centres for Academic Development, or equivalent, have a long history of supporting quality teaching in the university context, their role, structure and underlying mission vary greatly across higher education institutions. It is well-documented that some of these centres are subject to constant flux, with seemingly endless reorganisation in efforts to integrate new learning technology better, establish closer partnerships with faculties and justify their strategic value to institutions (Holt, et al., 2011; Sugrue et al., 2018). Set against this backdrop, the COVID-19 crisis put an even greater spotlight on the value of Centres for Academic Development, with many so-called third-space professionals (Whitchurch, 2009) playing a crucial role in the rapid pivot to Emergency Remote Teaching (Marin, et al., 2022; O'Toole, 2022). However, this attention also brought to the fore new questions about how best to support faculty colleagues in designing effective blended, hybrid and online learning environments and curricula. Therefore, it is timely to ask what does a contemporary Centre for Academic Development look like in the post-COVID era? How should it go about its work? Should it solely be staff-facing, or engage with students too? What is the relationship between academic development and support for learning technology? How should a centre engage with faculties in supporting more creative and innovative use of new digital technologies? Where does the Scholarship of Teaching and Learning fit? And crucially, how should it evidence its value and impact within the institution?

This paper explores these questions in the context of academic development and learning technology support at Dublin City University (DCU). It describes some of the challenges the Teaching Enhancement Unit (TEU) has faced since the pandemic and how it is attempting to navigate, steer a path and redefine its identity in a changing organisational context set against a new Teaching and Learning Strategy. The paper does not promise a bright new model of academic development for other institutions to follow, as the main objective is to reveal the messy reality of supporting new digital approaches for teaching, learning and assessment. To this end, the paper raises more questions than answers as we critically reflect on the role of a contemporary Centre for Academic Development from an insider's perspective.

Keywords:

Centre for academic development, academic development, teaching enhancement, digital education.

References

European Universities Association. (2022). Leadership and organisation for teaching and learning at European universities. Final report from the LOTUS project. Brussels. https://eua.eu/downloads/publications/final%20lotus%20report_december%202022_fin.pdf

Holt, D., Palmer, S., & Challis, D. (2011). Changing perspectives: teaching and learning centres' strategic contributions to academic development in Australian higher education. International Journal for Academic Development, 16(1), 5-17, DOI:10.1080/1360144X.2011.546211

Marin, L. F., Valgardson, B. A., & Watson, E. (2022). Evaluation in the time of crisis: evidencing value at a centre for teaching and learning during the Covid-19 pandemic, International Journal for Academic Development, 27(2), 135-147. DOI: 10.1080/1360144X.2022.2082437

O'Toole, S., O'Sullivan, I., O'Brien, E., & Costelloe, L. (2022). From nice to know to "newfound popularity": academic developers' perceptions of how COVID-19 has changed their role. International Journal for Academic Development, 27(2), 207-211, DOI: 10.1080/1360144X.2022.2082438

Sugrue, C. et al. (2018) Trends in the practices of academic developers: trajectories of higher education?. Studies in Higher Education, 43(12), 2336–2353. DOI: 10.1080/03075079.2017.1326026

Whitchurch, C. (2009). The rise of the "blended professional" in higher education: A comparison between the United Kingdom, Australia and the United States. Higher Education, 58(3), 407–418. DOI: 10.1080/13583883.2010.501685

SYNCHRONOUS ONLINE TEACHING: EXPLORING NEW HORIZONS

Szilas Nicolas, Nguyen Tuong-Vy Tiffany, Lam Yong Xin, Le Thi Kim Oanh Hélène, University of Geneva, Switzerland

Abstract

Synchronous online teaching has been experimented for more than a decade (Yamagata-Lynch, 2014; Kreie, Johnson, and Lebsock, 2017) but relatively rarely used in practice among the broad spectrum of modalities used in online education. It is nevertheless a promising approach to distance learning, as it may alleviate the risk of isolation and rupture with the system due to the absence of face-to-face contact (Rinaudo, 2018). The COVID-19 pandemic changed everything: it became a major way of teaching and learning. Nevertheless, because the transition was sudden, teachers merely transposed their in-class lectures to the online modality, which created a cumbersome and stressful learning context. Consequently, after COVID-19 restrictions, universities and schools went back to in-person courses, considering synchronous online lectures as poor replacements for normal lectures.

However, there are other ways to set up synchronous online courses, by rethinking distance in education not just as a way to avoid people travelling (or contaminating) but as a unique opportunity to improve teaching quality. Rather than erasing the respective places of students and teachers (modality of talking heads (Read, Barnes, and Wilson, 2022)), we acknowledge that distance is unique, binding together two different locations. In physical classes there is limited space, forcing students to sit in one place and the teacher in another, while travelling with the students remains difficult. To overcome this limitation, one can use the potential of synchronous online teaching to create a unique learning environment, as illustrated in two examples within a course in Educational Technology with 200 students.

The documentary modality

Most university courses don't allow an audience to take part in the practices directly in the field, because of spatial and monetary constraints and the difficulty to accommodate the complexity of setting up interactions with a professional to a large audience. We move away from traditional lectures in favour of teaching in an authentic environment by developing a mode of transmission of knowledge that is dialogic and dynamic. The documentary course focuses on filming and interviewing an expert in their workplace. The students can interact with them through questions transmitted synchronously by video conference. For example, we interview an elementary school teacher using an interactive whiteboard in his class.

The filmed hands modality

Teaching through video conferencing does not have to be limited to talking heads and slides. Filming and broadcasting the manipulation by the teacher of tangible artifacts and tri-dimensional objects (in our case, Lego elements) to explain various concepts in real time can offer another perspective on the course material. Automatizing the display and animation of information on a physical or virtual flat classroom board is no longer necessary if the device can make the tiny space of the desk visible to hundreds of distant students. The teacher can process the animation, making the course livelier. A camera with a fixed axis but a movable angle is used to show the speaker's hands so that they can give a close-up demonstration to online students.

Keywords:

Synchronous online teaching, Online modality, Online distance learning, Documentary, Filmed hands, Covid-19.

References

Kreie, J., Johnson, S., & Lebsock, M. (2017). Course Design and Technology For Synchronous Interaction in an Online Course. *Information Systems Educational Journal (ISEDJ)*, 15(5).

Read, D., M Barnes, S., & J Wilson, P. (2022). Student perspectives on online lectures during the Covid-19 lockdown. *New Directions in the Teaching of Physical Sciences*, *17*(1). https://doi.org/10.29311/ndtps.v0i17.3950

Rinaudo, J.-L. (2018). *La téléprésence en formation.* ISTE éditions.

Yamagata-Lynch, L. C. (2014). Blending Online Asynchronous and Synchronous Learning. *International Review of Research in Open and Distributed Learning*, *15*(2), 189-212. https://doi.org/10.19173/irrodl.v15i2.1778

USING LEGO® SERIOUS PLAY® FOR ENGAGING ONLINE STUDENTS IN CAREER IDEATION

Ken McCarthy, Margaret Tynan, South East Technological University, Ireland

Abstract

This short paper outlines a case study of using LEGO® Serious Play® methodology to engage a group of online students in career ideation. LEGO® Serious Play® is a facilitated process that uses LEGO® bricks to encourage participants to build and share metaphors and stories that facilitate creative thinking and problem-solving.

The study was conducted with a group of 11 online students enrolled in a graduate-level course in business systems analysis. The LEGO® Serious Play® session was conducted synchronously in a video conferencing environment (Zoom), with participants logging in from various locations in Ireland. Identical LEGO® kits were distributed to each participant beforehand and an online board (Padlet) was used to capture photographs of the models they built.

The session was designed to help students reflect on their careers to date and reflect on the skills they have learned from their course with a view to progressing their careers. The facilitator introduced the topic and provided a set of prompts for students to use as they built with LEGO® bricks. Participants were encouraged to share their constructions and explain the thinking behind them.

Data were collected through observations, photographs, and student and facilitator reflections. The findings indicate that LEGO® Serious Play® was an effective tool for engaging students in the online environment and career ideation. Participants reported feeling more connected to the course content and to each other as a result of the session. They also reported increased confidence in their ability to ideate about career progression with specific reference to the course content and the skills that they have been building.

The study concludes that LEGO® Serious Play® can be a valuable addition to the toolkit of online educators looking to engage students in active, collaborative learning. Further research is needed to explore the impact of this methodology on different types of learners and in different contexts.

Keywords:

Online Teaching, LEGO® Serious Play®, Ideation, Career Development, Pedagogy, Group Facilitation, Innovative Teaching, Digital Tools.

References

Dann, S. (2018). Facilitating co-creation experience in the classroom with Lego serious play. Australasian Marketing Journal, 26(2), 121–131. https://doi.org/10.1016/j.ausmj.2018.05.013

James, A. (2023). The value of play in he: A study. play and creativity for complex learning, from https://engagingimagination.com/the-value-of-play-in-he-a-study-free-book/

Martin-Cruz, N., Martin-Gutierrez, A., & Rojo-Revenga, M. (2021). A LEGO® serious play activity to help teamwork skills development amongst business students. International Journal of Research & Method in Education, 45(5), 479–494. https://doi.org/10.1080/1743727x.2021.1990881

McCusker, S. (2019). Everybody's monkey is important: LEGO® serious play® as a methodology for enabling equality of voice within diverse groups. International Journal of Research & Method in Education, 43(2), 146–162. https://doi.org/10.1080/1743727x.2019.1621831

Roos, J., & Victor, B. (2018). How it all began: The origins of LEGO® Serious Play®. International Journal of Management and Applied Research, 326–343. https://doi.org/10.18646/2056.54.18-025

Wheeler, A. (2023). LEGO® serious play® and Higher Education: Encouraging Creative Learning in the academic library. Insights the UKSG Journal, 36. https://doi.org/10.1629/uksg.611]

HOW TO ENABLE COLLABORATION FOR IMPLEMENTATION OF OPEN, FLEXIBLE, AND DISTANCE EDUCATION IN A NORDIC CONTEXT

Ebba Ossiannilsson, Ossiannilsson Quality in Open Online Learning (QOOL) Consultancy, Sweden; John Dalsgarö, Undervisningsstyrelsen, Faroe Islands; Jörgen Grubbe, Flexible Education Denmark, Denmark; Kaisa Honkonen, The Association of Finnish eLearning Centre, Finland; Sólveig Jakobsdóttir, University of Iceland, Iceland; Ebba Köber, Flexible Education Norway, Norway

Abstract

This concise paper and session discuss how to establish a regional network and task force in open, flexible, and distance learning. The insights for participants taking part in this session are how to build collaborative work in a region, in this case the Nordic region as well as the autonomous territories, such as the Faroe Islands so far. The network aims to create a better digital future for all through open, flexible learning and distance education, focusing on the potential and opportunities for the futures through digital transformative education and the next generations of educators and learners, which alos are in line with the EDEN DLE 2023 conference. NordFlexOn is a Nordic network for Open, Flexible and Distance Learning (OFDL), established by ICDE in 2019. Professionals from digital schools, universities, and other educational institutions decided to establish a Nordic network for OFDL at a meeting in Lillehammer on April 13, 2019. A core group got informally together at an EDEN conference in 2018 where the idea came up and did some groundwork with discussions and a survey among Nordic professionals of OFDL which revealed high interest for such a. network. The International Council for Open and Distance Education (ICDE) agreed to host NordFlexOn for an initial period of four years (2019 - 2023). The NordFlexOn network initiative has been endorsed by the national associations in the OFDL area. It was agreed that network members should have a connection to their national OFDL organization and/or ICDE. In four of the countries (Denmark, Finland, Norway, and Sweden), there are already associations in OFDL that have been operating for years, and in Iceland there are plans to establish one. NordFlexOn can be an important forum to share information and research to strengthen the operation and membership of these associations and can provide opportunities to synchronize important events including conferences and webinars. The development of the network NordFlexOn was interrupted due to the COVID-19 pandemic. Now the opportunity has come to revive NordFlexOn and use it to launch a Nordic Taskforce as part of the ICDE Global Advocacy Campaign for OFDL.Through knowledge exchange, networking and project coordination, the network aims to:

- Identify potential and current challenges to OFDL adoption and development in the Nordic region
- Advocate for high quality OFDL in the Nordic countries and beyond
- Facilitate cross-national collaboration and dissemination of practise- and research-based knowledge on OFDL across the Nordic region.

The network is open to all relevant individuals and associations in the Nordic countries of Denmark, Finland, Sweden, Iceland, and Norway, as well as the autonomous territories of the Faroe Islands and Greenland and the autonomous region of Åland and can be used free of charge. The NordFlexOn currently have country leads from 6 countries. Regarding Nordic added value, we at NordFlexOn believe that it is important to emphasize that Nordic transnational cooperation must be strengthened. We are so similar that we understand each other. At the same time, we are also so different that we can learn a lot from each other. The establishment of this network and how it works is something completely new. The knowledge is shared in the partner networks both at the institutional level and to individuals working with OFDL.

Keywords

NordFlexOn, ICDE, Nordic countries, Open flexible distance education, Open flexible distance learning

References

ICDE. (2023). NordflexOn. https://www.icde.org/projects-and-activities/nordflexon/

ICDE. (2022). ICDE Global advocacy Campaigne. https://www.icde.org/global-advocacy-campaign/

EXPRESS YOURSELF: USING VIDEO IN ASSESSMENT

Colum Foley, James Byrne, DCU Business School, Ireland

Abstract

This presentation discusses designing and implementing the use of video both in the presentation of material and the assessment of learning, in three contrasting modules in Dublin City University Business School. It seeks to outline the technical challenges presented, the opportunities offered, and the difficulties encountered through the use of this method of assessment. Student feedback is also considered.

MT314 is an undergraduate Project Management module. Students were asked to submit a reflection on the module as part of an Undergraduate Final Year Programme.

- Typically, the module has 200- 250 students
- Students were tasked to submit an individual reflection (5 minutes or less) on a Group assignment that they had completed, using Unicam (or a similar technology), or alternatively to submit a written submission.

Table 1: Project Management Video Submissions

MT314							
Year	Students	Submission	Written	Recorded	%	Male Recorded	Female Recorded
2020/21	199	197	187	10	5	4	6
2021/22	251	245	222	23	10	12	11

MT583 is a postgraduate Operations Management module. Students were tasked to source module related video material illustrating innovation or sustainable practices.

- In the first iteration of this task no marks were awarded for the submission although a prize was awarded for the best submission. Only 41% submitted.
- 5% of total assignment marks were awarded for this task in the second iteration, 100% submitted.
- In both iterations, the top submissions were filtered, and students voted for their top video.

Table 2: Operations Management Video Submissions

MT583					
Year	Students	Submission	%	Male	Female
2020/21	46	19	100	27	19
2021/22	53	53	100	35	18

MT5219 is a Postgraduate Dissertation module.

- Students were given the option to use Unicam (or a similar technology) to submit a reflection in video format, on their work, detailing their methods, findings, and conclusions. This offered the opportunity to assess oral presentation skills, a criterion measured to meet AOL (Assurance of Learning) standards recorded as part of the AACSB (Association to Advance Collegiate Schools of Business) accreditation process. Students were required to submit a reflection in video format, on their work, detailing their methods, findings, and conclusions.
- This offered the opportunity to assess oral presentation skills, a criterion measured to meet AOL (Assurance of Learning) standards recorded as part of the AACSB (Association to Advance Collegiate Schools of Business) accreditation process.
- Previously this was done in real time online
- Unicam, PowerPoint, and a variety of recording sources were used

Table 3: Dissertation Video Submissions

MT5219						
Year	Students	Submission	Recorded	%	Male	Female
2021/22	28	19	19	100	10	9

Across the board, this shows a reticence to engage with video assessment unless induced to do so.

Keywords:

Video, Business assessment, video presentation,

References

Frederiksen, J. R., Sipusic, M., Sherin, M., & Wolfe, E. W. (1998). Video portfolio assessment: Creating a framework for viewing the functions of teaching. *Educational Assessment, 5*(4), 225-297.

Jopp, R., 2020. A case study of a technology enhanced learning initiative that supports authentic assessment. *Teaching in Higher Education, 25*(8), pp.942-958.

Sotiriadou, P., Logan, D., Daly, A., & Guest, R. (2020). The role of authentic assessment to preserve academic integrity and promote skill development and employability. *Studies in Higher Education, 45*(11), 2132-2148.

UNIVERSITY EXAMINATIONS: HOW NEW GENERATION LEARNERS DESIGN THEIR OWN REVISING PROCESS

Anne-Dominique Salamin, HES-SO, Switzerland
Zhan Liu, HES-SO Valais-Wallis, Switzerland

Keywords:

Learning process, Students, Revision, Collaboration

Context

In a research project dedicated to learning instruments for new learners, we asked students to express their revising process for examination. Thus 105 academic students, enrolled in a bachelor's degree in economics or a master's degree in computing science, distributed in groups of 3-4 people, worked together on designing a common way for revision. We then generalized the results in a workflow.

Results

The most frequent activity mentioned takes place before revising the theoretical concepts. The second global process consists in making a revision summary collectively. Arandes&all (2018) identify three phases in reviewing for exams. 1) linking information together 2) organizing information 3) recalling information. This last phase, as identified by Zimmerman (2000), is the most effective in preparing. In the generalized diagram below, the common process of all groups shows that their method is essentially organization (phase 2) and recall (phase 3).

Survey

At the end of the process, all groups answered the following question: "How are group revisions for exams carried out?". Out of 33 groups, 28 groups reported revising collectively, while 5 groups preferred individual revision. Collective revision consists in exchanging notes, asking each other questions and redoing exercises. The revision is done as a group, in a common, physical, or virtual place. At a distance, one person shares their screen and does the exercise. The others help and guide him/her to find a solution together.

Findings

We found that the average revision process involves four phases: 1) gathering learning materials, 2) developing a revision plan, 3) redoing exercises, 4) producing summaries.

Phase 1 consists in finding out what is expected for the examination. Phase 2 deals with comparing each other's plannings and amending it to produce a common one. In phase 3, the group does the exercises together. In phase 4, summaries are produced, and the groups challenge each other through common quizzes. They only address the teacher, considered as a simple resource among others, in phase 3-4, if a clarification is needed.

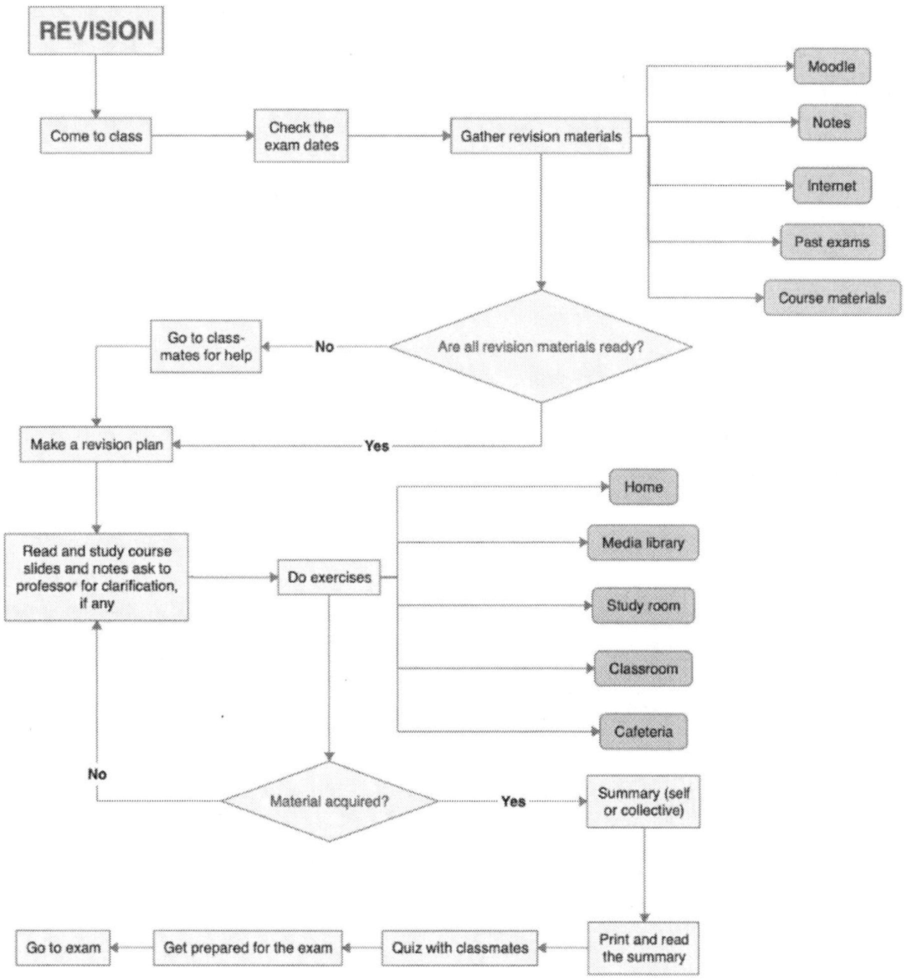

Figure 3 : Generalized revision flow chart

Conclusion

Intuitively, our assumption was that the students would start the revision process by producing summaries before carrying out the exercises, moving from theory to practice, and will revise mostly individually. The opposite occurs. This result can help both students and teachers to unveiling the average revision process, which is generally unexpressed, and emphasizing the value of the collective and the effective role of theoretical concepts in learning.

References

Arandes R., Bornet di Vorgeat T., Renaud L.-D., Richard E., Poscio P., Tormey R., and Hardebolle C. (2018) *How do science and engineering students approach revisions? A self-regulated learning tool for supporting the transition from secondary to higher education.* 46th SEFI Annual Conference, Danemark.

Zimmerman, B. J. (2000). *Attaining self-regulation: a social cognitive perspective.* Handbook of self-regulation. Academic, M. Boekaerts, P. R. Printrich and M. Zeidners, San Diego, CA.

REMOTE WORK AND WELLBEING AMONG PARENT-TEACHERS: DOES WORK AND FAMILY CONFLICT MEDIATE THE ASSOCIATION BETWEEN ORGANIZATIONAL SUPPORT AND TEACHING SELF-EFFICACY?

Eyal Rabin, Shira Goldberg, Ina Blau, The Open University of Israel, Israel

Abstract

Remote work during the COVID-19 pandemic posed a threat to people's wellbeing and was particularly difficult for teachers who were parents of young children. This group had to take care of their children, who were studying remotely from home because of the pandemic, while adjusting their teaching to distance learning through technological means.

The research literature has demonstrated that the transition to remote teaching threatened teachers' wellbeing. Teachers who were parents to young children reported that as a result of working from home, they had higher levels of conflict between family and work (Loscalzo, 2021), high levels of employment pressure (Chitra, 2020), high levels of stress, and low levels of teachers' self-efficacy (Rabaglietti, 2021). On the other hand, findings indicated that teachers who reported a high level of organizational support had lower levels of work-family conflict and family-work conflict (Aragasi & Pangandaman, 2021). The term "family-work conflict" refers to the fact that family and household care may interfere with work life, while the term "work-family conflict" refers to work pressures that may interfere with family life.

In accordance, this research aims to investigate the role of work-family conflict and family-work conflict in the context of digital teaching, as mediators of the relationship between organizational support and teaching self-efficacy among parent-teachers. A representative sample of 472 teachers who experienced remote work during the pandemic, and who are parents to young children (aged 0-12), completed a retrospective survey. The instruments included both quantitative scales, from previous studies with minor adaptations to the context, and open-ended questions.

The findings revealed negative relationships between organizational support, family-work conflict and work-family conflict, and sense of teaching self-efficacy. A mediation model showed that in the context of digital teaching, family-work conflict and work-family conflict mediated the relationship between organizational support and teaching self-efficacy.

This study contributes to our understanding of the effect of work-family conflict experienced among teacher-parents, and remote workers in general, when shifting their work to remote work from home. It has important implications for coping effectively with family-work conflicts in both emergency and routine times. This can foster wellbeing in digital or hybrid work in general, and in the context of hybrid teaching in particular.

Keywords:

work and family conflict, organizational support, teachers' self-efficacy, parent-teachers, Covid-19, emergency remote work.

References

Aragasi, N. A., & Pangandaman, H. K. (2021). Coping style, anxiety level, organizational support, and work commitment of educators during the COVID-19 pandemic in the Philippines: A mixed-methods study. *Belitung Nursing Journal*, *7*(4), 267-276. https://doi.org/10.33546/bnj.1393

Chitra, A. (2020). Study on impact of occupational stress on job satisfaction of teachers during Covid-19 pandemic period. *Global Development Review*, *4*(2), 52-62.

Loscalzo, Y. (2021). The Impact of Workaholism and Work Engagement on Distant Learning and Work-Family Conflict During the COVID-19 Lockdown. *Amfiteatru Economic*, *23*(58), 752-769.

Rabaglietti, E., Lattke, L. S., Tesauri, B., Settanni, M., & De Lorenzo, A. (2021). A balancing act during covid-19: teachers' self-efficacy, perception of stress in the distance learning experience. *Frontiers in psychology*, *12*, 644108. https://doi.org/10.3389/fpsyg.2021.644108.

IMPROVING EQUITY OF EXPERIENCE IN DISTANCE EDUCATION FOR STUDENTS WITH CHALLENGES ACCESSING ONLINE LEARNING ENVIRONMENTS

Fiona J. Aiken, Christopher Hutton, The Open University, UK

Abstract

There is a legal requirement (Equality Act, 2010) to provide students who have declared disabilities with reasonable adjustments which address their learning needs. An Advance HE report on making reasonable adjustments (Falsinger & Bryford, 2010) recommends including 'resources available'. Reading on screen can lead to difficulties focusing, e.g., when reading through text interspersed with images and links (Habib et al., 2012). This can also mean studying takes longer, which itself can be a barrier due to the impact on workloads and can negatively affect quality of life leading to stress and anxiety (Lambert & Dryer, 2018). Accessibility can be improved for students with barriers to studying online-only materials through producing printed versions of the materials ("print packs"). Typically, print packs improve accessibility for students with a range of declared disabilities (e.g., sight conditions; chronic migraine; chronic physical pain or fatigue).

This research evaluates the use, utility, and efficacy of print packs as a reasonable adjustment to some disabled students and students in secure environments (SiSE) on Earth and Environmental Science modules. We investigated (2021/22) how students used print packs and the problems and benefits associated with them, through scrutiny of institutional data, a student survey, and focus groups with Associate Lecturers tutoring the students, and student support staff.

Institutional data for a large, year 1 science module over 2 presentations revealed higher submission rates and performance among SiSE using print packs compared with the whole module cohort; however, the same metrics were lower than the whole cohort for students using print packs as an adjustment for a disability (Figure 1).

Figure 1: Comparison of two years' submission rates and scores for the first assessment on a module for the whole cohort (n = 1536 for 2019/20 and 1731 for 2020/21); students in a secure environment (n = 11 and 14 resp.); and students using a print pack for a declared disability (n = 35 and 21 resp.)

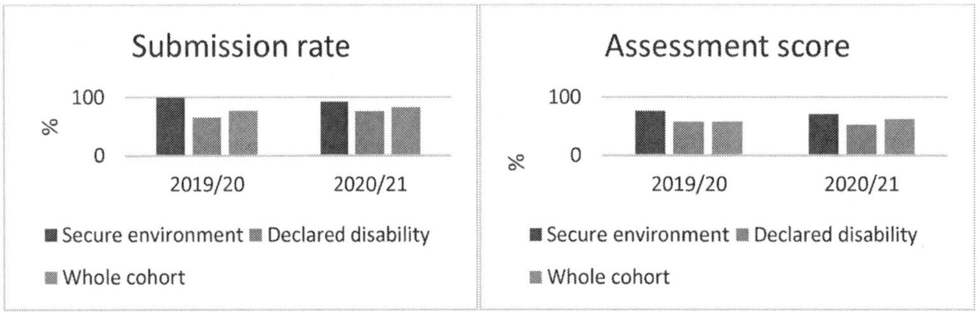

An online survey of students using print packs (13 responses / 43, 30%) highlighted that the majority use them for over half their study time (Figure 2). Comments revealed students blended study of the printed materials with shorter periods of access to interactive online content and synchronous / asynchronous tuition. 23% reported having received advice on how to make best use of print packs.

Figure 2: Survey of disabled students' (n = 13/43, 30%) percentage of weekly study time using print packs.

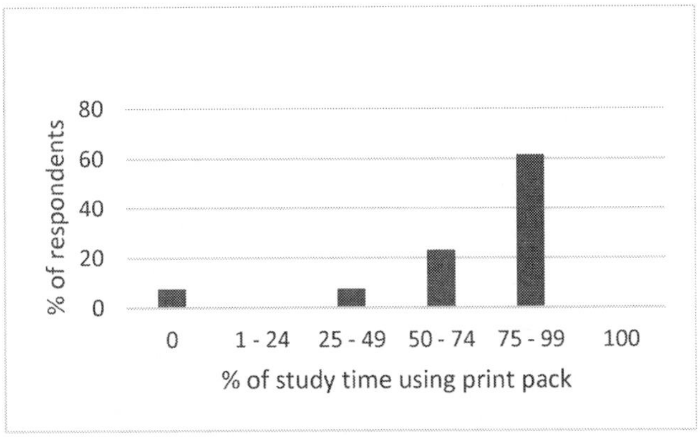

Focus groups with Associate Lecturers working with SiSE, and advisors from the Student Support Team who advised students with disabilities, identified a number of challenges for the two distinct groups (Table 1).

Table 1: Summary of main themes from focus groups.

SiSE	Students with a disability	Both groups
• Blended use often impossible due to no computer access • Poor interactivity • Lack support and information for Associate Lecturers	• Blended use with online materials usually effective • Few complaints or problems received from students • Adaptations usually possible where necessary	• Late postal delivery • Poor organisation of packs

We subsequently designed an intervention for the academic year 2022/23 and will communicate our findings at the conference.

Keywords

Disability; adjustment; online; printed resources; accessibility.

References

Aiken F.J., & Hutton C. (2022) Evaluating the effectiveness of printed materials as an alternative to online resources. Paper presented at the Advance HE Teaching and Learning conference, Newcastle-upon-Tyne, 5-7 July. https://www.advance-he.ac.uk/sites/default/files/2022-07/Day%202%20-%20Teaching%20and%20Learning%20Conference%202022_0.pdfEquality Act (2010) Equality Act 2010. The Stationery Office, London. www.legislation.gov.uk/ukpga/2010/15/contents

Felsinger A., & Byford K. (2010) Making reasonable adjustments in Higher Education, Advance HE report, [online] Available at file:///C:/Users/fja2/Work%20Folders/Documents/ESTEEM/Print%20pack%20project/managing-reasonable-adjustments-in-higher-education_1578587125.pdf (Accessed 23/02/2023)

Habib, L., Berget, G., Sandnes, F.E., Sanderson, N., Kahn, P. Fagernes, S. and Olcay, A. (2012). Dyslexic students in higher education and virtual learning environments: an exploratory study. *Journal of Computer Assisted Learning*, 28, 574-584. https://doi.org/10.1111/j.1365-2729.2012.00486.x

Lambert, D.C. & Dryer, R. (2018). Quality of Life of Higher Education Students with Learning Disability Studying Online. *International Journal of Disability, Development and Education*, 65(4), 393-407. https://doi.org/10.1080/1034912X.2017.1410876

WHAT IS NON-TOKENISTIC SUSTAINABILITY IN A DISTANCE LEARNING CURRICULUM?

Paul Astles, Hayley Johns, Kathleen Calder, James Openshaw, The Open University, UK

Abstract

Defining non-tokenistic sustainability in a distance learning curriculum felt somewhat overwhelming. Curriculum design (CD) has many competing requirements, but it felt important to find a place for it, as there is increasing evidence that students are demanding stronger connections to sustainability and the climate crisis in university courses (THE, 2021, Unite group, 2021 and Carr-Shand, 2022). Key to our work is the idea that any actions should not be tokenistic but meaningful for colleagues and students who are engaging with our learning materials. Our awareness of tokenism was reinforced by students' responses to an internal 'Question of the Month' survey related to sustainability. As members of the Open University's (OU) Learning Design team, we are well-placed to support our academic colleagues and have developed a bank of resources (see appendix) to guide academics and production staff. We are now at a wider consultation stage, seeking feedback on further resources that would help embed and support sustainability in curricula. Since the OU signed the UN Global Compact in 2018 (The Ten principles: UN global compact, n.d.,.), it has been working to connect with sustainable practices. Our vision was to create opportunities to inform colleagues about practical actions that they could take to connect with sustainability in design and production.

We have learned that not everyone is on the same page or ready to engage with the concept of sustainability. Therefore, we have decided to pitch our initial work at provoking colleagues' curiosity, rather than attempting to get all the answers. The OU is the largest distance learning provider in the UK, supporting over 200,000 students, so our actions are likely to differ from those in traditional higher education environments. However, we can still learn from each other. In sharing the resources outlined here (see appendix) we aim to inspire conversations around engaging with sustainability within the curriculum. Sustainability is complex and bringing people on a journey towards a shared understanding of what it means to be sustainable within the context of a distance learning curriculum is equally complicated. Future scholarships will be focused on reflecting on that journey and considering how best to move forward to support our colleagues with practical advice about how to connect with sustainability.

Keywords:

Sustainable development, sustainability, non-tokenistic, distance learning, curiosity, practical actions, learning design

References

Carr-Shand, S. (2022, April 29). *Climate change crisis should be embedded in education, say students and staff.* Climate Action. Retrieved February 28, 2023, from https://blogs.bath.ac.uk/climate-action/2022/04/29/climate-change-crisis-should-be-embedded-in-education-say-students-and-staff/

Prepare for student sustainability demands to go through the roof. THE Campus Learn, Share, Connect. (2021, October 19). Retrieved February 28, 2023, from https://www.timeshighereducation.com/campus/prepare-student-sustainability-demands-go-through-roof

Survey: Students call for strong action on climate change. Unite Group. (2021, October 15). Retrieved February 28, 2023, from https://www.unitegroup.com/articles/survey-students-call-for-strong-action-on-climate-change

The Ten principles: UN global compact. The Ten Principles | UN Global Compact. (n.d.). Retrieved February 28, 2023, from https://unglobalcompact.org/what-is-gc/mission/principles

Appendix

This overview explains the graphics we have created and how to use them. The resources in this appendix are the output of the first phase of our work in this area and help you to think about sustainability within module design and the curriculum. They have been designed so that a range of people can engage with them despite the stage they may be at when thinking about sustainability. If you would like access to a PDF version of the resources, please scan the QR code at the end of the appendix or follow the hyperlink that is just next to it (**Resource 8**).

Resource 1 A flow chart that helps you consider the possibility of embedding sustainability into module design and lets you know that there is support available from Learning Design if you wish to explore further.	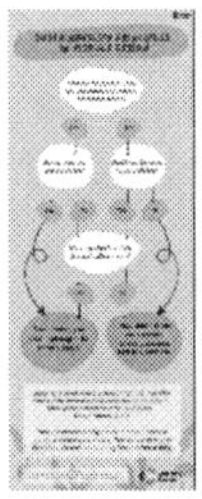
Resource 2 A honeycomb design to provoke your curiosity and raise awareness of other sources of information within curated areas, such as pedagogical approaches and teaching methods, and ethical and social considerations. Links can be selected to explore that information further.	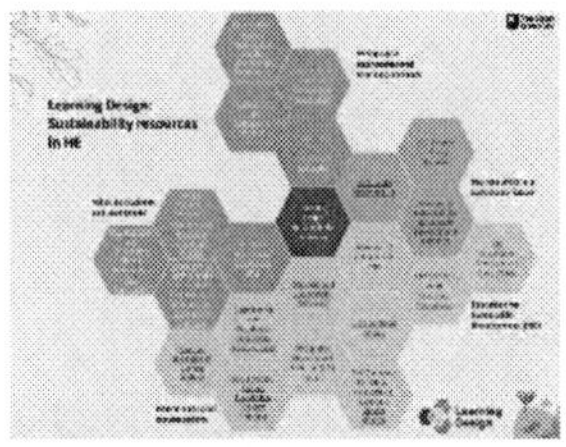
Resource 3 A resource that helps to narrow down some of the focus relating to sustainability areas that you could explore. This is not an exhaustive list of everything that sustainability means within curriculum design, but it provides a starting point to structure your thoughts.	
Resource 4 This resource informs you of the executive summary 'Education for Sustainable Development Guidance' by QAA and Advanced HE and provides a link to the paper. The summary has a framework that helps you to incorporate sustainability within your HE context and curricula.	
Resource 5 This graphic informs you that there are existing resources on OpenLearn under the categories of 'explore', 'empower' and 'do'. Each of these categories contains articles, interactive content, and free courses for you to explore and consider whether link to them or re-use some of the content.	

Resource 6 These are a series of three graphics that represent the UNESCO competencies that can be connected to learning outcomes. The areas of focus are 'Ways of Practising' and 'Ways of Thinking' and 'Ways of Being' If you are considering how activities in your courses can connect to more sustainable ways, this can be a useful place to understand this. For example, if you have a collaborative activity, you could look at the resource 'Ways of Practicing' and the learning outcomes that link to the key competency of collaboration and consider how to use in your context. After reflecting, you may want to explicitly connect to these competencies and learning outcomes, or you may prefer to have activities related to them.	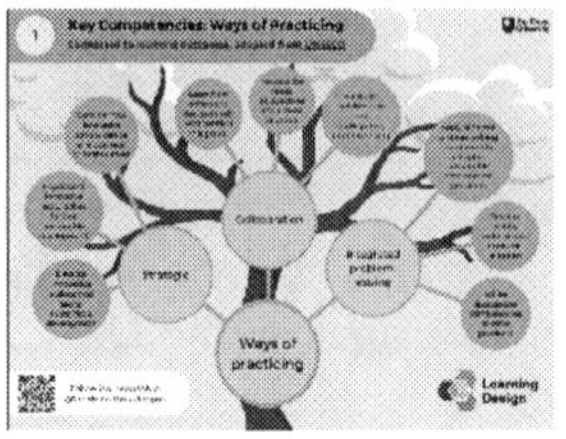 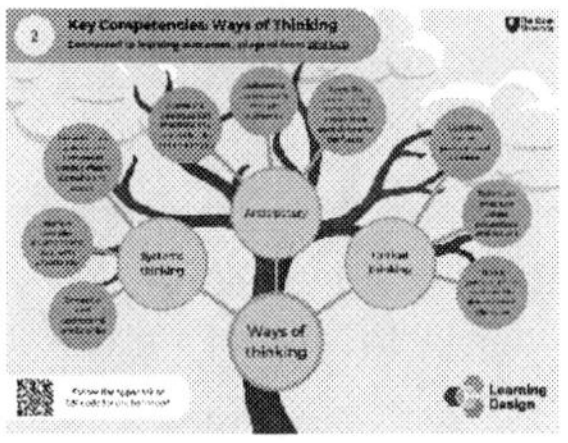 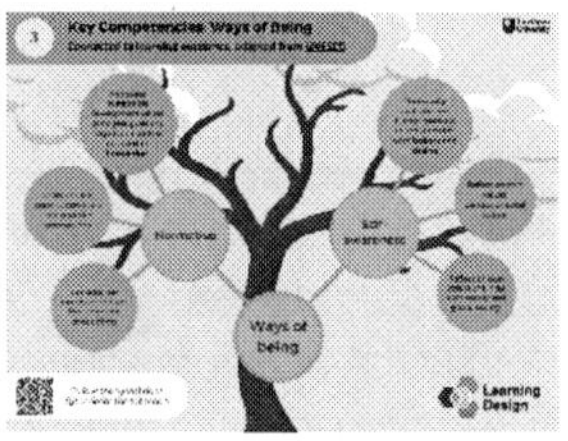
Resource 7 This resource emphasises the importance of the student voice in design. At the OU, colleagues have various means to enable students to represent themselves in the design process. The Curriculum Design Student Panel is a prime example of this, and colleagues can explore how to use that panel with the information in this resource. The purpose of this is to consider how to use the student input most appropriately in relation to sustainable thinking. This could be connected to sustainable content, but also content within the material that relates directly to sustainability. It could be to do with the skills related to a task or the learning outcomes that you are using. All these things could be considered in different ways using the student panel process and involving students as sustainability representatives in the curriculum design.	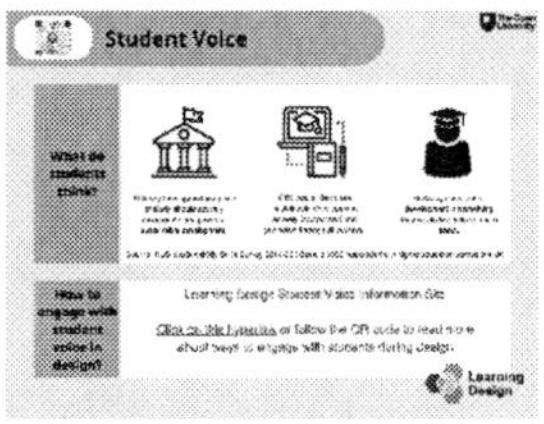
Resource 8 This hyperlink will take you to a page that contains PDF version of the images above. You can also access them via the QR code on the right..	

INTERNATIONALISATION AT A DISTANCE (IAD): A CONCEPTUAL FRAMEWORK FOR THE INCLUSION OF DIVERSE PERSPECTIVES FROM DISTANCE LEARNERS

Palitha Edirisingha, University of Leicester, UK; Phil Wood, Nottingham Trent University, UK

Abstract

This paper addresses the focus track of the conference "equity, diversity and inclusion' for digital education'. It presents the development of a new conceptual framework on *Internationalisation at a Distance* (IaD).

Internationalisation of higher education (IHE) is not new; 'its popularity [was] soaring ... since the early 1980s' (Knight, 2013: 85). However, much of the discussions of IHE are about 'internationalisation' of campus-based programmes from 'Internationalisation Abroad', i.e., students moving to another country to study, and 'Internationalisation at Home, i.e., introducing 'international' dimensions on campuses at home (Knight, 2004). A largely ignored third category of internationalisation is Internationalisation at Distance (IaD) (Ramanau (2016), which is gaining traction due to increasing use of digital technologies in education (Mittelmeier et al., 2021; and Gemmel et al., 2015). In IaD, students experience some elements of internationalisation in their studies while remaining where they live and/or work. Research and conceptual developments of IaD is still scarce.

Our research investigates how do distance learners experience internationalisation of education, and what elements of internationalisation do they experience, if any at all. Based on qualitative approaches to collecting data from a distance learning course at the University of Leicester, we explore the above research questions using two methods.

1. Short autobiographies of students depicting their professional and educational journeys and how these influence their experience on their present study programme.
2. Semi-structured interviews with 12 course participants exploring their autobiographies in-depth and their experiences of internationalisation in their current programme.

Much of the previous research reported literature on IaD (eg., Mittelmeier et a., 2021) are based on the perspectives of students who are enrolled in distance learning programmes while residing in their own home countries. A significant majority of our respondents live and work in a third country (i.e., a country that is different from where they have had their formative learning and living experiences) giving them a unique position to offer diversity of perspectives relevant to key elements and dimensions of IaD.

The conference presentation will outline an emerging conceptual framework of internationalisation at a distance that could be used to promote stronger diversity and inclusion of distance learners in their internationalisation experience of learning.

Keywords:

Internationalisation at Distance, Internationalisation in Higher Education, Inclusivity in Distance Learning.

References

Gemmell, I., Harrison, R., Clegg, J. and Reed, K., 2015. Internationalisation in online distance learning postgraduate education: A case study on student views on learning alongside students from other countries. *Innovations in Education and Teaching International,* 52(2), pp.137-147.

Knight, J., 2013. The changing landscape of higher education internationalisation - for better or worse? Perspectives: *Policy and Practice in Higher Education*, 17(3), pp.84-90.

Knight, J., 2004. Internationalization remodelled: Definition, approaches, and rationales. *Journal of Studies in International Education*, 8(1), pp.5-31.

Mittelmeier, J., Rienties, B., Gunter, A. and Raghuram, P., 2021. Conceptualizing internationalization at a distance: A "third category" of university internationalization. *Journal of Studies in International Education*, 25(3), pp.266-282.

Ramanau, R., 2016. Internationalization at a distance: A study of the online management curriculum. *Journal of Management Education*, 40(5), pp.545-575.

(LESS-)DIGITAL PEACE EDUCATION FOR DISPLACED POPULATIONS

Kyungmee Lee, Melis Cin, Lancaster University, UK

Abstract

With a growing number of displaced populations worldwide, many being severely affected by different regional, national, and inter-national conflicts, the importance of peace education has never been greater. However, the displaced, destabilised and often disconnected and disabled nature of their everyday lives poses a difficult challenge to peace educators (Cin & Doğan, 2021). Despite the transformative potential of emerging digital technologies for different educational contexts and the urgent needs of displaced populations for such potential, displaced populations can be the last to access and benefit from digital technologies (Lee, 2017; 2021). If we want equity, diversity, and inclusion at the heart of digital education, better futures enabled by digital technologies should be discussed and imagined from those marginalised (dis-)places.

To address this pressing issue, a group of researchers specialised in different areas of educational settings, distance education, peace education, and refugee education, have collaboratively explored the complex challenge faced by peace educators in a refugee camp in a unique cultural and political context. This paper presents the preliminary findings from our collective efforts to explore a range of transformative possibilities different digital tools can bring into the design and implementation of authentic peace education in the concerned camp.

Our qualitative research employs a dialectical scenario-based inquiry, which begins with deconstructing the complex challenge in our peace education context by identifying a set of problems that constitute the challenge. Unique digital (and less-digital) approaches to addressing and alleviating each problem are envisioned and concretised as a format of living scenarios. We further critically and systematically analyse each scenario and identify emerging contradictions subsequently introduced by the digital approaches. Those contradictions serve as problems, a starting point for another cycle of dialectical scenario-based inquiry, and the cycle recurs until innovative and actionable scenarios are developed. This study is the first phase of our large-scale project, aiming to transform peace education for displaced populations using (less-)digital technologies.

As the title suggests, based on our preliminary findings, we argue for a balanced and critical perspective on the transformative power of emerging digital technologies and embrace (less-)digital realities and changes to serve the authentic needs and conditions of marginalised populations. For example, more traditional distance education models, which utilise less-digital tools, should secure a place in our digital education ecosystem for all.

Keywords:

(Less-)digital education, peace education, refugee education, displaced populations, dialectical scenario-based inquiry

References

Cin, F. M., & Doğan, N. (2021). Navigating university spaces as refugees: Syrian students' pathways of access to and through higher education in Turkey. *International Journal of Inclusive Education, 25*(2), 298-312.

Lee, K. (2017). Rethinking the accessibility of online higher education: A historical review. *The Internet and Higher Education, 33*, 15-23.

Lee, K. (2021). Openness and innovation in online higher education: A historical review of the two discourses. *Open Learning: The Journal of Open, Distance and e-Learning, 36*(2), 112-132.

POTENTIAL OF BIOGRAPHIC, NARRATIVE RESEARCH TO UNDERSTANDING NEW FUTURES

Lisa Moran, Zeta Dooly, PJ Wall, South East Technological University, Ireland

Abstract

The emergence of new education policies based on data, learning analytics, tertiary market demand and access is not easily understood in our communities, even though many citizen consultation processes are administered online.

Much research captures tensions in global societal discourses about AI with particular reference to Ireland. Hitherto, there is scant social scientific research on societal attitudes towards AI; its value and limitations in education, citizen fears and emotions about AI technology which requires redress. Furthermore, there are even fewer studies that actively leverage knowledge from different professional groups (scientists, artists, educationalists, AI experts, sociologists, teachers) and citizens (e.g., older people, families who are members of 'hard to reach' groups and AI leaders) to understand individual and collective understandings of AI in education at primary, secondary, third and fourth level.

This paper highlights the challenges on understanding the socio-cultural legitimacy of AI in Irish society yielding data that is highly relevant for government with regards to the structure of targeted information campaigns, communication with/to different citizen groups and usage of social media platforms and other media to enhance citizen attitudes towards AI.

These challenges can be overcome using an innovative methodological approach to link the needs of communities, governments and citizens which are multi-faceted and difficult to untangle with the speed that AI technology is developing and delivering educational solutions globally and nationally.

There is a lack of societal awareness and understanding in relation to the potential benefits and limitations of AI, which can lead to misperceptions, heightened sense of risk, inertia and resistance to its adoption. Governments and organizations can work together to raise awareness about AI through education and outreach initiatives aimed at different communities (e.g., older people, children) but this necessitates greater knowledge about citizen perceptions of AI, information campaigns targeted at improved accessibility, usability and societal 'buy in' to AI and exposure to AI technologies that combine scientific expertise with artistic expression and skills.

This research promotes a collaborative approach, non-confrontational approach that invokes open dialogue, transparency, citizen participation, and the sharing of resources and knowledge through the use of biographic narrative methodology.

Keywords:

Education, Sustainability, Biographic Narrative, Futures literacy

GUIDELINES FOR EQUITY, DIVERSITY, AND INCLUSION (EDI) IN OPEN EDUCATION CENTERING ON AFRICA AND LATIN AMERICA CONTEXTS

Carina Bossu, Francisco Iniesto, The Open University, UK

Abstract

Equity, diversity, and inclusion (EDI) has been a topic of recent debate within the Open Education (OE) community, and some would argue that it has underpinned the OE discourse since the beginning. However, access to free and online resources alone, such as Open Educational Resources (OER) cannot be considered equitable, diverse, and inclusive. In fact, the large majority of OER are only available in English, which limits access and reach for many learners around the world (Bossu et al., 2023). The Global OER Graduate Network (GO-GN) is a network of PhD candidates around the world whose research projects include a focus on open education. These doctoral researchers are at the core of the network; around them, over two hundred experts, supervisors, mentors and interested parties connect to form a community of practice. EDI has been driving the GO-GN agenda since its foundation in 2013, but it was only in 2018 when its first projects directly related to EDI was developed; the first one had a focus on EDI in Open Education in Africa, followed by a second project which focused on Latin America. One of the aims of these projects was to increase representation from these communities within GO-GN, as despite attempts, most of GO-GN participants are from Global North/developed countries. Another aim was to reach those who could potentially benefit the most from being part of this network (Rodés & Iniesto, 2021).

In this presentation, we will briefly explore key aspects of these two EDI projects. We will also present, the GO-GN EDI Guidelines, which is an evidenced-based document that contains set of guiding principles that prompts questions and raises issues to be considered by higher education institutions, individuals, and in particular for GO-GN, and other similar initiatives wishing to create a more equitable, diverse, and inclusive open education environment so that it can benefit those who need it the most. Although the EDI guidelines were informed and contextualised by some of the regions of the Global South, it can be changed and adapted to suit different EDI and open educational contexts.

Keywords:

GO-GN, EDI, Equity, diversity and inclusion in OE, Open Education, EDI recommendations, EDI implementation.

References

Bossu, C.; Iniesto, F.; Vladimirschi, V.; Jordan, K. & Pete, J. (2023). *GO-GN Guidelines for Equity Diversity and Inclusion in Open Education with a focus on Africa and Latin America.* Global OER Graduate Network. https://go-gn.net/gogn_outputs/edi-guidelines/

Rodés, V., & Iniesto, F. (2021). Research in Open Education in Latin America: towards an agenda of collaboration between networks. In *2021 XVI Latin American Conference on Learning Technologies (LACLO)*, Arequipa, Peru. IEEE, pp. 462-465. DOI: 10.1109/LACLO54177.2021.00061

THE SDGS AND MICROCREDENTIALS, HAND IN GLOVE?

John Scahill, Carmel Heaney, Frances O Donnell, Atlantic Technological University, Ireland

Abstract

The sustainable development goal (SDG) framework places education in a central role as a catalyst for transformational change. The SDG agenda calls for a multidisciplinary approach to interpreting and responding to the myriad challenges presented by climate change and the mammoth task of creating a just and equitable society for all to enjoy and prosper in.

Third level institutions have an important role to play as recognised drivers of global, national, and local innovation, economic development, and societal wellbeing.

Micro-credentials offer a flexible and accessible alternative for learners to undertake short, accredited programmes of study and was considered an ideal vehicle for the development of a suite of non-discipline specific SDG related modules and programmes.

To this end a multi-disciplinary team was formed in the ATU to design a suite of SDG related micro-credential modules that focusses on the regional application and implementation of the SDGs.

The team created a level-6 20 credit Special Purpose Award (SPA) made up of 4 x 5 credit modules around the themes of partnership, people, planet and prosperity. The delivery mode is online and primarily asynchronous, but also includes direct engagement with teaching staff for assessment feedback and as such can be considered to have an element of blended/synchronous delivery. The programme focusses on the use of RLOs (reusable-learning-objects) and the content and delivery design consider the principles of universal design for learning (UDL).

The programme is designed to provide students with an opportunity to undertake an accredited qualification in the SDGs, in addition to their primary programme of study, further preparing them for the "work of the world". It is designed with the ultimate aim of being available to both students and staff in ATU (and beyond) who want to engage with the SDGs and explore what they are, why they are important and how to achieve them.

The programme is currently being trialled on a diverse group from outside of the student body of ATU. The programme was advertised on the ATU life-long learning platform as a CPD offering from the school of Engineering. The initial cohort of 19 students consisted of people form a wide range of backgrounds, disciplines and educational achievements (ranging from level 6 to level 10, with 80% having a level 8 or higher qualification).

Feedback from the group is being obtained through, surveys, semi-structured interviews and analysis of the on-line content produced by the students. Key questions that are being explored are delivery mode, student engagement, prior educational achievement, disciplinary influence.

The feedback will be used to finetune the design of the programme prior to its roll out across a number of campuses in ATU.

The project was funded under the HCI Pillar 3 funded project Higher Ed 4.0

Keywords:

UN Sustainable Development Goals, micro-credentials, inter-disciplinary, on-line asynchronous.

DIGITAL CITIZENSHIP IN SCHOOLS: WHO, HOW, WHERE AND WHEN?

Sólveig Jakobsdóttir, Skúlína Hlíf Kjartansdóttir, University of Iceland, Iceland

Abstract

Digital citizenship has been regarded as highly important focus area of education for young people who have constant online access through digital tools including tablets and smartphones, see for example the European Schoolnet (http://www.eun.org/focus-areas) and the ISTE association (https://www.iste.org/areas-of-focus/digital-citizenship). The concept of digital citizenship has been evolving and been defined and interpreted in various ways. It can encompass a wide range of topics including character education, online reputation, rights and responsibilities, online communications and netiqutte, health and wellbeing, online safety and security and media literacy (see e.g., Ribble, 2011). For schools that want to have digital citizenship education as part of their curriculum there are many challenges and questions.

- Who should give such lessons?
- How should they be delivered?
- Where should they be placed in the curriculum – in which subjects?
- When – in which age groups/years, to what extent in terms of number of lessons per week or year?

In this presentation we will provide an overview of the experiences of an Icelandic school district with nine schools which decided to place an emphasis on digital citizenship when all students in grades 5 to 10 were provided with tablet computers (iPad) for 1:1 learning in 2015. The results are a part of an evaluation study (Jakobsdóttir & Kjartansdóttir, 2023) on the effects of tablet integration on teaching and learning in the schools. Survey among teachers (n=425, 86% participation rate) revealed that about 29% thought that their students' knowledge and competences in relation to digital citizenship had shown little or no increase and another 29% were not sure. On the other hand, only 15% thought they had increased highly and 26% considerably. Interviews with teachers and support staff revealed that teachers were not confident to teach about digital citizenship and would rather ask members of the district support team to come in to introduce and discuss issues with students. Members of the support team thought this was not ideal because they did not know the students involved and the underlying problems. Learning materials are needed in this area as well as better preparation for teachers in their basic training and in access to continuing education courses about digital citizenship. Also, the national curriculum in ICT needs to be renewed. Swimming has long been a big part of the Icelandic culture and currently the national curriculum requires weekly swimming lessons for students at the primary and lower secondary level. It may be time to require weekly lessons in digital citizenship in a similar fashion to help students learn to "swim" and avoid "drowning" in our developing digital landscape. Digital citizenship is an important part of our current life skills.

Keywords:

Digital citizenship, schools, tablet computers.

References

Jakobsdóttir, S., & Kjartansdóttir, S. H. (2023). *Spjaldtölvur í grunnskólum Kópavogs: matsrannsókn [Tablet computers in Kópavogur schools - evaluation study]*. https://doi.org/10.33112/SGKM2040

Ribble, M. (2011). Digital citizenship in schools (2. ed.). ISTE.

THE CONTRIBUTION OF OPEN EDUCATION FOR IMPROVING CAUSES OF DEATH CERTIFICATION PRACTICES

António Moreira Teixeira, Universidade Aberta, Portugal; Amadeu Borges Ferro, Escola Superior de Tecnologia da Saúde de Lisboa, Portugal; Sara Brandão, USF São Julião, ACES Lisboa Ocidental e Oeiras, ARSLVT, Portugal; Maria do Carmo Teixeira Pinto, Universidade Aberta, Portugal; João Paz, Universidade Aberta, Portugal

Abstract

As recently demonstrated during the COVID-19 pandemic, mortality data provide a better understanding of epidemiological trends and the impacts of health policies within a population. The accurate and timely way information on causes of death is recorded, coded and published is therefore critical. Most countries apply the recommendations issued by the World Health Organization, in the International Statistical Classification of Diseases and Related Health Problems, currently in its 11th revision, [ICD-11] (WHO, 2023).

In the European Union, however, the quality of data on causes of death differs considerably between member states. Despite using an official online platform for registering death certificates since 2014 (Law 15/2012), which speeds up considerably the processing of statistical updates on death causes (DGS, 2013), Portugal records a relatively high proportion of deaths attributed to poor conditions or other codes unnecessary in public health analyses, the so-called 'garbage codes' (Fihel & Muszynska-Spielauer, 2021). This is mainly due to inappropriate certification practices by many medical doctors unaware of the fact. However, to retrain a wide community of practitioners scattered around the country in a speedy way represents a massive challenge for public health authorities. Due to the limited resources available, using traditional in presence learning formats does not seem sustainable.

In the framework of the European CODA-EU project (https://coda-eu.site.ined.fr/en/), supported by the Erasmus+ program, an international multidisciplinary team of experts from medical, social and education sciences designed a Multilingual MOOC on certification on the causes of death. It targets medical doctors, medical students and other health professionals for whom the competencies in cause-of-death certification are important and need to improve their knowledge on the recommendations and rules set by WHO for this purpose.

The MOOC "Certification of the Causes of Death" was produced in 4 different versions adapted to the specific national context and regulation framework of the member countries of the consortium (France, Poland, Greece and Portugal) and delivered in each country's respective language. The MOOC takes approximately 3 hours to complete and consists of 3 main modules, as follows:

1. Legal and organisational aspects of death registration in each country,
2. International Statistical Classification of Diseases and Related Health Problems,
3. Most common errors in the certification of causes of death.

The course also includes prior knowledge and final assessments, an introduction, cases studies (scenarios to train the ability to determine the appropriate causes of death) and additional references. A certificate is provided for those who complete the final assessment with a 50% or higher mark.

The first iteration of the MOOC in Portuguese was launched in April 2023. It attracted 369 participants, of which 95 passed the final exam and obtained the respective certificate of completion. 40% of the approved participants reached a mark of 80% or over. The profile of the participants was quite diverse and representative of the medical community. It included experienced medical doctors, medical students and even representatives from the Ministry of Health. Consequently, the age of participants ranged from 19 to 66 years old.

The feedback collected from the participants demonstrates high satisfaction with this short but impactful learning experience. The quality of the content and the flexibility of the learning experience, combined with the accessibility and openness of the course were considered most appropriate to the learners' profile and professional context. Moreover, representatives from the Portuguese Ministry of Health have recognised the contribution of this MOOC and of other future dedicated open education provision for the timely updating and improving of medical staff competences in certification of causes of death.

Acknowledgement

The authors acknowledge CODA-EU, an Erasmus+ project funded by the European Commission (2020-1-FR01-KA203-080629). This publication reflects the views only of the authors.

Keywords:

Certification of Causes of Death; Open Education; MOOC; eLearning course.

References

Fihel, A. & Muszynska-Spielauer, M. M. (2021). Using multiple cause of death information to eliminate garbage codes. *Demographic Research*, Vol. 45 (JULY - DECEMBER 2021), pp. 345-360 (18 pages) https://www.jstor.org/stable/48640782

Orientação nº 020/2013 da Direção-Geral de Saúde (2013). Certificado de óbito eletrónico – Utilização do Sistema de Informação dos Certificados de Óbito (SICO). https://www.dgs.pt/directrizes-da-dgs/orientacoes-e-circulares-informativas/orientacao-n-0202013-de-31122013-pdf.aspx

Lei nº 15/2012 do Ministério da Saúde (2012). *Diário da República*: Iª série, nº 67 (Lei de implementação do SICO). https://files.dre.pt/1s/2012/04/06700/0171601718.pdf

World Health Organization (2023). ICD-11 - International Classification of Diseases for Mortality and Morbidity Statistics. Eleventh Revision. https://icdcdn.who.int/icd11referenceguide/en/html/index.html

THE USE OF NATURAL LANGUAGE PROCESSING (NLP) TO GAUGE LEARNER SENTIMENTS

Ontiretse Ishmael, Etain Kiely, Ikechukwu Ogbuchi, Cormac Quigley, Donal McGinty, Atlantic Technological University, Ireland

Abstract

Qualitative data-analysis methods provide rich descriptions of subjects' thoughts, feelings, and lived experiences but may be time-consuming for education researchers(Daniel & Harland, 2018) due to the heterogeneous nature of the data which tends to have high volume and complexity. Natural language processing (NLP) is a machine learning technique that uses artificial intelligence (AI) based algorithms to analyse textual data. This presentation offers strategies on how to develop different models to promote the use of text-based data analysis techniques. The analysis of human language data from survey documents is made possible by the use of various NLP approaches including Latent Sematic Analysis (LSA) and Latent Dirichlet Allocation (LDA). In this study, LDA is used for modelling topics to analyse students' sentiments on the feedback assessment given to them regarding their performance on the module. The application of NLP in education environments to provide meaningful and useful feedback to lecturers on students' sentiments is explored. The study presents the steps, algorithm and findings so that other practitioners can apply this model to their education setting. The findings of year 1 maths module (n=194) revealed 90% of students have positive sentiments, 7% are neutral, 3% are confused by the personalized feedback forms.

Keywords: Qualitative data, NLP, students, sentiments, LDA

References

Alhojely, S. (2016). Sentiment Analysis and Opinion Mining: A Survey. *International Journal of Computer Applications, 150*(6), 22–25. https://doi.org/10.5120/ijca2016911545

Daniel, B. K., & Harland, T. (2018). Qualitative data analysis. *Higher Education Research Methodology, 15*(1), 98–110. https://doi.org/10.4324/9781315149783-10

Lin, C., & He, Y. (2009). Joint sentiment/topic model for sentiment analysis. *International Conference on Information and Knowledge Management, Proceedings*, 375–384. https://doi.org/10.1145/1645953.1646003

R, N., S, P. M., Harithas, Pramath. P., & Hegde, V. (2022). *Sentimental Analysis on Student Feedback using NLP & POS Tagging. Icecaa*, 309–313. https://doi.org/10.1109/icecaa55415.2022.9936569

Rakhmanov, O., & Schlippe, T. (2022). Sentiment Analysis for {H}ausa: Classifying Students{'} Comments. *Proceedings of the 1st Annual Meeting of the ELRA/ISCA Special Interest Group on Under-Resourced Languages, June*, 98–105. https://aclanthology.org/2022.sigul-1.13

Shute, V. J. (2009). Simply Assessment. *International Journal of Learning and Media, 1*(2), 1–11. https://doi.org/10.1162/ijlm.2009.0014

EASING OF PANDEMIC RESTRICTIONS – EFFECT ON DIGITAL CONTENT?

Jane Boyd, The College of Law, Australia

Background

During the pandemic, many institutions (including The College of Law) increased their percentage component of digital learning content to 100%. Whilst then necessary, it is now time to decide whether it is still appropriate, while recognising the supremacy of digital content.

There is very little current research in this area. We therefore need to revert to the classic debate regarding digital saturation.

Table 1: Relevant issues considered in this paper

Element	Pros	Cons
Economics	No bricks and mortar needed, cheaper courses for students	Large development and maintenance costs, Lecturer training costs
Convenience, Flexibility, and Isolation	Work in own time in varied locations	Isolation, requires "adult learners"
Screen exposure	Digital literacy	Increased exposure to screen time
Student learning capability and outcomes	A given huge field not encompassed in this presentation	
Technical issues	Nil	Expense, disruption, need for extended student and lecturer support
External Regulators requirements	Consistency with other like providers	Compulsory

My paper is based on 35+ years teaching experience in a post graduate institution. The College of Law is in the business of providing post-graduate Practical Legal Training (PLT) in all eight Australian jurisdictions (New South Wales, Australian Capital Territory, Victoria, Queensland, South Australia, Western Australia, Northern Territory and Tasmania) and in New Zealand. This involves approximately 6,500 students annually. In addition, each year the College of Law enrols approximately 1,500 master's students across Australia and New Zealand, has approximately 1,000 enrolments in post graduate short courses in Australia, and dozens of students in College of Law Asia and College of Legal Practice United Kingdom. All these courses include digital learning, with anywhere from 15% to 100% of the course being delivered online.

My proposal centres around recognising the importance of digital delivery for the majority of our courses, whilst recognising that it is difficult to deliver our courses with 100% digital content. My thesis is that they should consist of blended learning with face-to-face content used for the soft skills components (in our case Interviewing, Problem Solving, Advocacy, Ethical Decision Making, Wellbeing in Practice and Dispute Resolution). This constitutes 6.7% to 3.3% of course time, dependent on whether enrolment is full-time or part-time. The remainder is digital content. The Covid-19 pandemic provided us with a valuable yardstick to measure the efficacy of 100% digital content. Historically, pre-pandemic, soft skills were taught in face-to-face workshops. I believe that this should be partly reinstated with some of the converted to digital content retained.

Our history of digital learning

The College of Law was an early adopter of online learning components, first delivering a course via CD Rom and email in 1998. As technology developed, so did our means of delivery. In 2002 we moved to web-based delivery. In 2004 we broadened our delivery to multiple Australian jurisdictions. In 2008 we commenced our first iteration of the learning portal which hosted all student and lecturer material. In 2015 we transferred our learning management system to Canvas. We continue to operate in Canvas, notably because it allows simple embedding of external digital content into courses. So, it is fair to say the College of Law has been proactive in the use of digital resources.

Figure 1: Timeline of digital learning development at the College of Law

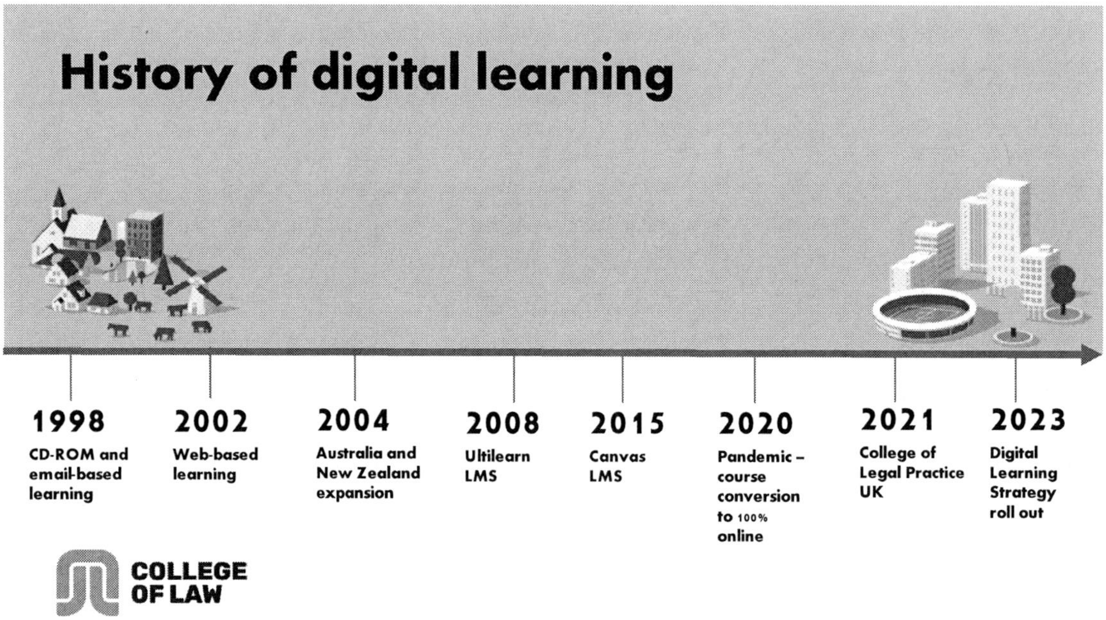

As a result of the Covid-19 pandemic, our 2020 course conversion centred on the conversion of face-to-face teaching components to virtual workshops using Zoom, Microsoft Teams and HTML5 (H5P) interactive books. This was a rapid response on 1 weeks' notice. The hasty changeover assisted our recognition that this conversion may not necessarily provide the best learning outcomes for our students encouraging us to analyse our digital content. It became apparent that not all content is easily adapted to digital delivery.

From there, we decided to develop a digital learning strategy which took into account what we had learned from our amendments to course delivery due to the pandemic. In short, training in vocational skills is difficult without face-to-face teaching. It can of course be underpinned by digital resources, but physical presence was necessary to effectively teach some components.

Our Digital Learning Strategy

Our Digital Learning Strategy aims to ensure that our products and services are continuously improved and digitally transformed to retain high value and viability in the current and future legal education market. It is designed to align people, processes and technology. The increased incorporation of technology presents us with opportunities to equip students with new skills necessary to survive in a tech-dominated world, preparing them to be digitally literate and technologically savvy beyond the classroom. At the same time, we need to understand the associated risks in relation to privacy, cyber-security, plagiarism (which I am sure will be the subject of many papers) and copyright. The increase in the use of AI also presents benefits and dangers and I am sure other papers will be focusing on this.

Figure 2: Key components of The College of Law digital learning strategy

We have also adopted a Careers Skills Framework to overlay our digital learning strategy. This is graphically illustrated below.

Figure 3: The College of Law Careers Skills Framework

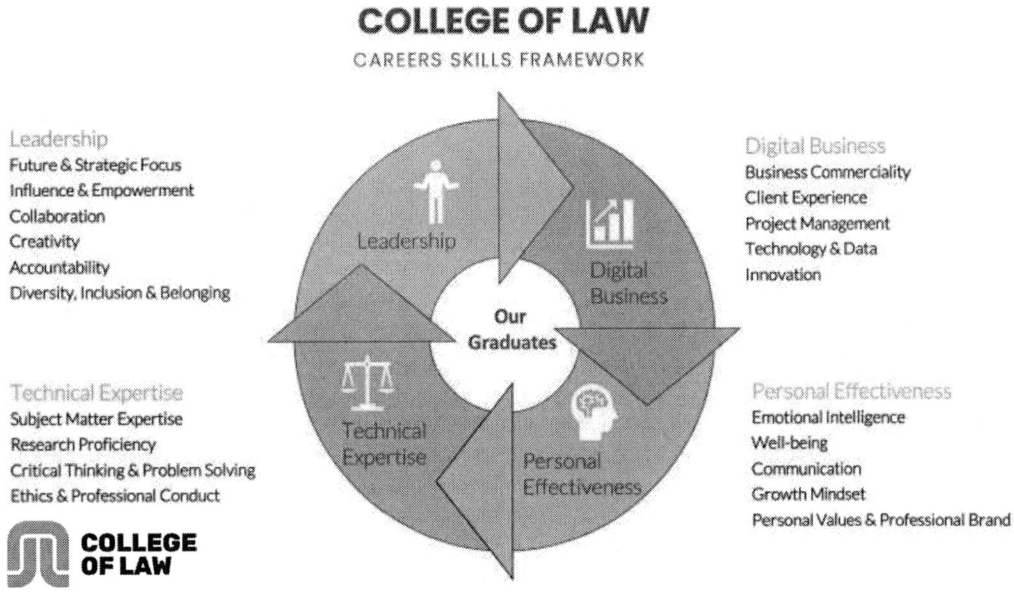

We have chosen to adopt EdTech and LegalTech within our existing Canvas Learning Management System, rather than attempting to create tailored designed software. I suggest that we should use LegalTech products widely used in the legal services industry and suitable to be made available to learners as sandboxes. This meets the needs of students, providing them with authentic experience as they get to engage with established programs used in the real world of legal practice. It is also more time and cost effective. Examples include:

PEXA	Josef	SILQ	Forage virtual internships	EdTech
• E-conveyancing platform used in practice	• Legal automation (bot) platform	• Legal practice management and trust account software	• College of Law and Forage partnership to offer virtual internships for NewLaw professional roles	• Curriculum Management System • Padlet • Canvas (LMS) • Learning Analytics Platform

PEXA is a national Electronic Network Operator for conveyancing. Electronic conveyancing is now mandatory in most jurisdictions. Students get to practice, discover and interact with the real software used by Australian lawyers all while in a safe environment. The PEXA sandbox component has proved incredibly popular with students. This has encouraged us to consider further integration of the sandbox environment in other areas.

External Regulation

As in most educational establishments, we are subject to multiple external regulators dictating various standards which affect our course accreditation.

As we enter a post-pandemic world, admitting authorities are expecting a return to teaching some areas of the course in the real rather than virtual classroom. At the same time our enrolment statistics show a continued preference for online courses. However, our student satisfaction data also indicates that students appreciate at least some face-to-face teaching. The regulator's requirements and students' expectations need to be balanced.

An extraordinarily brief summary is:

TEQSA (Tertiary Education Quality and Standards Agency) expects:

- Quality online content
- Use of LMS and instructional design to engage learners and enhance the learning experience.

Local admitting authorities expect:

- Potential re-introduction of face-to-face skills teaching

Students expect:

- Flexibility
- Accessibility
- Interactivity
- Engaging content
- Current and relevant content
- Access to subject matter experts
- Support when required (24/7)

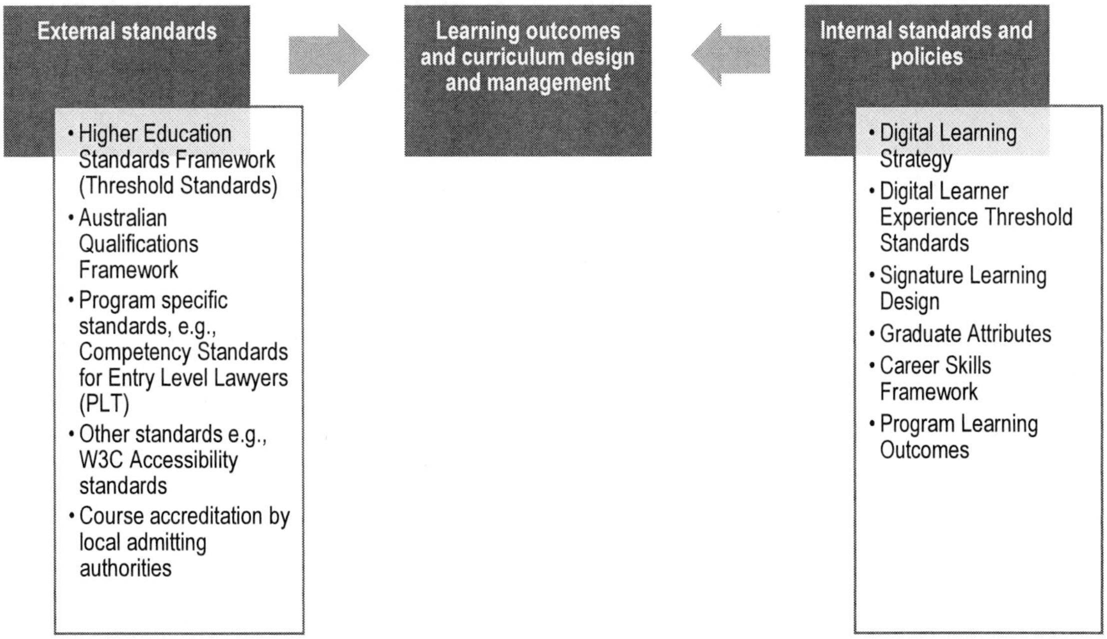

Conclusion

Digital learning is here to stay but is not an appropriate delivery method for all types of course content. Blended learning is the way of the future for many courses.

It is more time and cost effective for us to adopt and include existing EdTech and Legal Tech rather than creating bespoke programs which come with lengthy time delays and at a vast cost. It is also capable of delivering an authentic experience and allows us to incorporate sandbox methodology in our courses.

Keywords: Blended learning, EdTech, LegalTech, Sandbox

References

Ippolito, P. (2022, May). *Predicting the future of law during a pandemic.* Paper presented at APLEC Conference, Sydney.

Klift, S. (2022, May). *Regulating Australian legal education and training*. Paper presented at APLEC Conference, Sydney.

Law Admissions Consultative Committee. (2015, July 1). *Competency standards for entry level lawyers.* https://www.lawcouncil.asn.au/files/web-pdf/LACC%20docs/Competency_Standards_for_Entry-Level_Lawyers_-_1_July_2015.pdf

Mottershead, T. (2022, May). *Lawyer competencies in a digital legal world.* Paper presented at APLEC Conference, Sydney.

Mottershead, T. (Host). (2022, October 30). Getting started with legaltech projects – What's new in 2022? (No. 156) [Audio podcast episode]. In *Centre for Legal Innovation*. https://www.cli.collaw.com/podcast/2022/11/14/episode-156-getting-started-with-legaltech-projects-whats-new-in-2022

Salyzyn, A. (2020, December 18). *A taxonomy for lawyer technological competence.* Slaw - Canada's online legal magazine. https://www.slaw.ca/2020/12/18/a-taxonomy-for-lawyer-technological-competence/

WHO ARE YOU (AND WHAT DO YOU DO)? BEING AND DOING LEARNING DESIGN.

Eamon Costello, Mark Brown, Orna Farrell, James Brunton, Enda Donlon, Ruby Cooney, Dublin City University, Ireland

Abstract

The role of Learning designer now represents the fastest growing job in higher education. This initiative aims to shines a light on key aspects of this phenomenon. A wave of recruitment of digital learning designers occurred during the pandemic (Decherney & Levander, 2020). These workers were heralded as online learning's "first responders". Nonetheless the role and experiences of these professionals still exists in the shadow of the teacher and student narratives. Significant gaps exist in our understanding of these vital brokers, or "third space" professionals, including what their professional and career needs are (Whitchurch et al, 2021). In particular, there is a dearth of research into professional identities of learning designers in Ireland and the UK post-pandemic (Costello et al 2022; McDonald, Forthcoming). This initiative hence proposes to conduct a comprehensive survey of digital learning designers in UK and Irish universities and answer following three research questions:

What are the key skills and competencies of digital learning designers in contemporary Higher Education (HE) environments?

What contributions are digital learning designers making to HE missions and how well is this being recognised?

What gaps and opportunities exist for continued professional development of learning designers?

This project draws upon related work (Altena, 2019) into the lived experiences of learning designers which looks at their work and identity through the lens of being and doing. In addition to the survey the project is also collecting testimonies of learning designers via video interviews to showcase the everyday idea of learning design.

References

Altena, S., Ng, R., Hinze, M., Poulsen, S., & Parrish, D. (2019). "Many hats one heart": A scoping review on the professional identity of learning designers. ASCILITE Publications, 359-364.

Costello, E., Welsh, S., Girme, P., Concannon, F., Farrelly, T., & Thompson, C. (2022). Who cares about learning design? Near future superheroes and villains of an educational ethics of care. *Learning, Media and Technology*, 1-16.

Decherney, P., & Levander, C. (2020). The hottest job in higher education: Instructional designer. *Inside Higher Ed.*

McDonald J. K. *(Forthcoming)* The Everydayness of Instructional Design and the Pursuit of Quality in Online Courses. *Online Learning*

Whitchurch, C., W. Locke and G. Marini (2021). "Challenging Career Models in Higher Education: The Influence of Internal Career Scripts and the Rise of the 'Concertina' Career". Higher Education 82(3): 635-650.]

IF YOU BUILD IT, THEY MIGHT OR MIGHT NOT COME: HOW WE BECAME REPOSITORY DETECTORISTS

Irene O'Dowd, Ann Byrne, Emberly Davey, Hibernia College, Ireland

Abstract

The creation of an institutional repository for research and scholarly content was a key priority for our institution's research committee, and upon its rollout we waited for the submissions to roll in. And waited. And waited. Eventually, facing up to the reality of our anticipated deluge of artefacts proving to be an occasional drip, we took matters into our own hands.

Developing faculty and staff engagement with a new open-access institutional repository (IR) is a challenge often underestimated during IR implementation projects. The idea that "if you build it, they will come" does not reflect the reality of establishing a successful IR in a third-level institution (Ferreira et al., 2008). Factors that hinder the adoption of open-access IRs are many and varied, and a multi-pronged approach is required both to gain an understanding of these factors and develop a strategy to address them (Narayan and Luca, 2017; Tmava, 2022). For those involved in IR implementation projects, having surmounted the considerable hurdles of securing approval and funding for an IR and then developing the platform, the need for the development of such a strategy often comes as quite a surprise. However, it is arguably the most important part of ensuring a successful IR implementation.

In this presentation, the genesis and continuing evolution of our own IR engagement strategy will be reflected upon, and our learnings shared for the benefit of those at a similar or earlier stage of the open-access IR journey. Crucial to our professional journey has been the process of replacing the hubristic "if you build it" metaphor with one suggesting a more incremental and infinitely less glamorous approach to the problem. Inspired by a popular television series (Crook, 2014-2022), we reflect on the role of IR administrators less as architects and more as *detectorists*.

Informed by the reflective model of Experience, Reflection, Action (Jasper, 2013) and guided by Holliday's (2017) thinking on the power of metaphor in theory and practice, we present a story of lofty idealism giving way to scuttling skullduggery; of the painful metaphorical journey from building a magnificent baseball stadium to squelching through a muddy field with a metal detector. It is also a story of how we were (almost) desperate enough to dress up in fish onesies and jump into the Liffey.

Keywords:

Institutional repositories; open access; engagement; research; metaphors; critical reflection

References

Crook, M. (2014–2022). *The detectorists* [TV series]. Channel X; BBC Four.

Ferreira, M., Rodrigues, E., Baptista, A.A., and Saraiva, S. (2008) Carrots and sticks: some ideas on how to create a successful institutional repository. *D-Lib Magazine*, 14(1/2). Retrieved from https://www.dlib.org/dlib/january08/ferreira/01ferreira.html

Holliday, Wendy (2017) Frame works: using metaphor in theory and practice in information literacy. *Communications in Information Literacy*, 11(1), Article 12. Retrieved from http://pdxscholar.library.pdx.edu/comminfolit/vol11/iss1/12

Jasper, M. (2013) *Beginning reflective practice*. 1st ed. Andover: Cengage Learning, pp.1-6.

Narayan, B. and Luca, E. (2017) Issues and challenges in researchers' adoption of open access and institutional repositories: a contextual study of a university repository. *Information Research*, 22(4). Retrieved from http://InformationR.net/ir/22-4/rails/rails1608.html

Tmava, A.M. (2022) Faculty Perceptions of Open Access Repositories: A Qualitative Analysis. *New Review of Academic Librarianship*. DOI: 10.1080/13614533.2022.2082991

UNDERSTANDING STUDENT READINESS FOR ONLINE LEARNING: LESSONS FROM A SYSTEMIC LITERATURE REVIEW

Elaine Beirne, Mark Brown, Conchúr Mac Lochlainn, Mairéad Nic Giolla Mhichíl, Dublin City University, Ireland

Abstract

This paper reports what is known about student readiness for online learning. It draws on the COVID-19 experience and is based on the premise that learning how to learn online is now a crucial life skill; it must not be left to chance. As part of the Erasmus+ DigiTeL Pro project, the paper establishes that student readiness for online learning has a long history. However, different conceptions of the concept exist with a lack of consensus in the literature.

The paper then describes a systematic analysis of the literature published during the global pandemic, focusing on student readiness (Beirne et al., 2022). This study sought to answer three main research questions: i) What research has been published reporting student readiness for online distance learning during the COVID crisis? ii) How strong is the "learner voice" in COVID- related research reporting on student readiness for online distance learning? iii) What lessons can be taken from the COVID-related literature on student readiness for new digital education models?

A brief description of the literature search methodology is provided, with a sample of over 40 relevant publications identified. The related data extraction template and analysis techniques are shared along with a descriptive profile of the literature. Overall, the paper confirms a previous finding that a lot of emergency remote research was conducted during the COVID-19 crisis (Bond et al., 2021), alongside what became known as Emergency Remote Teaching (Hodges et al., 2020). Notably, with few exceptions, there is limited evidence of previous student readiness literature on online learning informing how higher education institutions (HEIs) responded during the pandemic. There is even a risk of some research literature undoing or reinventing what is already known.

Secondly, the findings raise questions about the current conception of readiness and new and emerging domains that must be better understood in supporting online learners in the post-pandemic future, including the implications for those undertaking micro-credentials. The importance of the educational context and the notion of relational readiness is discussed in efforts to support learners and promote student success. Thirdly, the study argues that most of the survey-based research published on the student COVID-19 experience is not a good proxy for encapsulating the learner's voice, with important implications for the methodological design of future research. Hence, a significant gap remains in telling the student story of their learning experience and personal readiness for online learning in their own words.

Finally, the value of the student's voice is briefly illustrated through the experience of a free online course developed during the pandemic to help bridge the readiness gap and translate contemporary theory and research into practice. The paper concludes with a challenge to HEIs committed to a learner-centred approach to heed the lessons from this experience by developing digital supports and resources with a stronger underlying ethos of 'for learners by learners'. The paper underscores the value of working in partnership with students to help develop new online solutions to the challenges and opportunities posed by new digital education models in the Age of Artificial Intelligence.

Keywords:

Student readiness, online learning, literature review, COVID-19, learner voice

References

Beirne, E., Mac Lochlainn,C., Brown, M., & Nic Giolla Mhichíl, M. (2022). Student readiness for online learning: A systematic literature review. European Association of Distance Teaching Universities (EADTU). https://digitelpro.eadtu.eu/images/IO5A1_Student_Readiness_for_Digital_Learning_Literature_Review_FINAL_250822_1.pdf

Bond, M., Bedenlier, S., Marín, V.I., & Händel, M. (2021). Emergency remote teaching in higher education: Mapping the first global online semester. *International Journal of Educational Technology in Higher Education, 18 (50).* https://doi.org/10.1186/s41239-021-00282-x

Hodges, C., Moore, S., Lockee, B., Trust, T., & Bond, A., (2020). The difference between emergency remote teaching and online learning. *Educause Review,* 27th March. https://er.educause.edu/articles/2020/3/the-difference-between-emergency-remote-teaching-and-online-learning

OPENING A NEW PAGE ON FOO-FOO THE SNOO: REMIXING THE DIGITAL EDUCATION PLAYLIST

Mark Brown, Dublin City University, Ireland

Abstract

This paper critically reflects on the 7th edition of the annual NIDL top 10 "good reads" in digital education. In telling the story of open scholarship through the lens of the 2022 curated playlist of good reads, the paper illustrates several new and emerging trends in literature. It also reveals the diverse nature of open scholarship. Reflecting on seven years of this exercise, participants are invited to consider how we can better engage busy educators in critically reading and reviewing the published literature to bridge theory and research with good practice and back again. Metaphorically speaking, taking inspiration from Dr Seuss (1978), the intention is to look beyond "Foo-Foo Snoo" by exploring new digital possibilities for engaging time-poor educators, researchers and policymakers in critical analysis of the literature. In response to this challenge, potential new initiatives designed to spotlight fresh reads and develop a "readers collective" in the field of digital education are presented for consideration. Constructive feedback is sought on ways to extend the "top 10" initiative to foster critical conversations that help keep abreast of the burgeoning literature, including developing a digital education journal club. A brief synopsis of educational research on journal clubs is provided as we consider how to open a page on "Foo-Foo Snoo" through more engaging and innovative platforms to support critical professional reading.

Keywords:

Scholarship, scholarship of teaching and learning, digital education, critical reading

References

Dr. Seuss (1978). *I can read with my eyes shut.* Random House, Inc., New York.

National Institute for Digital Learning. (2023). *Top 10 good reads from 2022: From theory to practice and back again.* 16th January. Available at https://nidl.blog/2023/01/16/top-10-good-reads-from-2022-from-theory-to-practice-and-back-again/

GASTA PAPERS

MICROCREDS INNOVATE: NOVEL UNIVERSITY-ENTERPRISE COLLABORATION FOR MICRO-CREDENTIALS

Emma Francis, David Corscadden, Jools O'Connor, Irish Universities Association, Ireland

Abstract

Micro-credentials have the potential to reimagine university-led innovation for enterprise, supporting agile and flexible upskilling and reskilling opportunities. The Council Recommendation on a European approach to micro-credentials for lifelong learning and employability (Council of the European Union, 2022) aims to empower leaners to acquire, update and improve their knowledge, skills and competence, support the preparedness of micro-credential providers and foster inclusiveness and equal opportunities. Therefore, there is a need for micro-credentials to be recognised by academia and employers, in turn necessitating closer collaboration. Notably, the pace of digital transformation and Sustainable Development Goal commitments are both driving the evolution of novel, collaborative approaches to help close skills gaps and address socio-economic shifts.

MicroCreds is an ambitious project (2020-2025) led by the Irish Universities Association working with seven partner universities collaborating to develop, pilot and evaluate the building blocks required for a transformation across lifelong and life-wide learning, through micro-credentials. MicroCreds is working in partnership with learners and enterprise to transform the thinking and engagement structures with university learning. MicroCreds is funded by the Irish Government with four distinct, interconnected Pillars.

Key to our Enterprise Pillar has been the development of a dynamic model of enterprise engagement for micro-credentials, positioned to identify emerging skills needs, informing and evolving micro-credentials in development. MicroCreds Innovate is a sustainable model for data-informed university-enterprise collaboration for micro-credentials. The structure provides facilitated space to explore enterprise-informed development in a focused way, expanding upon universities' capacity to anticipate, understand and respond to developing skills needs. MicroCreds Innovate focuses on priority skills needs for the economy particularly in high-productivity growth sectors, responding to digitalisation and the future world of work. The presentation will outline key insights from MicroCreds Innovate, exploring challenges and opportunities revealed by the co-creation of micro-credentials addressing such high-level skills gaps between enterprise and universities.

Keywords:

Micro-credentials. Lifelong learning. Enterprise engagement. Skills gap analysis. Sustainable engagement.

References

Council of the European Union. (2022). Council Recommendation on a European approach to micro-credentials for lifelong learning and employability (9237/22). https://data.consilium.europa.eu/doc/document/ST-9237-2022-INIT/en/pdf

RE-DESIGNING ONLINE LEARNING TO MEET THE NEEDS OF FUTURE LEARNERS

Mohsen Saadatmand, Ulla Hemminki-Reijonen, University of Helsinki, Finland

Abstract

Digital learning is transforming in an unprecedented way with the impact of frontier technologies. The question is how higher education is creating such learning formats to prepare learners with future skills for the 4th industrial revolution (World Economic Forum). By applying a learner-centered design approach (Saadatmand, 2017) in Global Campus project at the University of Helsinki, we strive to harness pedagogical and technological innovations to design and develop digital learning formats that meet the needs of the future learners.

Keywords:

Online learning, sustainability education, digital transformation, learning design, XR, AI

Summary

The Global Campus project develops international online learning by experimenting and implementing emerging technologies such as XR and AI with a focus on sustainability education. Our learning innovation is multifold:

- Develop discipline-specific sustainability courses with innovative methods such as immersive 360 environments and AI-generated media,
- Create opportunities for students to apply their knowledge and improve their sustainability competencies in virtual reality
- Develop interactive MOOCS and micro-learning formats using simulations.

Knowing that participatory methods, immersive learning environments and art-based pedagogies are recommended for innovative climate change education (Hemminki-Reijonen& Logadóttir, 2021), the visually appealing, engaging virtual learning experiences are being designed together with students and teachers.

References

Education 4.0 Framework, World Economic Forum. Retrieved from https://initiatives.weforum.org/reskilling-revolution/education-4-0

Hemminki-Reijonen, Ulla & Logadóttir, Halla H., (2021). Reinventing Climate Change Education. Harvard Kennedy School Belfer Center. Arctic Initiative. https://www.belfercenter.org/publication/reinventing-climate-change-education

Saadatmand, M., (2017). *A New Ecology for Learning: An Online Ethnographic Study of Learners' Participation and Experience in Connectivist MOOCs* (Doctoral dissertation). University of Helsinki, Finland. Retrieved from https://helda.helsinki.fi/handle/10138/184138

STOP IN THE NAME OF MICRO-CREDENTIALS - FAUX-PAS AND SOLUTIONS

Mairéad Nic Giolla Mhichíl, Dublin City University, Ireland

Introduction

Micro-Credentials are everywhere, since the publication of the European Commission's Recommendation (2022) the hype around micro-credentials has reached new levels in Europe. But let's be clear micro-credentials are not the cure to everything in education and training and indeed many other policy areas too! This Gasta is based on the crowd sourced observations of the common issues and problems that DCU's micro-credentialing team encountered. They are derived from our knowledge and experience gained through DCU's research focus on micro-credentials and from our own practice. DCU has supported a number of institutions, both nationally and internationally to engage with micro-credentials and we are currently involved with implementation across a myriad of projects within our own University both nationally through the MicroCreds project and through the European Consortium of Innovative University's Alliance. We are not naming or shaming or indeed calling out or drawing attention to any specific initiative to point to deficits, as some sort of proverbial self-named and self-proclaimed micro-credential paragons of virtue. Our objective in reality is to highlight some common pitfalls with getting involved in the current micro-credential craze to help institutions reflect on these issues and ultimately to successfully engage with micro-credentials. Let's begin and look at the following top three issue for institutions as they start on their micro-credential journey:

1. Don't promise the Sun, Moon and Stars
2. Don't assume that industry knows what they want or understands us!
3. Don't repackage current offerings as micro-credentials… unless you…

Faux-Pas & Solutions

With respect to the first point, institutions really need to clarify why and to what purpose they are engaging with micro-credentials. What rationale do they have for committing to short form learning and does it actually make sense strategically and operationally for them to do so beyond the draw of funding opportunities. In DCU, before we started our micro-credential and short form learning journey, (many moons ago at this stage), we actively engaged in an exercise very explicitly to call out and really understand why and how micro-credentials aligned with DCU's strategic objectives. In a review we did of the literature some time back for the European Commission employability drivers were dominating the scene with some aspirations by universities to increase flexibility of provision and promote access to higher education (Desmarchelier & Cary, 2022). Priorities do change in every organisation. As our university has evolved and the onset of a new strategic plan and process, we have conducted this exercise both at the top and with individual Faculties to ensure continued alignment.

Delving into the real impact of the development of micro-credentials is a worthwhile exercise as most university and HEIs systems and processes are based on long form learning, when you start to unpack some of these issues, potentially micro-credentials are not the right road for your institution. There is also a temptation to think that a university or HEI can and should offer micro-credentials across all disciplines, whilst it is not impossible but is it advisable? Furthermore, there is a huge focus on skills across the multitude of grey and academic literature written about micro-credentials. One of the major unique selling points universities and HEIs bring to teaching and learning is our research focus and context i.e., research informed teaching, we should not forget this as the rhetoric for skills, skills and more skills is constantly drummed out. This is not said to be elitist but to recognise that higher education micro-credentials should be different and differentiated on this basis, focusing not only on higher-order skills, but knowledge and competences. When a HEI is thinking about the subject range of its micro-credentials it should also put into the equation particular research and teaching strengths that lie within that institution.

Moving on to the second point which relates directly to the relevancy of micro-credentials. Micro-credentials are identified as being an attractive and suitable proposition for upskilling employees, cross-skilling into new sectors as a means to address identified skills gaps through more focused provision. Consistently the rhetoric around micro-credentials points to this, whilst we are not disputing the importance of this in the broader sense, there is a fundamental and indeed healthy tension which needs to be considered. More often than not, assertions are made which are quite broad in nature. Having worked with industry partners there is a clear and definitive requirement to ensure that we are speaking the same language. Whilst this issue is not new it is certainly magnified as part of co-creation and co-construction that HEIs engaging with industry in the process of developing and sometimes delivering micro-credentials. To address this issue in DCU we have developed an industry collaboration framework which broadly categorises how and what industry collaboration and co-construction should look like to meet our threshold of industry relevance with respect to DCU micro-credentials. By calling out a framework *"the ask"* becomes clearer and it also can be moulded to shape the requirements and needs, whilst we are all clear about what we are all talking about. This is particularly useful for smaller enterprises who potentially do not have the resources to engage with this type of work for very long, therefore being explicit and clear with them saves time for all and allows us to fine tune our offerings. One of the golden inputs from our perspective is working with industry to define the real-world business or industry applications for particular micro-credentials, this in our mind is part of the secret sauce of making micro-credentials tangible learning experiences which ultimately address the needs of learners and our industry partners. In DCU we have been doing a lot on transversal skills, with a Director of Transversal Skills appointed as part of the Human Capital Initiative DCU Futures programme to re-imagine undergraduate education in DCU. What we have learned is that the term transversal skills are potentially quite alienating. Is it soft skills or power skills? Whichever you choose perhaps is immaterial for this paper, but there is a clear need to translate into industry terms and applications what exactly you mean by these particular skills. Talking with industry will help you to achieve and contextualise this.

The third point is we which we think needs to be called out explicitly by institutions, and it relates specifically to the repackaging of current content as micro-credentials and the process by which micro-credentials are developed and delivered within your institution. One of the reasons that micro-credentials are resonating and gaining such traction across education and within industry is the potential they hold to be different. As previously mentioned, their relevancy is a key hallmark of their implied potential, collaboration with industry and other stakeholders is implicit in their make-up, it therefore behoves that those developing and creating micro-credentials ensure that these characteristics are a key part of their design and make-up. In DCU as part of our quality assurance process all micro-credentials must meet threshold levels on eight characteristics these include collaboration and relevancy. Therefore, even if a smaller credit offering has been previously quality assured, it must undergo an evaluation to ensure that it meets these levels in DCU. To DCU this is a really important step in the mainstreaming of this offering type within the institution we see it as a key step in narrow view of "micro-credentials" to a more holistic approach to micro-credentialing or the process of developing, delivering, learning, collaborating and teaching short form learning offerings for credit. Without such a process it would be quite easy to repackage all or any of our offerings as micro-credentials and essentially fall into the emperor's new clothes trap! Our advice to institutions is to set out what is micro-credentialing and micro-credentials in your institution beyond pure definitions and establish processes and thresholds which ensure that your institution can stand over this offering type and be successful.

Keywords:

Micro-credentials, panacea, skills higher education, emperor's new clothes.

Summary

Hopefully, there are some useful reflection points in the above for all those institutions think about starting or are in the start-up phase of their micro-credential journey. This advice hopefully prompts reflection and ensuing consideration of (i) the drivers, (ii) the process and the basis for collaboration and development that micro-credentials can bring to an institution and prompts some much-needed rules of engagement, therefore, *Stop in the Name of Micro-Credentials!*

References

European Council (2022). *Proposal for a Council Recommendation on a European approach to micro-credentials for lifelong learning and employability*, [Available at https://eur-lex.europa.eu/legal-content/EN/ALL/?uri=CELEX:52021DC0770], Last access: March, 2023.

Desmarchelier, R., Cary, L.J. Toward just and equitable micro-credentials: an Australian perspective. *Int J Educ Technol High Educ* **19**, 25 (2022). https://doi.org/10.1186/s41239-022-00332-y

VIRTUAL SCENARIO-BASED LEARNING (VSBL) AS AN INTEGRATIVE AUTHENTIC ASSESSMENT APPROACH

John Meegan, Elva Casey, Hibernia College, Ireland

Project Summary

The purpose of this study is to explore the use of a virtual scenario-based learning simulation as an integrative authentic assessment (MacArthur, 2021) approach for a Master of Education in Primary Education professional program. The simulation will bridge the gap between real-world practice experiences and academic and professional studies, allowing for consistent, efficient, and transparent assessment practices.

Authentic Assessment

The concept of authenticity can be highly beneficial as it encourages us to consider the lasting value of the tasks we assign, and promotes genuine, higher-level learning that enables students to comprehend complex ideas and apply them effectively to new situations.

Virtual Scenario-Based Learning

Virtual scenario-based learning (VSBL) is a relatively new method of instruction that has not been widely used in initial teacher education (Dieker et al., 2014). VSBL provides an opportunity for student teachers to practice classroom management, lesson planning, and teaching students with varying needs in a controlled and safe environment (Kaufman & Ireland, 2016).

Method

An Educational Design Research (EDR) (McKenney & Reeves, 2018) approach has been chosen for this project as it entails a collaboration between stakeholders to simultaneously develop both new theoretical insights and practical solutions to serious teaching and learning challenges.

References

Centre for Applied Special Technology (2011): https://www.cast.org/

Dieker, L. A., Rodriguez, J. A., Lignugaris/Kraft, B., Hynes, M. C., & Hughes, C. E. (2014). The potential of simulated environments in teacher education: Current and future possibilities. *Teacher Education and Special Education*, 37(1), pp-pp: 21-33.

McArthur, J. (2021). Rethinking student involvement in assessment'. Working Paper 58. *Oxford: Centre for Global Higher Education*. Available at: working-paper-58final.pdf (researchcghe.org)

McKenney, S., & Reeves, T. C. (2018). *Conducting educational design research*. Routledge.

NO MORE, THE POOR RELATION! CAMPUS IS FOR THE ELITE, ONLINE EDUCATION IS FOR EVERYONE!

Brian Mulligan, Education Futures, Ireland

Abstract

We are now well past the point of having demonstrated the merits of online learning and it should now become the dominant form of tertiary education. Not only is online learning as good, if not better than campus teaching (Paul et al., 2019), it has demonstrated the potential to be much cheaper (Hanson et al., 2022). Given the economic challenges of pensions and healthcare, due to demographic change in the developed world, and the unaffordability of mass tertiary education in the developing world, it is imperative that we grasp this opportunity to massively reduce unit costs in tertiary education. For the majority of students, tertiary education is a path to gaining knowledge, understanding, skills and work. Only a minority become primary knowledge creators. Universities may well be the place for that elite. For the rest of us, a combination of work-based and online learning will be the most effective, and only affordable means of both personal and professional development in the future.

Keywords: work-based learning, online education, work-integrated

References

Hanson, M., (2022) "Cost of Online Education vs. Traditional Education" *Education Data Initiative* https://educationdata.org/cost-of-online-education-vs-traditional-education

Intelligent.com, (2023) "34% of companies eliminated college degree requirements to increase number of applicants in

Paul, J., Jefferson, F., (2019) "A Comparative Analysis of Student Performance in an Online vs. Face-to-Face Environmental Science Course From 2009 to 2016" *Frontiers* https://www.frontiersin.org/articles/10.3389/fcomp.2019.00007/full

FORMATIVE ASSESSMENT: HACKING GRADES IN ESL LEARNING USING AUDIOFEEDBACK

Maria Isabel Mansilla, European University Miguel de Cervantes (UEMC), Spain

Abstract

Formative assessment has been a challenge that can be tackled using technology. Audio feedback paired with a self-assessment rubric as means to provide students support in their learning process in Moodle has provoked a new learning environment.

Keywords:

Audio feedback, self-assessment, rubric, Moodle.

Formative (Self)assessment

For many ESL teachers, grading is the most hideous activities we have to perform. Responding to student work requires a huge amount of time, particularly when you are teaching a foreign language. Our students worry about assessment, but learning should be made more visible. Technology has made assessment possible without being a punishment. The traditional summative assessment performed by an end-of-unit test does not help students becoming independent learners controlling their improvement towards proficiency.

One of my biggest challenges as an ESL teacher was providing feedback to my students' classwork. I spent hours, returning work covered in comments from top to bottom. I was exhausted, my students were overwhelmed. That feedback was ineffective and it wasn't responsive to my student's needs. In order to solve this issue I prepared a self-assessment rubric where learning objectives where clearly stated. Formative assessment is a learning strategy where self-assessment enhances the learning process as:

- Students track their progress and learn to "self-grade".
- Teachers provide meaningful feedback
- The learning process can be revised using digital tools providing different snapshots of the learning process

Talk it Through: Audio feedback

Recording my voice on the task uploaded, focusing on the rubric has been my feedback tool. Audios are up to five minutes long. We use the Moodle platform to provide this but most major learning management systems have integrated audio feedback mechanisms into their platforms.

Conclusion

Audio feedback complements self-assessment rubric this academic year so my results are not available yet. However, most of my students have really responded, saying that it feels much more like they are having a conversation with me. While evaluating student work is a significant time investment, focusing on specific learning objectives paired with audio feedback can help you be more responsive to students' specific needs, enabling their learning enhancement.

References

Begmatova, K. (2022). *The Role of Rubrics in Self-and Peer Assessment at the University* in Humanising Language Teaching https://www.hltmag.co.uk/aug22/role-of-rubrics

Sanckstein, S. (2015) *Hacking Assessment: 10 Ways to Go Gradeless in a Traditional Grades School* , Hack Learing Series.

FLEXIBLE LEARNING AND VIRTUAL REALITY

Gizéh Rangel-de Lazaro, Josep M Duart, Universitat Oberta de Catalunya, Spain

Abstract

From a pedagogical perspective, virtual reality (VR) resources are accessible tools for developing active and student-centred learning methods (Bates et al., 2020; Radianti et al., 2020). In recent years, defined by the COVID-19 pandemic, we have witnessed a boom in applying these emerging technologies, which have been key at the educational level (Hernandez-de-Menendez et al., 2020). Furthermore, there is a greater interest in creating flexible learning spaces at the educational level. Different ways of configuring a classroom are sought to integrate diverse teaching methods, including adaptive pedagogies and novel learning approaches. Here, we propose a didactic experience focused on designing and organising flexible learning spaces using immersive VR resources.

Objectives

- To design and regulate learning spaces interactively using VR and 2D resources.

- To analyse how students apply information and communication technologies to design flexible classrooms as learning spaces.

- To develop creative thinking to provide knowledge and solutions when using VR resources in flexible learning environments.

Keywords:

Immersive learning, emerging technologies, online higher education, adaptive learning technologies.

Summary

Digital resources applied to the creation of flexible learning spaces could be as effective as non-digital ones if inserted within a sound pedagogical approach with well-defined training objectives and guidelines. Thus, the purpose is not to replace traditional techniques with digital tools. However, consider them for the genuine benefit they can offer.

References

Bates, T., Cobo, C., Mariño, O., & Wheeler, S. (2020). Can artificial intelligence transform higher education? International Journal of Educational Technology in Higher Education, 17(1). https://doi.org/10.1186/s41239-020-00218-x

Hernandez-de-Menendez, M., Escobar Díaz, C., & Morales-Menendez, R. (2020). Technologies for the future of learning: state of the art. International Journal on Interactive Design and Manufacturing, 14(2), 683–695. https://doi.org/10.1007/s12008-019-00640-0

Radianti, J., Majchrzak, T. A., Fromm, J., & Wohlgenannt, I. (2020). A systematic review of immersive virtual reality applications for higher education: Design elements, lessons learned, and research agenda. Computers and Education, 147, 103778. https://doi.org/10.1016/j.compedu.2019.103778

TEACHING BACKWARD: USING BACKWARD LEARNING DESIGN TO PLAN A BLENDED COURSE

Ana Marques, Limerick and Clare Education Training Board, Ireland

Abstract

I work as an educator in the LCETB and have been teaching the Work Experience module (L4) for a few years. The module helps learners to appreciate diversity in the workplace, adjust to expectations of the working world, set personal, educational, and career goals, make informed career decisions, and gain relevant knowledge and skills.

Recently, I have been working on designing a blended learning course for L5 combining face-to-face with online T&L (Teaching and Learning) The aim is to provide a flexible learning experience that enhances engagement, provides access to learning resources, and encourages self-directed learning and collaboration. The course includes synchronous and asynchronous activities tailored to meet the individual learner's needs.

In this Gasta presentation I talk about an essential element of blended learning course design which is Understanding by Design (UbD) or Backward Design. This approach involves identifying desired learning outcomes and planning my teaching strategies, assessment methods, and learning activities that align with these outcomes. By using Backward Design, the learning objectives are clearly defined, and the course materials and activities are relevant and meaningful to my learners. Backward Design helps me create cohesive and effective learning experiences aligned with learning outcomes and enhances my learner's assessment.

Keywords

Asynchronous, backward design, blended learning design, e-tivities, multi-modal, synchronous.

Summary

This is a Gasta presentation about using Backward Design in a Blended Learning Course to plan my teaching strategies, assessments, and activities aligned with learning outcomes to make them meaningful and assessable.

References

Bergmann, J., & Sams A. (2012). *Before you flip, consider this.* Phi Delta Kappan, 94(2), 25-29.

Salmon, G (2003). E-Moderating. *The Key to teaching and Learning Online.* Routledge.

McTighe, J and Wiggins, G (1998). *Understanding by Design.* ASCD.

THE MYTHOLOGY OF CHATGPT

Darragh Coakley, Munster Technological University, Ireland

Abstract

The generative AI tool ChatGPT has recently caused a moral panic of sorts within Higher Education. In this presentation, ChatGPT is examined through the lens of several mythologies and figures in folklore, to contextualise some of the commentary and fears which have been expressed regarding its impact on Higher Education. In particular, the fear which educators have expressed about the impact of ChatGPT and similar tools on the process of assessment; the reactions to, and proposals to overcome, same within Higher Education Institutions and the underlying causes associated with the appeal of ChatGPT to students within the context of Higher Education systems are examined through comparison to a range of ancient and/ or recent mystical narratives. Finally, a series of lessons which may be extracted from analysis of these legends of the past, and how these same lessons may guide Higher Educations' response to ChatGPT and similar tools, are presented in an effort to highlight some key considerations for the future.

Keywords:

ChatGPT, Artificial Intelligence, Instructional Design, AI education, Assessment, Higher Education

Summary

According to Midgley (2003), "Myths are not lies. Nor are they detached stories. They are imaginative patterns, networks of powerful symbols that suggest particular ways of interpreting the world. They shape its meaning.". As ChatGPT and generative AI tools have come recently to the fore of media attention, there has been a wide range of discussion and commentary on same from those involved in Higher Education – from the trivial to the hysterical. Drawing upon lessons and figures from historical folklore can help us to interpret the mythology being presented and to draw valuable conclusions for the future.

Identifying and exposing creatures, such as Pùcas and changelings, who would secretly replace an original with a sinister copy has always involved obscure rituals. Similarly, the suggestion of reverting to more archaic means of assessment, from only written or oral exams (Ahsan et al, 2021; Zawacki-Richter et al, 2019; Cotton et al, 2023; Zhai, 2022), to combat the use of ChatGPT for written assessments should bear cautious scrutiny. Further consideration to this approach is noted by Hesiod who, concluding the story of Pandora's box, warns: "So is there no way to escape the will of Zeus". There is no putting the evils back into the box. Attempting to simply ignore the presence of these tools in higher education as a means to combat them serves no purpose. By moving students backwards in terms of assessment and activity, they will be even less prepared to navigate this new world. Further to this, much as Voldemort is monikered "He Who Must Not Be Named", an unspoken element in this discussion points to the limitations of current educational systems which prioritise the productivity and points offered by ChatGPT rather than genuine learning.

References

Ahsan, K., Akbar, S., & Kam, B. (2022). Contract cheating in higher education: a systematic literature review and future research agenda. *Assessment & Evaluation in Higher Education, 47*(4), 523-539.

Cotton, D. R., Cotton, P. A., & Shipway, J. R. (2023). Chatting and Cheating. Ensuring academic integrity in the era of ChatGPT. https://edarxiv.org/mrz8h/

Midgley, M. (2003). *The myths we live by*. Taylor & Francis.

Zawacki-Richter, O., Marín, V. I., Bond, M., & Gouverneur, F. (2019). Systematic review of research on artificial intelligence applications in higher education–where are the educators?. *International Journal of Educational Technology in Higher Education, 16*(1), 1-27.

Zhai, X. (2022). ChatGPT user experience: Implications for education. https://papers.ssrn.com/sol3/papers.cfm?abstract_id=4312418

BREAKING THE MOULD FOR A NEW GENERATION OF LEARNERS – PUTTING THE VOICE OF LIFELONG LEARNERS ON THE AGENDA

David Corscadden, Emma Francis, Jools O'Connor, Irish Universities Association, Ireland

Abstract

As we navigate a post-COVID19 world, we face a rapidly changing society that requires learners of all ages to amass new and updated skills in short, focused, and agile ways. Lifelong learning is a key mechanism for individuals to engage in formal education to upskill and address specific needs.

To encourage uptake in lifelong learning the 2021 OECD Skills Outlook report recommends that the learner's needs should be placed at the centre and addressed at all stages of the education process. Opportunities such micro-credentials have the potential to reimagine and reframe the relationship between learners and universities, but they also pose significant challenges to traditional systems and internal processes created for fulltime undergraduate and postgraduate courses.

MicroCreds is an ambitious five-year project lead by the Irish Universities Association with seven of its founding universities collaborating to develop and implement the building blocks necessary to transform lifelong learning in Ireland through micro-credentials. A learner focus is a core strategic element of the MicroCreds project and subsequently is at the forefront for partner universities as they embed lifelong learning pathways in their local education systems.

To truly put the learner at the centre of education their needs must be properly understood and correctly addressed throughout the student cycle. From the application process, through to on-boarding and subsequent course delivery, we need to break the mould to better suit the specific needs of lifelong learners who are potentially only engaging with formal education for a short, fixed amount of time. To understand the needs of lifelong learners in an Irish context the MicroCreds project has embraced both quantitative and qualitative UX research. This presentation will explore how we have used UX to design a new national platform for micro-credentials where the needs of learners were a cornerstone to its development.

Keywords:

Lifelong Learning, Micro-credentials, Upskilling, Higher Education, Learner Engagement, UX Design, Flexible Learning, Learner Focused

References

OECD (2021), OECD Skills Outlook 2021: Learning for Life, OECD Publishing, Paris, https://doi.org/10.1787/0ae365b4-en.

SUPPORTING SUSTAINABILITY IN ONLINE DISTANCE LEARNING DESIGN: OUR JOURNEY TO CONNECT COLLEAGUES WITH NON-TOKENISTIC SUSTAINABILITY ACTIONS

Paul Astles, Kathleen Calder, Hayley Johns, James Openshaw, The Open University, UK

Abstract

The Open University's (OU) Learning Design (LD) team has been working on an approach to support academics to embed sustainability in curriculum design, within the OU's modular, mostly online, distance learning context. In this presentation, we will share our journey so far: how the LD Sustainability workstream began and what we have produced; how we are forging links with our OU colleagues and what we have learned from them; and finally, where we see our work fitting into existing projects and initiatives, and how we want to develop our work.

We collated a range of resources, from the UN's Sustainable Development Goals (United Nations (n.d.)) and Education for Sustainable Development in action (AdvanceHE (n.d.)), to ethical and social considerations around incorporating sustainability in the curriculum (UCU (2021)), cataloguing the information and where it could prove relevant to our own work. From there, the team created infographics to share with academics and production staff, to support them with meaningful sustainability work.

Via internal and external social media, the LD workstream has forged links with other teams around the OU to learn more about their work. From these connections, we have identified sustainability work that can feed into existing projects on learning outcomes, student voice, and the wider HE environment, so that we can demonstrate to colleagues the links between sustainability and institutional plans, to build trust in and promote the value of our work.

Keywords:

Learning design, sustainability, curriculum design, distance learning, online learning, asynchronous learning, sustainable development, ethical, social, social media, higher education

Summary

This presentation aims to highlight our journey from collating information, to connecting with colleagues, to supporting meaningful progression in embedding sustainability into curriculum design.

References

AdvanceHE (n.d.). Education for Sustainable Development in Higher Education. Retrieved from https://www.advance-he.ac.uk/teaching-and-learning/education-sustainable-development-higher-education

UCU (2021). Decarbonise & decolonise 2030. Retrieved from https://www.ucu.org.uk/decarbonise+decolonise

United Nations (n.d.). The 17 goals. Retrieved from https://sdgs.un.org/goals

"GLOBAL PLAY2LEARN": CHALLENGE BASED TRANSDISCIPLINARY LEARNING

Etain Kiely, Mossy Kelly, Ontirestse Ishmael, Jennifer Gallagher, Natalie Nokuvimba Chiyaka
Atlantic Technological University (ATU), Ireland

Abstract

This truly diverse ATU student partnership team of multiple nationalities (Ukraine, Botswana, Malyasia, Nigeria and Ireland) aims to promote cultural equality and diversity across multiple years and programmes of study (PhD, Masters, Years 1,2 and 4 in Science and Computing). These students are members of the ATU - Global Play2Learn Academy which promotes challenge based, transdisciplinary sharing and learning using technology. A case study will share how an ATU PhD research student travelled to South Africa as an invited speaker to contribute to a "Girls in Tech" camp. The student led project implemented a parallel sustainability investigation between ATU Galway students and the team in South Africa using low-cost agriculture microbit kits to collect environmental data. Real time data was collected in both locations and stored in ATU Galway's Dataverse for visualisation and analysis. The study shares how hands-on play and learning in context can influence transferable skills such as problem solving, creative thinking, learning analytics, programming, and sustainability. The Global Play2Learn Academy enables authentic dialogic interactions to promote personalised, diverse, inclusive, fun and challenging learning opportunities.

Keywords:

Challenge based, transdisciplinary, play, sustainability, diversity.

TRANSFORMING THE STUDENT EXPERIENCE THROUGH LEARNER EMPOWERMENT WITH NTUTORR, A NATIONAL TECHNOLOGICAL UNIVERSITY TRANSFORMATION PROJECT SUPPORTED BY #NEXTGENERATIONEU

Carina Ginty, Atlantic Technological University (ATU), Ireland; Moira Maguire, Dundalk Institute of Technology (DKIT), Ireland

Abstract

Ireland's technological sector, combining new technological universities and institutes of technology, have formed a partnership to develop and deliver on the National Technological University Transformation for Recovery and Resilience (NTUTORR) programme. This programme, which is EU funded and overseen by the HEA, proposes to utilise the national scale and scope of the sector to deliver a best-practice suite of initiatives and opportunities for the learner, for staff development and supported by necessary enabling technologies.

This presentation will focus on Stream 1 of the NTUTORR project and share how it aims to transform the student experience and address the key challenges arising out of the pandemic including equality, access, community empowerment and climate action. The student empowerment theme of the NTUTORR project is informed by Transforming our World: The 2030 Agenda for Sustainable Development (United Nations, 2015), the National Access Plan (2022-2026), the EU Digital Education Action Plan (2020-2027), and the findings from Next Steps (National Forum, 2021), which considers what the Irish HE sector has learnt from the experience of COVID-19 and what this means for the future for learning and teaching in Ireland.

"THE FUTURE" IS BULLSHIT

Donna Lanclos, Munster Technological University, Ireland

Abstract

The edtech world has recently been alight with references to Machine Learning and Large Language Model tools often referred to as "generative AI." We are being told by the companies selling these tools that these represent the future—of writing, of art, of education, of work. I am here to call bullshit on those claims, in the academic sense of the word, Let's talk about what bullshit is, what it means to our practices, and what kind of bullshit things like ChatGPT (and our reactions to them) signal about our practices in education, and our attitudes towards work and life both in and out of universities. I want to make an argument for shaping and choosing futures, not accepting those that are handed to us by venture capitalists. That begins with paying careful attention to our present, and to the most vulnerable people in our communities, and what is necessary for them to have futures, not just the most privileged. The future being sold to us might be bullshit, but the one we can create is only going to be bullshit if we let that happen.

Keywords:

The Future, Machine Learning, Autonomy, Bullshit.

References

Bender, Emily M., Timnit Gebru, Angelina McMillan-Major, and Shmargaret Shmitchell. "On the Dangers of Stochastic Parrots: Can Language Models Be Too Big? 🦜." In *Proceedings of the 2021 ACM conference on fairness, accountability, and transparency*, pp. 610-623. 2021.

Bergstrom, Carl T., and Jevin D. West. *Calling bullshit: The art of skepticism in a data-driven world.* Random House Trade Paperbacks, 2021.

Gilliard, Chris. "Challenging Tech's Imagined Future." Just Tech. Social Science Research Council. March 2, 2023. DOI: doi.org/10.35650/JT.3050.d.2023.

Graeber, David. (2018). Bullshit jobs: A theory. New York, NY: Simon and Schuster.

Fiesler, Casey "The Black Mirror Writers Room: The Case (and Caution) for Ethical Speculation in CS Education" CU InfoScience, Medium, March 4 2022, retrieved 6 April 2023 https://medium.com/cuinfoscience/the-black-mirror-writers-room-the-case-and-caution-for-ethical-speculation-in-cs-education-5c81d05d2c67

Forlano, Laura (2021) "The Future is not a Solution," Public Books, October 18, 2021 https://www.publicbooks.org/the-future-is-not-a-solution/

Frankfurt, Harry G. *On bullshit.* Princeton University Press, 2005.

Kohn, Alfie (2023) "I've never been able to improve on the management theorist Frederick Herzberg's timeless 10-word maxim: "Idleness, indifference, and irresponsibility are healthy responses to absurd work." (Teachers/parents: Feel free to substitute "worksheets" for "absurd work."). (2023, March 25). https://sciences.social/@alfiekohn/110083807127046096.

Perrigo, Billy (2023) "Exclusive: OpenAI Used Kenyan Workers on Less Than $2 Per Hour to Make ChatGPT Less Toxic" Time Magazine, January 18, 2023, https://time.com/6247678/openai-chatgpt-kenya-workers/

Quintarelli, Stefano (2019) "Let's forget the term AI. Let's call them Systematic Approaches to Learning Algorithms and Machine Inferences (SALAMI). Nov 24, 2019, https://blog.quintarelli.it/2019/11/lets-forget-the-term-ai-lets-call-them-systematic-approaches-to-learning-algorithms-and-machine-inferences-salami/

EXPLORING THE INTERSECTION OF THE SCHOLARSHIP OF TEACHING AND LEARNING (SOTL), DIGITAL EDUCATION, AND STUDENTS AS PARTNERS: STRATEGIES FOR ENGAGING AND EMPOWERING LEARNERS

Melanie Hamilton, University of Saskatchewan, Canada; Karla Wolsky, Lethbridge College, Canada

Abstract

The Scholarship of Teaching and Learning (SoTL) is an increasingly important field in the future of digital education in higher education. SoTL research focuses on the systematic examination of teaching and learning practices with the aim of improving student outcomes (Felten, 2013; Frieberg; Simmons 2016, 2020; Poole & Simmons, 2013). The integration of technology in education has resulted in a need for an understanding of its impact on teaching and learning. SoTL research can provide valuable insights and reframe the most effective use of digital tools in enhancing student engagement and critical thinking skills, as well as the changing role of instructors and institutions. In addition, SoTL often takes a 'Student as Partners' (SaP) approach to creating research projects, which allows for our future academics to co-create the research, adding their perspective on what is possible in academia (Bonney, 2018; Felten,2013)

Keywords:

SoTL; Students as Partners; Digital Education; Student Engagement; Critical Thinking

Summary

In this Gasta presentation, we will discuss how the utilization of SoTL research can inform and improve the development of digital edification and initiatives (Sipes et al, 2020). As such, it is crucial that we invest in SoTL research to ensure that digital education is effective, appropriate, accessible, and inclusive for all students.

1. What is SoTL?
    a. Definition
    b. Why SoTL is important in higher education.
2. How to engage in SoTL
    a. 4M framework
    b. Micro-level SoTL
3. How SoTL can help enhance digital education research in the classroom
    a. Opportunities for inter- and intra-disciplinary collaboration
4. Students as Partners in SoTL Research
    a. How to engage students as partners in your research project
    b. Benefits of Students as partners

References

Bonney, K. M. (2018). Students as partners in the scholarship of teaching and learning. *International Journal for the Scholarship of Teaching and Learning, 12*(2). https://digitalcommons.georgiasouthern.edu/ij-sotl/vol12/iss2/2/

Felten, P. (2013). Principles of good practice in SoTL. *Teaching & Learning Inquiry, 1*(1), 121-125. https://www.researchgate.net/publication/259734804_Principles_of_Good_Practice_in_SoTL

Friberg, J. (2016). Might the 4M framework support SoTL advocacy?

https://illinoisstateuniversitysotl.wordpress.com/2016/07/11/might-the-4m-framework-support-sotl-advocacy/

Poole, G., & Simmons, N. (2013). Contributions of the scholarship of teaching and learning to quality enhancement in Canada. In R. Land & G. Gordon (Eds.), *Enhancing quality in higher education: International perspectives* (pp. 118-128). Routledge. https://doi.org/10.4324/9780203590218

Simmons, N. (2016). Synthesizing SoTL institutional initiatives toward national impact. *New Directions in Teaching and Learning, 146(1)*, 95-102. https://doi.org/10.1002/tl.20192

Simmons, N. (2020). The 4M framework as analytic lens for SoTL's impact: A study of seven scholars. *Teaching and Learning Inquiry*, *8*(1), 76–90. https://doi.org/10.20343/teachlearninqu.8.1.6

Sipes. S. M., Minix, A. L., & Barton, M. (2020). Building a social network around SoTL through digital space. *To Improve the Academy, 39*(1). http://dx.doi.org/10.3998/tia.17063888.0039.108

POSTER ABSTRACTS

TRANSFORMING ACADEMIC LITERACY IN AN ONLINE WORLD: UNDERSTANDING THE P WORD!

Helen Kaye, Zoe Worth, The Open University, UK

Abstract

Acquiring academic literacy is a vital skill but may be difficult to achieve. This study gave first year students the opportunity to view and respond to a similarity report on a draft of their own work prior to submission for marking. This resulted in 43 draft submissions with high levels of similarity. However subsequent editing reduced similarity in 72% of cases with 56% of final submissions reduced to levels that would be unlikely to trigger investigation for academic misconduct.

For students new to university the requirement to "write in your own words" is challenging, particularly when using electronic sources. Students may view online content as legitimate material to copy and draw on without needing acknowledgement. Less confident writers may use published wording because it "says it better than I could". Educators may contribute to inadvertent plagiarism by encouraging students to take notes and express the idea in their own words to address the topic in their writing. Copy and pasting offers an easy shortcut to notetaking, but educators may neglect to explain its risks and exactly how to express and reference an idea "in your own words". Consequences of plagiarism are often disciplinary, punitive action, though there may be positive effects of proactive target training (Newton, Wright and Newton 2014). Research related to the self-reference effect suggests that contextualising and personalising material improves learning (Hartlep and Forsyth 2000). The current project empowers students to develop academic literacy skills through checking and revising their own draft work for inadvertent plagiarism.

Students on six level 1 modules spanning a range of subject areas were given access to Turnitin (https://www.turnitin.com). Audio -visual and written materials were developed to supplement the provision by Turnitin LLC and explain the software in the context of the students' studies. An online forum staffed by Turnitin experts was available throughout the study. Students were provided with sample marked-up materials, but crucially assignments they themselves prepared could be submitted to Turnitin, on receipt of the marked up copy students were supported to identify instances of plagiarism and revise their drafts as necessary before submitting for marking

A total of 544 students on 5 of the modules uploaded a draft of their assignment to Turnitin prior to submitting their work for marking. 43 of the drafts yielded similarity scores greater than 25%, a value that would be likely to trigger further investigation of potential plagiarism. Of those 43 drafts, 31 had lower similarity scores when the assignment was submitted for marking, 24 were reduced to less than 25% match, a level unlikely to initiate further investigation.

Enabling students to check their work has substantial benefits. Primarily students have an opportunity to gain valuable skills in academic literacy and an enhanced understanding of academic integrity. This improves academic success, promotes self-confidence and contributes important employability skills. Students also avoid the stress and disruption of investigatory and disciplinary procedures. Our evidence suggests that students are able to edit their writing effectively and those who engage with this enjoy the opportunity. An ongoing goal is to ensure that this does lead to an enhanced understanding of how to write in their own words.

Keywords: Academic literacy, plagiarism, enabling students

References

Hartlep, K. L., & Forsyth, G. A. (2000). The Effect of Self-Reference on Learning and Retention. Teaching of Psychology, 27(4), 269–271.

Newton, FJ , Wright J.D & Newton J.D (2014) Skills training to avoid inadvertent plagiarism: results from a randomised control study. Higher Education Research & Development , 33 (6), 1180-1193.

USING VIRTUAL LABORATORIES AS TRANSFORMATIONAL TOOLS TO AUGMENT STEM PRACTICAL TEACHING & LEARNING: A MULTI-INSTITUTIONAL STUDY IN IRELAND

Bridget Kelly, Sinead Loughran, Ronan Bree, Bernard T. Drumm, Caoimhin S. Griffin, Arjan van Rossum, Dundalk Institute of Technology; Aoife Morrin, Dublin City University; Brian Murphy, Technological University of The Shannon; Eric Moore, University College Cork; Marwa Aly, Carmel Breslin, Frances Heaney, Denise Rooney, Maynooth University, Ireland

Abstract

In this multi-institutional project, involving academic, student and enterprise partners, we have implemented virtual laboratory resources (VLRs) in a blended approach to enhance the STEM practical teaching and learning environment. Here, we provide details of the aims, objectives and initial findings of the project as well as details on the VLRs we have utilised. We show how the partnership approach to co-create content and provide transformative feedback has helped shape the direction of the project in a student-led and industry-informed way.

We investigated how these VLRs have impacted student transferable skills and employability via practical-based pedagogy across Ireland. In 2021/2022 at Dundalk Institute of Technology, students (years 1-4) across a range of programmes were surveyed on their experiences/opinions of VLRs. Students consistently commented that VLRs work best as a pre-lab activity, to link with lecture material and complement practical theory. Feedback from focus groups identified many positives around the teaching and learning experiences in using VLRs, but also highlighted some limitations.

Overall, our findings suggest that VLRs should primarily be used to supplement in-person teaching as opposed to replace face-to-face labs. This example of a digital transformation has potential to augment student transversal skills development and generate more work-ready graduates.

DIGITAL INTERACTIVE FICTION IN THE HUMANITIES

Irene J.C. Lubbe, Kaitlin A. Lucas, Flora Ghazaryan, Juan Manuel Rubio Arévalo, Central European University, Austria

Abstract

What is history and how is it different from storytelling? Can a historian reach an objective truth? In this poster presentation, these and other related questions are explored through a pedagogical tool known as interactive fiction (IF).

IF, or "Choose Your Own Path" books, is a genre of narrative games which leads students through a branching story or scenario. The choices students make in the game directly influence their future choices and the story outcomes. Purposefully incorporated in the humanities classroom, IF can be used for rich storytelling, discussion, and reflection (Ahmad, et al, 2021; Plass, et al 2015).

Our CEU team — a technologist, faculty developer and two doctoral students —embarked on a journey to explore how IF could be incorporated into our university's interdisciplinary bachelors' program through the creation of two digital games. This poster summarizes our six-stage game development process, including the materials, tools, and approximate time needed. It also shares our games— "The Four Cities: A story of Outremer in the 12th Century" and "The Richest and Most Favoured Rayahs of the Sultan: The Case of Düzoğlus"— with suggested lesson plans. Furthermore, it discusses the uses and limitations of emerging AI, including Midjourney Bot, for generating multimedia used within digital game-based learning projects.

Keywords:

Interactive Fiction, History, Midjourney Bot

References

Ahmad, M., Noor, R.M., Roswati, A.R., Nurul, A., Chua, R.Z., & Cho, M.S. (2021). Journal of Physics: Conference Series, 1793 (1). DOI: 10.1088/1742-6596/1793/1/012069

CEU (Central European University): Yehuda Elkana Center for Teaching, Learning and Higher Education Research. Digital Interactive Fiction. https://elkana.ceu.edu/digital-interactive-fiction

European Distance and E-Learning Network (2023). Upcoming Conferences. http://www.eden-online.org/eden-events/upcoming-conference.html

Plass, J. L., Homer, B. D., & Kinzer, C. K. (2015). Foundations of game-based learning. *Educational Psychologist*, 50(4), 258-283. DOI: 10.1080/00461520.2015.1122533

RE-IMAGINING ASSESSMENT AND FEEDBACK FOR STUDENT SUCCESS IN ATU: STUDENTS AS PARTNERS INSPIRING ASSESSMENT TRANSFORMATION AND FEEDBACK PRACTICES.

Emma McDonald, Carina Ginty, Mary Mcgrath, Kevin Cunningham, Atlantic Technological University, Ireland

Abstract

This project is a collaboration between the Teaching and Learning Centre and six faculties in Atlantic Technological University (ATU). It focuses on three themes including: Assessment; Feedback; and Academic Integrity. The project also forms part of a Master's in Education study by research. The study is supported by the National Forum for the Enhancement of Teaching and Learning in Ireland. The aim of this study is to explore the current assessment and feedback practices in place across six programmes in ATU and identify areas that could be re-imagined, helping to improve the overall learning experience for students. The student voice is a key factor in this project and the student experience data gathered will be used to inform positive changes to assessment and feedback practices. Through this project questionnaires and focus groups were carried out with students on each programme to gather data on their experience covering the three themes. The questions designed focused on a variety of topics within these three themes. The main findings from this project to date showed students are satisfied with the variety of assessments offered but highlighted the need to enhance feedback practices. The next phase of this research will aim to build on these findings.

CO-TEACHING: AN UNDULATING JOURNEY!

Irene J.C. Lubbe, Yurgos Politis, Central European University, Austria

Abstract

This study contributes to the literature on team-teaching, a complex and challenging task that can lead to rewarding experiences or highly stressful situations. This is especially true when newly acquainted colleagues from different backgrounds team-teach a new course, in an unfamiliar institution, in a new country, during a pandemic. This situation creates interesting conversations, challenges, and opportunities, resulting in valuable lessons learned.

We conducted a single case-study analysis using brutally honest self-reflective reports. We used an autobiography writing style for data collection, based on grounded theory and Braun and Clarke's thematic analysis methodology to identify six main themes. These included deep personal emotions and feelings, from guilt and irritation to patience, back-up, and safety-nets. Other themes focused on organizational components, role differentiation, relationships, and experiences, and the added value for the students.

This poster provides practical tips for novice and established lecturers who want to engage in team-teaching. We offer suggestions on how to exit (or continue) this endeavor with your sanity in check, happy students, and new professional relationships forged. Our analysis provides insight into the benefits and challenges of co-teaching and highlights the importance of open communication, flexibility, and mutual respect between co-teachers.

Keywords:

Co-teaching; diversity; team-teaching; reflective analysis; university teaching; professional relationships; student

experience

References

Braun V, Clarke V. (2006). Using thematic analysis in psychology. Qualitative Research Psychology, 3(2).

Clarke A. (2003). Situational analysis: grounded theory after the postmodern turn. Symbolic Interaction, 26(4).

Griffin E, Ledbetter A, & Sparks GG. (2018). A first look at communication theory (10th ed). McGraw-Hill.

Hang Q, & Rabren K. (2009). An examination of co-teaching: perspectives and efficacy indicators. Remedial and

Special Education, 30(5).

Lubbe, J.C. & Politis, Y. (2023, March 1). Finding synergy in diversity during interprofessional team-teaching. Advances in Online Education: A Peer-Reviewed Journal, Volume 1 (3). Pp.219-232

Lock J, Clancy T, Lisella R, Rosenau P, Ferreira C, & Rainsbury J. (2017). The lived experiences of instructors co-teaching in higher education. Brock Education Journal, 26(1).

Lock J, Rainsbury J, Clancy T, Rosenau P, & Ferreira C. (2018). Influence of co-teaching on undergraduate student

learning: a mixed-methods study in nursing. Teaching and Learning Inquiry. 2018;6(1).

Pratt S. (2014). Achieving symbiosis: Working through challenges found in co-teaching to achieve effective co-teaching

relationships. Teaching Teacher Education. 2014;41.

OPTIMISING LMS WITH LARGE LANGUAGE MODELS

Ahmad Fdawi, Matthew Waters, Dublin City University, Ireland

Abstract

Large language models (LLMs) like GPT-3 (Generative Pre-trained Transformer 3) have gained attention for their ability to generate and understand natural language, making them valuable tools for enhancing the learning experience (Rudolph et al., 2023). In this poster, we offer practical tips for maximising the educational benefits of this technology for teachers and students and provide guidance on integrating GPT-3 into the Moodle platform.

LLMs can be a valuable asset to teachers and students alike. For instance, teachers can use LLMs to create lesson plans, automatically generate exercises, and grade students' work by highlighting potential strengths and weaknesses (Kasneci et al., 2023) (Qu et al., 2021). Students, on the other hand, can use LLMs to assist with research and writing tasks, generate summaries and outlines of texts, better understand and analyse the material, and even support students who may be less willing to communicate (Tai & Chen, 2020). Additionally, LLMs can provide access to a broader range of educational resources (Baidoo-Anu & Owusu Ansah, 2023).

GPT-3 is an advanced AI by OpenAI. It's been trained on a vast amount of data from the internet to generate human-like text based on the input it receives. GPT-3 can be added as a plugin to Moodle (Learning Management System). It has the potential to assist students with a wide array of questions, enriching the learning experience. Custom questions and answers can be added to the database to offer tailored information unique to your students (Moodle, 2023). The image below demonstrates the OpenAI Chat block (GPT-3):

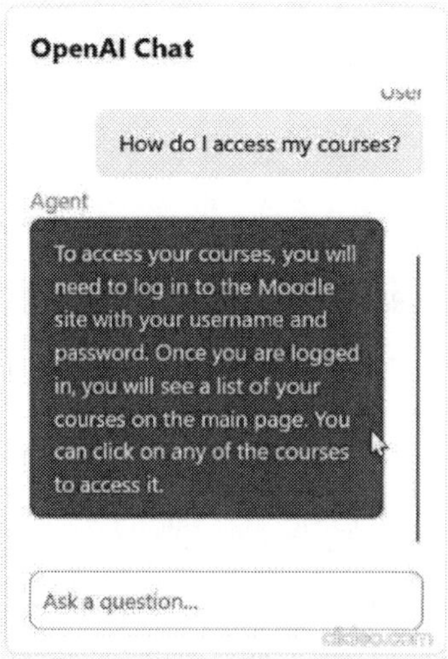

Example of OpenAI Chat block (GPT-3) (Moodle, 2023)

Keywords:

Large Language Models - Learning Management Systems - GPT-3 - ChatGPT - Moodle - Learning Experience - OpenAI Chat plugin - API key

Summary

This poster outlines the benefits and practical applications of integrating Large Language Models (LLMs), specifically GPT-3, into a Learning Management System (LMS), using Moodle as an example. For educators, LLMs can aid in lesson planning, generating exercises automatically, and grading students' work, providing insights into their strengths and weaknesses. For students, LLMs offer assistance with research, writing tasks, and comprehending material, and can help bridge communication gaps. The poster proposes empowering Moodle with GPT-3, enabling access to a broad range of information by asking questions and tailoring this information to meet the specific needs of students.

References

Baidoo-Anu, D., & Owusu Ansah, L. (2023). *Education in the Era of Generative Artificial Intelligence (AI): Understanding the Potential Benefits of ChatGPT in Promoting Teaching and Learning.* Available at SSRN 4337484.

Moodle. *"OpenAI Chat block"* Moodle plugin directory. Retrieved March 3, 2023, from

https://moodle.org/plugins/block_openai_chat.

Kasneci, E., Seßler, K., Küchemann, S., Bannert, M., Dementieva, D., Fischer, F., Gasser, U., Groh, G., Günnemann, S., Hüllermeier, E., & Krusche, S. (2023). *ChatGPT for good? On opportunities and challenges of large language models for education.* Frontiers in Education, 8, 834265.

Qu, F., Jia, X., & Wu, Y. (2021). *Asking questions like educational experts: Automatically generating question-answer pairs on real-world examination data.* arXiv preprint arXiv:2109.05179.

Rudolph, J., Tan, S., & Tan, S. (2023). *ChatGPT: Bullshit spewer or the end of traditional assessments in higher education?* Journal of Applied Learning and Teaching, 6(1).

Tai, T. Y., & Chen, H. H. J. (2020). *The impact of Google Assistant on adolescent EFL learners' willingness to communicate.* Interactive Learning Environments, 1-18.

DEVELOPING A COMMUNITY OF PRACTICE FOR INITIAL TEACHER EDUCATION STUDENTS USING THE COHORT APP

Frank Kehoe, Hibernia College, Ireland

Abstract

This research was focused on the Professional Masters in Post Primary Education (PME) at Hibernia College in Dublin. The PME in Post-Primary Education is a 120-credit award at Level 9 on the National Framework of Qualifications (NFQ). It is delivered over 24 months and is a blended learning programme, combining online and face-to-face delivery to develop professionals positioned to be leaders in the field of post-primary education.

The College introduced the Moxo Cohort app in 2021, a cloud-based portal to facilitate and upscale communication and collaboration between members of the Hibernia community. This research was focused on the use of the communication app in one specific module, 'Digital Technology for Teaching and Learning', This module is offered for students who hold less than 40 credits in a second subject or do not have a second subject. The module aims to give participants an understanding of the contemporary landscape with respect to digital technologies for teaching and learning. The research proposed if the app could facilitate the growth of a 'Community of Practice' (Wenger, 1999) within the student group taking this module which started in Autumn 2022.

A quantitative methodology was adapted, and results indicate that it was successful, although it is only in its first phase. It is an effective way to foster collaboration, knowledge sharing, and professional development within the module and with the community of students taking this option on the course. Additional support as recommended will be needed for further growth.

Keywords:

Community of Practice, Communication App, Blended Learning, Initial teacher training.

References

Wenger, E. (1999). Communities of Practice: Learning, Meaning and Identity. Cambridge: Cambridge University Press.

Serrat, O. (2008). Building Communities of Practice Development, American Quality Press.

ADVANCING GHANAIAN HIGHER EDUCATION DIGITAL COMPENTENCIES

Edward P.G. White, Tampere University, Finland, Jussi Okkonen Tampere University, Finland
Maart Laanpere Tallinn University, Estonia

Introduction and overview

The COVID-19 pandemic has exasperated inequality in Ghana by lowering living standards, and simultaneously increasing poverty and unemployment (Bukari et al., 2021). To overcome these structural issues and advance the current Ghanaian digital competencies in higher education, a partnership was established between the Ghanaian University of Cape Coast (UCC) and University of Education, Winneba (UEW) the Estonian Tallinn University (TU) and Finnish Tampere University (TAU).

The COVID-19 pandemic necessitated the use of online teaching and learning, which requires enhancing the competences of teaching staff and the acquisition of resources to aid in its implementation. Moreover, the digital literacies of both staff and students require systematic development. The adoption of hybrid or blended mode of instructional delivery in academic programmes caused significant discontinuity in delivery. The last two years have revealed several issues for efficient implementation of digital delivery including: inadequate teaching/learning facilities, equipment, e-resources, and high-cost of Internet connectivity. In addition, most of the faculty have inadequate technology competences and are unable to effectively develop online courseware and facilitate online teaching and learning.

To chart a path forward, the OPEKA questionnaire had been adapted for higher education teachers at UCC and UEW (Viteli, 2013). The questionnaire determines the usage of information, communication, and technology in teaching; whose outcomes provide micro, meso and macro-level changes to be implement. The outcomes will then be adapted into UCC and UEW digital learning policies to develop graduates with better suited skillsets for the current and future workplaces. Later on, higher education teachers from UCC and UEW will visit TLU or TAU, to job shadow teachers with similar profiles as their own. This will help to identify best digital practises to incorporate into their teaching approach and then bring them back to their relevant institutions where they can function as change agents.

Delivery of digital education provides greater access to educational resources to those who are living in remote areas or have physical impartments. This allows them to have access to the same educational material as their peers. This allows for inclusion to a wider array of student groups and therefore grater economic and social development. This opens a deeper discussion about the role of digital literacy and what it offers and what is views successful implementation.

References

Bukari, C., Essilfie, G., Aning-Agyei, M. A., Otoo, I. C., Kyeremeh, C., Owusu, A. A., Amuquandoh, K. F., & Bukari, K. I. (2021). Impact of COVID-19 on poverty and living standards in Ghana: A micro-perspective. *Cogent Economics & Finance*, *9*(1), 1879716.

Viteli, J. (2013). Teachers and use of ICT in education: pilot study and testing of the Opeka system. EdMedia+ Innovate Learning,

SUPPORTING SUSTAINABILITY IN A DISTANCE LEARNING CURRICULUM

Paul Astles, James Openshaw, The Open University, UK

Abstract

We have developed a suite of resources that help the audience focus on ways to connect to the sustainable development goals (United Nations, 2015). Key to our work is the idea that any actions should not be tokenistic but meaningful for colleagues and students who are engaging with our resources. We developed these resources into three stages of detail to bring the audience on a journey towards taking informed action. Stage 1 provides an opportunity to reflect on whether sustainability has been considered. Stage 2 outlines a range of resources grouped by theme alongside some suggested areas on where to begin to focus. Stage 3 infographics lead on from stage 2 and delve deeper into 4 areas of focus (1. Promoting competencies for sustainable development, 2. Engaging with existing resources, 3. Becoming more aware of what is happening within higher education, 4. Exploring opportunities to engage students in designing within the context of sustainable development).

Keywords

Sustainability, distance learning, informed actions, sustainable development goals, non-tokenistic, reflection, learning design.

Summary

Supporting sustainability in a distance learning curriculum is not something that can be achieved without careful thought and consideration. It is important to acknowledge that we need to support our colleagues and stakeholders to engage in meaningful discussion and reflection. It is this that has brought us to where we are with the resources that we have created within this poster submission. Further scholarship will focus on reflecting on our next steps with regards to supporting colleagues and stakeholders to take non-tokenistic actions relating to sustainability in the curriculum.

Reference

United Nations. (2015). The 17 Goals. Retrieved February 2, 2023, from https://sdgs.un.org/goals

AI PIONEERS: THE DISSEMINATION, EXPLOITATION AND SUSTAINABILITY STRATEGY DESINGNED BY EDEN DIGITAL LEARNING EUROPE

Carla García Iglesias, EDEN Digital Learning Europe, Spain; Gizéh Rangel-De Lazaro, Universitat Oberta de Catalunya, Spain; Josep M Duart, Universitat Oberta de Catalunya, Spain; Denise Whitelock, The Open University, UK

Introduction

The AI Pioneers project successfully started in January 2023 under the EU Erasmus+ program with 10 project partners from Italy, Portugal, Greece, Spain, Cyprus, Estonia and Germany. The project focuses on building a network of pioneers from the education sector who are actively involved in the field of artificial intelligence (AI).

This will involve trainers, stakeholders, policy makers and educational planners to promote the use and delivery of AI in VET and adult education. Here, we present the dissemination, exploitation, and sustainability strategy EDEN designed for Artificial intelligence in education and training (AI PIONEERS), which is funded by Erasmus+. This project aims to contribute to the skill of all educators in using digital technologies effectively in their teaching and training process by qualifying them as high-quality, contributing to the Digital Education Action Plan 2021-2027. This project aims to develop a reference network of trainers, stakeholders, policymakers, and educational planners to promote the use and teaching of AI in Adult Education and Vocational Education Training (VET).

Mission

AI Pioneers will act as reference points for designing and implementing future educational projects related to AI at regional, national and European levels.

Abstract

Here, we present the dissemination, exploitation, and sustainability strategy EDEN designed for Artificial intelligence in education and training (AI PIONEERS), which is funded by Erasmus+. This project aims to contribute to the skill of all educators in using digital technologies effectively in their teaching and training process by qualifying them as high-quality, contributing to the Digital Education Action Plan 2021-2027. This project aims to develop a reference network of trainers, stakeholders, policymakers, and educational planners to promote the use and teaching of AI in Adult Education and Vocational Education Training (VET). AI Pioneers will serve as reference points for designing and implementing future AI-related educational projects at the regional, national, and European levels. Moreover, it will produce recommendations, toolkits, and implementation guidelines at the organizational and systemic levels and disseminate and exploit the use of AI in education and training. The project's impact will be maximized through face-to-face and online dissemination activities. These activities will target engaging participants, mainstreaming, and implementing the results in other education providers, organizations, policymakers, and planners. In this context, EDEN Digital Learning Europe, responsible for the dissemination strategy of the AI PIONEERS project, has planned the following actions and channels of dissemination

- *To design the logo and the graphic identity, character and brand of the project using AI.*
- *To create Newsletters to promote the project results and activities, ensuring that AI PIONEERS reach the maximum number of people.*
- *To use social media platforms like AI PIONEERS Twitter and LinkedIn page. In addition, EDEN accounts on YouTube and Facebook.*
- *To network with institutions, professionals and academics interested in the AI PIONEERS project.*

• *To disseminate the project results in conferences with international or national audiences, including stakeholders (i.e., teachers and trainers, learners system administrators and service providers, schools training centre teachers' educators/ trainers of trainers, Educational policy makers NGO.)*

• *To create an interactive community of the Pioneers to discuss the project toolkit through alternative channels such as Telegram or WhatsApp.*

Keywords:

Dissemination, exploitation, communication, sustainability, promotion.

Summary

The dissemination, exploitation, and sustainability strategy designed by EDEN for AI PIONEERS also includes an inventory of activities to track and monitor all the actions, events and relevant data throughout the project concerning the dissemination plan. The following impact indicators can help us create a more detailed picture of the progress of dissemination actions and outputs.

• Social media followers, mentions, (re)tweets, replies, impressions, and outreach, among others.

• Newsletters impact: number of subscribers, number of downloads

• Number & target size of project-related press & social media coverage items (reports/mentions/dedicated articles)

We expect to include more dissemination outputs in future dissemination, exploitation, and sustainability strategy revisions. The resources developed during and after the project will be distributed with a Creative Commons Licence 4.0 or the most updated version. All software and content will be open access.

THE NEED FOR SCIENTIFIC JOURNALS TO CONTRIBUTE TO GENDER EQUALITY

Elsa Corominas, Josep M Duart, Universitat Oberta de Catalunya, Spain

Abstract

Nowadays, with a favourable regulatory framework and increased awareness, we can confidently state that there is true institutional commitment to gender equality. We are moving from words to deeds, that resources, budget allocations and institutional efforts are being dedicated to this issue.

Universities have three major challenges:

- Achieving gender equality in decision-making, incorporating more women into decision-making bodies & positions
- Working towards real equal opportunities in academic & teaching careers
- Incorporating gender perspective into research & teaching

Scientific journals guarantee that the results of research and the major breakthroughs in all knowledge areas are published as articles, regularly, flexibly, and relatively quickly, in structured texts of reasonable length, which have been validated by experts in the content field. Journals are key factors in science, academic careers, and scientific communication, and play a central role in the important issue of ensuring gender equality.

Laws, regulations, and recommendations are not enough, an effort and the desire to act are needed if the goal of equality is to be achieved. Sound science with a gender perspective is positive for society in general, so it must be adopted as part of the evaluation of research quality.

Keywords

Gender equity, research quality, scientific communication, scientific journals, equal opportunities, science, academic careers

References

Abadal, Ernest, & Da-Silveira, Lúcia (2020). Open peer review: otro paso hacia la ciencia abierta por parte de las revistas científicas. *Anuario ThinkEPI, 14.* https://doi.org/10.3145/thinkepi.2020.e14e02

Corominas Rodríguez, Elsa. (2023). The Need for Scientific Journals to Contribute to Gender Equality *[Blog].* http://etheblog.com/2023/01/27/the-need-for-scientific-journals-to-contribute-to-gender-equality/

Fressoli, Mariano, & De Filippo, Daniela (2021). Nuevos escenarios y desafíos para la ciencia abierta. Entre el optimismo y la incertidumbre. *Arbor, 197(799), a586.* https://doi.org/10.3989/arbor.2021.799001

López Lloreda, Claudia. Women researchers are cited less than men. Here's why—and what can be done about it https://www.science.org/content/article/women-researcherscited-less-men-heres-why-what-can-done

Sumner, Jane (2018). The Gender Balance Assessment Tool (GBAT): A Web-Based Tool for Estimating Gender Balance in Syllabi and Bibliographies. *PS: Political Science & Politics, 51(2),* 396-400. https://www.cambridge.org/core/journals/ps-political-science-and-politics/article/abs/gender-balance-assessment-tool-gbat-a-webbased-tool-for-estimating-gender-balance-in-syllabi-and-bibliographies/1D63629A4A52FC04AF9EAF94A67F6A9B

COMPLEX TRAJECTORIES PROMOTING STUDENTS' SUCCESSFUL TRAJECTORIES IN HIGHER EDUCATION INSTITUTIONS

Alfredo Soeiro, Vera Miguéis, Universidade do Porto, Portugal, Josep Duart, Universitat Obierta de Catalonia, Spain, António Teixeira, Universidade Aberta, Portugal, Helena Troiano, Universidad Autonoma de Barcelona, Spain, Alicia Villar, Universidad de Valencia, Spain, Janine Jongbloed, Université de Bourgogne, France, Chris Edwards, Open University, UK

Abstract

The Complex Trajectories Project focuses on understanding the complex trajectories of students at university and supporting those who navigate them. In the practical domain, the project aims to contribute to the establishment of a system of regular monitoring of student trajectories in order to adjust the development of policies supporting these trajectories at different levels of the system and university institutions.

The First part is where it is envisaged aiming to end up developing a methodology for analysing student trajectories that is transferable to other higher education contexts. In the second part we will carry out a collection of good practices in support of complex trajectories by exploring policies in the Higher Education Institutions (HEIs) that are partners in the consortium and in other HEIs in their nearby territories. In the third part, it is planned to transform the knowledge acquired from the two previous parts into training and decision-making support material. To this end, degree program evaluation indicators are constructed on the theme of trajectories. Two MOOCs are designed, one aimed at learning the longitudinal analysis of student trajectories, the other for advisors on measures to support complex trajectories. A handbook for advisors and other support materials are designed.

Keywords:

Drop-outs, student retention, student trajectories, university support, student advisor, training.

References

COMPLEX - Promoting Students' Successful Trajectories In Higher Education Institutions, https://web.fe.up.pt/~complext/index.html, accessed 31 March 2023